ENGLISH PLACE-NAME SOCIETY. VOLUME II.

THE PLACE-NAMES OF BUCKINGHAMSHIRE

By

A. MAWER *and* F. M. STENTON

CAMBRIDGE
AT THE UNIVERSITY PRESS
1925

PRINTED IN GREAT BRITAIN

PREFACE

IN presenting to the members of the English Place-name Society and to the public generally the first county volume it is the pleasant duty of the editors to place on record their indebtedness to those who by their ready co-operation and help have alone made their task a possible one.

Their mainstays have been three in number. Mrs Stenton has acted as general county organiser and has given invaluable help, not only in transcribing the place-name material from a large number of unprinted documents but also in the work of carding up and identifying the place-names themselves. Major J. de C. Laffan has been her untiring associate in the work and has also carried through the heavy task of constructing in duplicate a slip-gazetteer of all the place-names found on the 1-in. and 6-in. O.S. maps, thus providing the basis upon which the whole of the work is ultimately built. Mr A. Harman, of Aylesbury, with his wide and thorough knowledge of the topography and dialect of Buckinghamshire, has rendered services of the greatest value by his readiness to deal with all those questions of situation and pronunciation in which the man on the spot, who has lived in the district itself, is always the best guide, provided that he has eyes and ears such as Mr Harman has, and an untiring willingness to prosecute local enquiries.

Apart from these three helpers it would be invidious to make distinctions, and one can only enumerate one's debts and express one's deep obligation to the following:—The Council of the Buckinghamshire County Museum for the loan of a set of the *Records of Buckinghamshire* and to the Curator of the Museum for untiring readiness to help. Mr A. H. Cocks, for the use of a transcript of the early 14th cent. charter granting the Poynatts estate and for untiring patience and kindness in answering the numerous questions which the editors have put to him upon this matter and upon numerous others in connexion with the topography and archaeology of Buckinghamshire, upon which he speaks with such long-established authority. Miss M. A. Cook for extracting the forms from the unpublished Feet of Fines for Hy iii. Next to the Assize Rolls these have proved

the most useful material derived direct from unprinted sources. Mr G. Eland for the use of two early Bucks deeds in his possession and for help in answering various enquiries put to him by the editors. The Rev. Canon C. W. Foster for the use of his invaluable MS list of institutions to benefices in the Lincoln diocese and for checking against the MS the printed edition of the rolls of Bishop Hugh de Welles. Mr C. F. Hardy for forms from Ogilby's *Britannia*. Mr T. F. Hobson for forms from the 17th cent. transcript of deeds in the possession of New College. Mr Michael M. Hughes, for the use of his transcripts of the invaluable Buckinghamshire Assize Rolls for Henry iii. Mr Charles Johnson for forms from the Registers of John de Pontissara. The President and Fellows of Magdalen College for the loan of a volume of transcripts of North Marston, Thornborough and Westbury deeds in their possession, made by the Rev. W. D. Macray. Mr Wm. Page, General Editor of the *Victoria County Histories*, for having placed at the disposal of the Survey the MS material for the unpublished volumes of the *History of Buckinghamshire*, and, even more usefully and profitably, having allowed the editors the use of the uncorrected proofs of those same volumes. It will be clear at every turn how much the editors owe to this kindness. They alone however are responsible for the correctness of any information quoted from these uncorrected and unpublished volumes. Mr S. A. Peyton for the transcript of Terriers and other documents in the Bodleian which have provided invaluable material for the field-names of Buckinghamshire, for 17th and 18th cent. phonetic spellings of its place-names and demonstrated how valuable as a whole is the material to be found even in these later documents. Mr J. H. Sacret for extracting the Bucks material from the *Valor Ecclesiasticus*. Miss M. S. Serjeantson for transcribing the place-name material to be found in the Buckinghamshire Charters in the Bodleian and for extracting from the transcripts of the Merton College Deeds made by the late W. H. Stevenson all relevant Buckinghamshire material. Miss Edith Scroggs for much most useful work in checking forms derived from unpublished material in the Public Record Office. The Rev. R. Usher of Westbury for the loan of a privately printed copy of the Westbury Deeds in the possession

of Magdalen College and for other services. Miss Joan Wake for material derived from charters in the possession of Col. Stopford Sackville, cited as *Drayton Charters*.

The names of these helpers and of the work they have contributed will show in some measure the good fortune of the editors in compassing two of the aims which the promoters of the Survey have always had in view, viz. the active co-operation of a large group of scholars in the collection of material and the extensive use of early unpublished material. It remains to say how equally fortunate they have been in securing the help and criticism of other scholars in the interpretation of their material, especially in those cases which offered peculiar difficulties. During the course of the last year both editors had opportunities of personal conference with Professors Ekwall and Zachrisson and they have also had their written opinions on many of the *cruces*. Professor Ekwall's five months' stay in England gave opportunities of discussion such as can seldom arise, and the editors are specially indebted to him for his constant willingness to help.

The editors had hoped that this and other of their volumes would have benefited by the criticisms of W. H. Stevenson, but it was not to be. English place-name studies within fifteen months of the death of the late Dr Bradley have now suffered still further loss by the untimely death of a scholar who combined in a peculiar degree the varied learning of the historian, the palaeographer, the philologist and the topographer, and the editors can only pay their tribute of homage to one to whom both of them alike were deeply indebted.

A word should perhaps be said about the material used in the volume. So far as was possible references have been given which will enable those who may wish to do so to check the forms against the original as found in printed or MS document. This did not prove possible in the case of the forms derived from the Assize Rolls. The slips for these forms with the full references to the membranes of the rolls have been kept with all the other slips and are available for consultation at the headquarters of the Society. Those slips include a large number which had to remain unused because they were not immediately necessary for the explanation of the names in question.

This volume, like its predecessors, owes much to the kindness of Professors Ekwall and Tait in reading the proofs. They have saved us from many errors. For those that may remain we are alone responsible.

In issuing the first county-volume of the publications of the English Place-Name Society the editors are deeply conscious how many problems they have had to face and how uncertain are the solutions that they have suggested for many of them. Some of them will remain for ever insoluble. Others might have been brought nearer definite solution had it been possible to pursue special and detailed lines of investigation. Such investigations would however delay indefinitely the publication of the Society's volumes thereby effectively stopping what is after all most urgently needed for the solution of these and other problems, viz. the speedy publication of early and reliable material on which alone safe and certain conclusions can in the end be based.

A. M.
F. M. S

ST PANCRAS' DAY, 1925.

CONTENTS

MAPS

INTRODUCTION

The contrast which exists to-day between the north and south of Buckinghamshire was no less apparent in the Middle Ages. Despite the existence of wide stretches of woodland, the north of the county was in the main a land of villages, a representative part of the English midlands. The Chilterns were by no means uninhabited. A high proportion of the local names of this region must have arisen in the time before the Norman Conquest. But apart from ancient estates such as Missenden, High Wycombe, Chalfont, and Chesham, the Chiltern population was sparse and scattered, distributed among hamlets and farms rather than concentrated in villages. The isolation of the Chilterns can, indeed, be exaggerated. They were traversed by at least two important medieval roads, converging on London from Oxford and Aylesbury respectively. But under medieval conditions lines of travel had little effect on the country through which they passed, and the influence of London, which has done much and will do more to reverse the distribution of population between the north and south of the county, was scarcely felt in the Middle Ages. High Wycombe was a day's ride from the City.

There is therefore no real unity in the history of Buckinghamshire. The county itself is of late formation. It first appears in the year 1016, and it was probably created somewhat late in the previous century. When ealdorman Æthelred of the Mercians died in 910 or 911, a contemporary chronicler relates that king Edward 'annexed London and Oxford and the lands which belong thereto,' words which are not easy to reconcile with the existence of an intermediate shire centring on Buckingham. On mere geographical grounds it is not evident why Buckingham rather than Aylesbury should have been chosen for the central borough of the new shire. The explanation probably lies in topography. Buckingham stands in a corner of the county, apart from any known line of early travel, and is served to-day by roads which have little appearance of antiquity. But the hill on which it is placed, a peninsular site like Shrewsbury,

was by nature a defensible position, and as such it played its part in the wars of king Edward the Elder. It commanded the valley of the upper Ouse, promised security and offered a convenient market place to a considerable extent of fertile country. Under the conditions which prevailed before the Norman Conquest, there was not room for two boroughs in the shire, and Buckingham remained its head.

If the outline of early West Saxon history preserved in the Old English Chronicle may be trusted, the plain at the foot of the Chilterns was still in British occupation in the year 571. The Chronicle relates that in that year a certain Cuthwulf, whose name suggests that he belonged to the royal house of Wessex, fought with the Britons at a place called *Bedcanford* and took four 'towns,' Limbury[1], Aylesbury, Bensington, and Eynsham. *Bedcanford*, often in the past identified with Bedford, is really an unknown site. But the identification of Aylesbury is certain, and there can be no question that, according to West Saxon tradition, the Vale of Aylesbury, and indeed the region occupied by the *Cilternsætan* of the 8th century, was conquered during the great expansion of the West Saxons in the reign of Ceawlin, between 560 and 591.

This tradition has often been called in question by modern writers, generally because it has been felt improbable that the country between the Lea and the middle Thames could have remained British until so late a time. It may at once be admitted that no settled, peaceable, British life is likely to have survived in this region until the year 571. But it is not in itself improbable that the district to the north of the Chilterns may still have been debateable land, in which a sparse British population maintained a precarious existence, harried, perhaps, from time to time by the Saxons from beyond the Thames, but allowed to remain in occupation of its territory until the Saxons needed new land for settlement[2]. In any case, the question

[1] This identification is new, but the early forms of Limbury recently found in unpublished Beds. Assize Rolls make certain an identification suggested some time since by Dr G. H. Fowler. The early forms which are cited below under Lenborough are conclusive evidence against the identification of that place with the *Lygeanburg* of the Chronicle.

[2] The traces left by the British inhabitants of Buckinghamshire in the place-names of the county are few, but sufficient to disprove the extermination of the Britons. British words are contained in *Chetwode*, *Panshill*, *Brill*,

when the Saxon settlement of this region began is more important than the question when the British occupation ceased, and no evidence sufficient to disprove the Saxon tradition has yet been brought forward. In particular, the objects recovered from the somewhat numerous Saxon burial grounds in central Buckinghamshire seem quite compatible with a settlement beginning in or soon after the year 571. There is no archaeological evidence in this quarter of early Saxon settlements such as certainly existed in Berkshire, Surrey, and Middlesex. Central Buckinghamshire was undoubtedly settled by Saxons in the heathen time, but the extant traces of their settlement suggest the age of Ceawlin and his immediate successors rather than that of Cerdic and Cynric.

The same may be said of the place-names of this region. The surviving names *Oving* and *Wing*, and the lost Stoke *Halling* in Stoke Mandeville, would go far of themselves, apart from archaeological evidence, to prove a 6th century settlement of the district which centres on Aylesbury. But the local nomenclature of this district as a whole presents few early features. The name *Weedon* must have arisen in the heathen time. The personal names *Creoda* and *Horsa*, which underlie *Long Crendon* and *Horsendon* respectively seem to have passed out of use at an early date, and *Myrsa*, the personal name from which *Mursley* is derived, is certainly archaic and probably unique. But these are exceptions, and the place-names of central Buckinghamshire as a whole undoubtedly suggest a settlement appreciably later than that which produced the ancient local nomenclature of the region to the west, by the middle Thames.

No argument is needed to prove the late settlement of the Chilterns. The numerous local names of medieval or later origin tell their own tale. Nevertheless, even here the map reveals names which may go back to the 7th or even the 6th century. The personal name *Myssa* from which *Missenden* is derived, a

and *Brickhill*. The name *Brayfield* may contain the pre-English name of Yardley Chase, and in the 13th century a wood called *Morezyf* (sic) and *Moreyf* is mentioned in the neighbourhood of Westbury. This name is probably identical with the obscure, but certainly pre-English, name of Morfe Forest in Staffordshire (IPN 15). All these examples come from the centre and north of the county. If Datchet, like Chetwode, contains the Celtic *kēton*, 'wood,' it is an isolated example in the south.

later form of the ancient *Myrsa* of Mursley, does not seem ever to have been generally current in Old English personal nomenclature. The name *Æbba*, contained in the lost Chiltern place-name *Abfield*, has not been observed to occur later than the 9th century. More interesting, whatever the circumstances of its origin, is one remarkable name which suggests the late survival of a British population in the Chiltern valleys. Each part of the place-name Chalfont, OE *Ceadeles funta*, is of British origin. It does not follow that the name itself was British. *Ceadel* was one of the few British personal names adopted by the English invaders at an early time, and the word *funta* occurs in place-names which are certainly of English creation. Nevertheless, the ultimate Celtic origin of the name Chalfont suggests very strongly that intercourse between Britons and Saxons was possible when the name arose, and this signifies, what, indeed, is *a priori* probable, that the British inhabitants of a country which, like the Chilterns, did not invite early settlement might long remain unmolested there.

There is good evidence of heathen Saxon settlement in the angle of more open country between the Chilterns, the Thames, and the Colne. The great mound at Taplow covered one of the most richly furnished burials of the whole heathen Saxon time[1]. Little can be said at present as to the origin of the earliest Saxon settlements in this corner of the county, but they were probably independent of, and may well have been earlier than the West Saxon occupation of the plain north of the Chilterns. On geographical grounds, they are most naturally regarded as the work of the original Middle Saxons. The whole Saxon culture of the middle Thames valley was too homogeneous to allow sharp distinctions to be drawn between its West Saxon and Middle Saxon forms, and it is easy to overstrain the evidence of individual place-names. Nevertheless, there is one piece of linguistic evidence which from its nature cannot be conclusive, but undoubtedly suggests an early connexion between the Middle Saxons and the settlers of south-east Buckinghamshire. The name of Harlington in Middlesex, three

[1] It is almost certain that the personal name *Tæppa* from which Taplow is derived denoted the Saxon noble who was buried with this remarkable accompaniment of grave furniture.

miles from the Buckinghamshire border, represents an OE *Hygereding tun*[1]. The stem *Hyge-*, contained in the personal name *Hygered*, is rarely found in English place-names[2]. It is therefore remarkable that no less than three place-names in south Buckinghamshire, *Hitcham*, *Hedgerley*, and *Hughenden*, are severally derived from a personal name *Hycga*, a normal short form of a compound name containing the stem *Hyge-*. The juxtaposition of these names is a slight but definite piece of evidence in favour of an original connexion between Middlesex and south Buckinghamshire, and the three Buckinghamshire names themselves suggest interesting conclusions as to the Saxon settlement of this part of the county. It cannot be through chance that three separate places within a small area each bear names derived from an identical, and otherwise unknown, personal name. It is hard to avoid the conclusion that the same person gave his name to Hitcham, Hedgerley, and Hughenden or at least that different members of the same family gave their names to each of these places. In either case, these names amount to virtual proof that the southern slopes of the Chilterns were colonised from the early settlements on the Thames bank, of which Hitcham, OE *Hycgan ham*, is one.

In many ways, the early history of the north of the county, the districts round Buckingham and Newport Pagnell, is more obscure than that of the centre and south. There is no early tradition of its conquest, and the archaeological material which it has produced gives little convincing evidence as to the date of its settlement. For historical reasons it seems certain that the north of the county was settled by Angles, not Saxons. The indications of Anglian settlement supplied by place-names are slight but suggestive. Calverton in the north of the county and Chalvey in the south are each derived from the OE *c(e)alf*, 'calf,' but the initial *c* of Calverton is as definitely Anglian as the initial *ch* of Chalvey is Saxon. The OE *botl*, 'building,' is characteristic of Anglian local nomenclature. It has become the *Botolph* of *Botolph* Claydon, and it appears again in the medieval

[1] BCS 400 (original).

[2] It occurs again in Hewelsfield Gl (from OE *Hygeweald*) and Hibaldstow L (from OE *Hygebeald*), but the latter is probably derived from the name of Hygebeald, an early abbot in Lindsey.

place-name *Newbottle*, which denoted a site near Shalstone and Westbury. The stem *Ean-* which occurs in the personal name *Eanbeorht* from which Emberton is derived, was much more commonly used by Angles than by Saxons. How far towards the south this Anglian settlement extended is a question which cannot at present be definitely answered. Until new information comes to light, it may be suggested that the broken, wooded, country round Brill formed the boundary between the Saxons on the upper Thame and the Angles on the upper Ouse, and that towards the north-east of the county the high ground of Whaddon Chase formed a similar barrier[1]. To the north of this suggested frontier, the place-names give the impression of a settlement appreciably later than that of the Vale of Aylesbury. They include no archaic formations like *Oving* and *Halling*, and, on the other hand, they contain clear examples of a type of name consisting of a compound personal name in the possessive case followed by *tun*, which are characteristic of the western midlands. *Woolstone* and *Simpson*, OE *Wulfsiges-tun* and *Sigewines-tun*, resemble such typical Staffordshire names as *Darlaston* and *Admaston*, OE *Deorlafes-tun* and *Eadmundes-tun*. The name *Turweston*, OE *Thurulfes-tun* or *Thurfestestun*, proves that new village names could arise in this region after the Danish invasions of the 9th century, for the singular transformations which this name has undergone do not conceal its Scandinavian origin. On grounds of general history the Anglian settlement of northern Buckinghamshire is likely to have been late. It is in Northamptonshire and the districts to the north-west and south-east that, to judge from archaeological remains, the strength of the heathen Middle Angles lay.

In the reign of Henry I, as doubtless for the previous two hundred years, Buckinghamshire formed part of the Danelaw. With Bedfordshire, Cambridgeshire, Huntingdonshire, and the north-west of Hertfordshire, Buckinghamshire forms a definite part of the Danelaw of which the local nomenclature yields little evidence of Scandinavian settlement. In Northamptonshire, where the Scandinavian element was undoubtedly strong in the

[1] The suggestion sometimes made that the valley of the upper Ouse was settled by Saxons is probably influenced by the common identification of the *Bedcanford* of the Chronicle with Bedford.

10th century, the new settlers left the earlier English local nomenclature substantially unchanged. Hence, only sporadic traces of their presence may be expected to occur in Buckinghamshire. They appear from time to time in medieval field names, one of which, the *Krakuluesberh* mentioned in a 13th century document relating to Thornborough, reveals a Scandinavian personal name *Krakulf* which seems to be otherwise unknown. Among surviving place-names, the difficult but interesting name *Skirmett* affords the most definite evidence of Scandinavian influence in the county. There seems no doubt that the name descends from an OE *scir-gemot*[1]. The *scir* commemorated in the name was probably a group of Hundreds with a common court, such as appears on more than one occasion in 10th century Northamptonshire. But the medieval form of the name, with its initial *sk*, must be due to Scandinavian influence, and to produce so permanent a result this influence must have been strong. It is illustrated again in the name of the adjoining parish of Fingest, which is derived from an earlier *Thing-hyrst*. The word *thing*, which occurs in many local names in the northern Danelaw, is the usual Anglo-Scandinavian term for an assembly, and it is a safe assumption that the *thing* which gave name to Fingest was identical with the *scir-gemot* which is the origin of the name *Skirmett*[2]. The existence of an Anglo-Scandinavian population whose speech could modify the initial consonants of this name does not rest on mere conjecture. The first element in the name *Turville*, less than a mile from Fingest, is the Scandinavian personal name *Thyri*, and the details which are brought together below in the note on Brands Fee prove that as late as the 12th century Scandinavian personal names were still being used in the south of Buckinghamshire. In the first element of the name *Owlswick*, the medieval forms show a curious oscillation between the Scandinavian and OE personal names *Ulfr* and *Wulf*. The Scandinavian settlement of Buckinghamshire must have been

[1] Another p.n. containing OE (*ge*)*mot*, 'meeting-(place)' is to all appearances to be found in Landmoth (Y), DB *Landemot*.

[2] Dr G. H. Fowler's discovery that the meeting-place of Manshead Hundred in Bedfordshire was in the immediate neighbourhood of Tingrith (OE *þing riðig*) provides a close parallel to the contiguity of Skirmett and Fingest.

far less thorough than that of Northamptonshire, but it was thorough enough not only to compel the inclusion of the county within the Danelaw but also to make a genuine impression on local nomenclature.

The Norman Conquest, too, has left its mark upon the place-names of Buckinghamshire. The modern forms of the names *Cippenham*, *Linslade*, *Turweston*, and *Turville*, are due to the difficulty which Frenchmen felt in pronouncing existing English names. The articles which follow will show many cases in which this difficulty has had a temporary effect on pronunciation, but there were special reasons why its influence should be permanent in the four cases which have been quoted. Turweston is close to the Norman castle of Brackley, Cippenham to Windsor, Linslade is only separated by a stream from the important royal manor of Leighton Buzzard, and confusion was bound to arise between the place-name *Thyrefeld* and the name of the Norman family of *Turville* which is still preserved in the compound Weston Turville. A more obvious sign of French influence is afforded by the many cases in which the name of a French family has been attached to an earlier English place-name. Newport Pagnell, Clifton Reynes, Drayton Parslow, Stoke Mandeville, and the other names of this class which have been brought together in the list printed below (256), bear their witness to the dominance of a French aristocracy in Buckinghamshire in the centuries following the Norman Conquest. Few of these families have left material trace upon the soil of the county. Unlike its neighbour Bedfordshire, Buckinghamshire contains few examples of the private castle of the Norman time. In one and perhaps only one case is the presence of a Norman family attested at once by the surname which it has left to a village, by the surviving remains of its castle, and by documentary evidence. At Weston Turville there still exists, almost unmutilated, the motte and bailey in which in King Stephen's time the tenants of Geoffrey de Turville were required to do him service.

Among the Buckinghamshire place-names recorded in the 11th century, there are two which present difficulties of a somewhat unusual character. All the medieval forms of the name *Saunderton* suggest derivation from an original form

Sandheres-tun. The difficulty in this case is that not only is there no English example of the compound personal name *Sandhere*, but, except for one possible example in a p. n., the stem *Sand-* itself does not seem to have been employed in OE personal nomenclature[1]. If the name Saunderton contains the personal name *Sandhere*—and no other derivation can be suggested—this personal name must be of Continental Germanic origin. There is no intrinsic improbability in the suggestion that Saunderton contains the name of some immigrant from the Continent who sought the service of one of the kings of the 10th century and was rewarded by him with a grant of land, and some explanation of this kind is necessary if the name is not to be left unexplained. It is to some extent supported by the fact that similar problems are raised, and a similar explanation is required, by the more difficult name Amersham. The numerous medieval spellings of this name cannot be brought into any consistent relationship, but the majority of them suggest that they are derived from an OE *Agilmodes ham.* The personal name *Agilmod* cannot be English, and there are conclusive linguistic reasons why the name *Agilmodes-ham* cannot have arisen after, at latest, the end of the 8th century. All that can here be suggested is that the Agilmod of Amersham, like the Sandhere of Saunderton, was an immigrant from the Continent who at some time after the original settlement obtained a territorial position which led to the permanent association of his name with the place where he lived. It is possible that in the progress of the present Survey place-names presenting similar problems will appear in other counties, but at present, Saunderton and Amersham certainly possess the interest which belongs to the exceptional.

The place-names of Buckinghamshire, like those of other counties, make their contribution to Old English social history. The name Quainton is an important addition to the evidence which shows that women, before the Norman Conquest, could hold land and leave their names to their farms. The name of Walton by Aylesbury, an addition to the cases in which a *weala-tun* occurs close to some important and ancient estate,

[1] The *Sandi* of Saundby (Nt) is certainly a Scandinavian personal name.

supports the opinion that the *wealas* who appear in such a context should be regarded as the British servants belonging to an early manor rather than as a group of Britons whose ancestors had survived the English Conquest. Of greater interest are the cases in which the same Old English personal name is seen to be compounded in the names of different places in the same neighbourhood. The very remarkable group of names Hitcham, Hedgerley, and Hughenden, each derived from the personal name *Hycga*, seems to go back to the early time when a powerful settler might obtain a wide territory in a region not suited to the formation of village communities. The fact that a pre-Conquest charter mentions *Wottes broc* in the neighbourhood of Waddesdon, OE *Wottes dun*, and *Bican broc* in the neighbourhood of Beachendon, OE *Bican dun*, implies that some at least of the men who have left their names annexed to places were of more than peasant rank. Parallel cases are afforded by the appearance of a *Pichelesburne* in the neighbourhood of Pitstone, OE *Piceles-þyrne*, of *Hildesden* adjacent to *Hildesdun* (*v.* Hillesden *infra*), and it cannot well be an accident that *Adstock* and *Addington*, the names of two adjacent parishes, are each derived from the rare and early OE personal name *Aeddi*. A different but related problem is suggested by the proximity of the names *Beachendon* and *Bigstrup*. Beachendon is derived from the personal name *Bica*, Bigstrup, from a diminutive of this name, OE *Bicel*. It may at least be conjectured that Bica and Bicel were members of the same family. It is possible that Shalstone (Bk) and Shelswell (O), each derived from a personal name *Sceald*, contain the name of the same individual[1]. But only when similar cases have been discovered in other counties will it be possible to form a definite opinion on the significance of such names as these.

It remains that something should be said of the materials from which the early forms of the place-names which follow have been derived. No important religious house was founded in the county before the Norman Conquest, which means that few Buckinghamshire place-names can be interpreted in the light of Old English forms. It is therefore peculiarly unfortunate

[1] Other possible cases are Pitstone and Pitchcott, Hoggeston and Hogshaw. *v. infra*.

that the forms of Buckinghamshire place-names in the Domesday Survey are often demonstrably inaccurate. The Domesday spelling of a place-name in this county can never be allowed serious weight against the evidence of later forms. Moreover, Buckinghamshire is not one of the counties in regard to which numerous original charters of the 12th century compensate for the rarity of pre-Conquest material. The early grants to the alien priory of New(ing)ton Long(ue)ville, published by the Oxfordshire Record Society, and the original charters in favour of Biddlesden Abbey preserved in the British Museum, have proved valuable, but they do not form a body of early material such as exists for the study of local nomenclature in Northamptonshire and Lincolnshire. The workmanship of the early 14th century cartulary of Missenden is good, but it only covers a small portion of the county, the Biddlesden cartulary is late, and that of Snelshall is of little more than local interest. Of the unpublished sources which have been used for this book, the Assize Rolls of the 13th century have proved invaluable. They have often preserved evidence of forms which might, perhaps, have been inferred without them, but are never actually recorded in other sources. They have also yielded the earliest record of many names, obviously of pre-Conquest origin, but referring to small places, unmentioned in the scanty 12th century material. The information which they have given has shown that they should be regarded as one of the principal, though they have been hitherto one of the least considered, sources of material for place-name study.

NOTES ON THE DIALECT OF BUCKINGHAMSHIRE AS ILLUSTRATED BY ITS PLACE-NAMES

OE *æ* appears as [æ] in *Addington*, *Adstock*, and quite exceptionally as [e] in *Elsage*. In *Marsworth*, and in the local pronunciations of Haversham, Addingrove, Chalfont and Aston Clinton as [hɑˑʃəm] [ɑˑngrouv] [tʃɑˑfənt] [ɑˑstən], ME a from OE *æ* has undergone a characteristic lengthening to [ɑˑ], so also in Drayton *Parslow*, where ME *a* has become [ɑˑ].

OE *a* before *ld* is found sporadically in the forms of Weald, Westbury Wild and *Netherweld* and may possibly be Anglian, but the forms which ultimately prevail are those going back to WS *weald*. So also in field-name evidence we have *Welde* in Thornborough (*c.* 1250–60), *The Weald* in Cublington in 1680.

OE *ēo* appears as *u*, *o* in Muswell (one *e*-form), as *e* in the lost *Mesle* in Bledlow, as *o* in Muzwell, the difference being between the West and the Centre of the county.

OE *eo* normally develops to ME *e*, and this before *r* becomes *a* as in Hartwell and Hardicanute's Moat. Forms in *u* are only found sporadically. In these two names the influence of the common St Eng *herte*, *hart* was probably too strong to allow of the preservation of the *u*-forms. In Petsoe and Peterley the forms in *o* and *u* are much more persistent, probably because there was no word in St English to influence them. From field-name evidence we have also *Musewelle* in Thornborough (1246), *Flutmedebrok* (*ib.*) *c.* 1260 with long *eo* and *Nuþerende* (*ib. c.* 1250–60), *Mildenesturte* (*ib.*). These last forms are however only sporadic and the usual forms are *nether* and *sterte*.

OE *īe* is only found in the *Steeple* of Steeple Claydon. *e*-forms are the common ones, *u*-forms are found sporadically in the 14th and 16th cent. The influence of the ordinary word must be taken into account.

OE *o* has been unrounded to [a] in Crafton, Dadford, Dadbrook, Shabbington, Tathall End, Tattenhoe.

OE *y* appears as *i* in Biddlesden, Linford, Lillingstone, Tittershall, Missenden, Kimble, Hill (2), as *u* in Lude and

Mulducks but this statement does not indicate the whole history of the relation of the three possible developments of OE *y* to ME *e*, *i*, *u* (cf. IPN 136).

Taking the place-names from north to south we note

Biddlesden has *e*-forms from DB to 1394, *u*-forms from Hy ii to 1392 and once in 1522, *i*-forms from 1224 onwards, the forms being of approximately equal commonness.

Linford has *i*-forms from DB onwards and occasional *u* in the 13th cent.

Lillingstone has *i* in DB and onwards and occasional *u* in the 13th cent.

Cranwell has *e*-forms from 1185 to 1360 and *u*-forms from 1227–1326 with equal frequency, and *i*-forms from 1379.

Tittershall has *u*-forms in 13th and 14th cents.

Kimble has *e*-forms from DB onwards, the *e*-forms being much the commonest in the 13th cent. *u*-forms are sporadic in the 13th cent., lost in the 14th and found once in the 15th cent. *i*-forms are found from 1180 on, become fairly common in the 13th and 14th cents. and then finally prevail.

Missenden has *e*-forms from 1154 on and they are much the commonest in the 13th cent. The last example is found in 1535. *i*-forms are extremely rare from DB to 1400 and are of definitely late development. *u*-forms are found as early as 1200 and are the commonest in the 14th cent. They are not found after 1500.

Hughenden has *u* in DB and these forms are the commonest until 1400. After that they are sporadic till 1607. The *i*-forms are sporadic from 1125 on but they only become important quite late.

Lude has *e* in DB and then persistent *u*.

Iver has persistent *e* except for four early *u*-forms. The *i*-forms are quite late and seem to depend on raising of *e* to *i*.

In addition to these names we may note that there is definite evidence that the Buckinghamshire form for *brycg* was ME *bruge*, EModE *burge*. *v.* Honeyburge, Kingsbridge, Touchbridge. It should be noted that all these come from the west side of the county. So also *Burgemead* in Beachampton (1639). We have however Aley *Burge* in a Stoke Goldington Terrier of 1607.

It is impossible until the full evidence for the neighbouring counties has been worked out to determine the exact significance of this distribution of forms but one fact at least is clear, viz. that Buckinghamshire in its early days was definitely not an *i*-county. In this connexion it may be noted that the only forms that we have for the two examples of Hill in the county are *u*-forms and that a *Hully Broad* survived till 1674 in Gt Horwood.

In discussions of dialect-distribution a good deal of stress has been laid on the names containing OE *strǣt* as their first element but no conclusions of a definite nature can be drawn from a study of the early forms of Fenny, Stony and Water Stratford. It is clear that the identity of the first element in this name with the common word *street*, and the two forms *stret-* and *strat-* derived from it, was too readily recognised for the forms to develop uninfluenced by the standard speech or by other neighbouring or well-known places.

Buckinghamshire is an area in which there is a considerable tendency to voice *f* to *v*. This is found in the local pronunciation of Fingest as [vingəst] and in such a form as *Veny* Stratford for *Fenny* Stratford. Voicing of *f* to *v* also accounts for the large measure of confusion between names with the suffix *-feld* and those in *-ville*. *-ville* has replaced *feld* in *Turville* and the reverse process has taken place in Spinfield and Mansfield. The same process is seen in forms like *Blosefyld*, *Longfylde*, *Turfild* in Newton Blossomville and Longville, Weston Turville. The form *Darvell* from OE *deorfald* shows a similar change in Darrillshill. Further evidence is found in field-names in such forms as *Venforlong* in Aylesbury (*c.* 1240), *Vairhoc* in Westbury (*c.* 1236), *Voxlenmore* in Whitchurch (13th).

In the treatment of initial *c* in such words as *cealf*, *ceald* (*calf*, *cold*) one has the Anglian *c* in *C*alverton, *C*aldecote and *C*aldecotte in the north and middle of the county but *Ch*adwell in Stoke Hammond parish and *Ch*awley and *Ch*alvey in the south of the county. From field-name evidence we may note *Chaldewelle* in Bow Brickhill (1244), *Chadwell* in Akeley (1639), *Chaldewelle* in Thornborough (*c.* 1240), *Challwell* in Stewkley (1680), *Cheldewelle* in Edlesborough (1212). The only exception is *Kaldewelle* in Thornborough (*c.* 1260).

Characteristic of the dialect is the **loss of final *d* and *t* after a consonant**, as in Rockwell, [stɔkəl] for Stockholt, [wi·l] for Weald, and [hæmən] for *Hammond* in Stoke Hammond.

The **inflexional *n*** in the suffix of the weak adj. form long survived in Buckinghamshire though it has left no trace in the present forms of the place-names. See the history of the forms of Newton Blossomville and Longville and of the Claydons. So also we have *Smethenhill* in Emberton as late as 1639 and *Smithnell* in Dorney in 1706.

In two cases the modern editions of the O.S. maps obscure definite local dialect features. In Sheepcote Hill and Sheepridge, *Sheep-* has replaced the earlier and more correct *Ship-*, still preserved in local pronunciation. In Bourton and Nash Brake the local *breach*, preserved in *Breaches* Wood, has been replaced by an entirely different word.

An interesting feature of pronunciation, not necessarily dialectal, is the evidence which certain Buckinghamshire place-names give us for a **shifting of the stress** from the first syllable to the second, possibly under French influence. Such shifting can alone account for the pronunciation of OE *Wigrædesbyrig* as *Wraysbury*, for the very common *Shrington* for *Sherington*; it is further illustrated in the form *Tringeham* for Tyringham and it may help to account for the early loss of *t* in *Gayhurst* from *Gatehurst*. We may compare the development of Fringford (O) from *Færingaford* and Knowsley (La) from *Cenwulfesleah*.

ABBREVIATIONS

In addition to the abbreviations given in the *Chief Elements of English Place-names* (p. ix) the following have been used in the present volume.

AOMB	Augmentation Office Miscellaneous Books.
Abbr	*Placitorum abbreviatio*, 1811.
Abingd	*Historia monasterii de Abingdon*, 2 vols., 1858.
AC	*Ancient Charters* (Pipe Roll Soc.), 1888.
AD	*Catalogue of Ancient Deeds*. (In progress.)
AN	Anglo-Norman.
AddCh	Additional Charters in the British Museum.
Archd	Oxf. Archd. papers, Bucks (Bodleian).
Ass	Assize Rolls.
B	A. Bryant, *Map of the county of Buckingham*, 1826.
BM	*Index to the Charters and Rolls in the British Museum*, 2 vols., 1900–12.
Bodl	Bodleian Charters, *Buckinghamshire*. For any other county the abbreviation for the county is added after *Bodl*.
Bract	*Bracton's Note-book*, 3 vols., 1887.
BW	Browne Willis, *History and Antiq. of Buckingham*, 1755.
Ch	*Calendar of Charter Rolls*. (In progress.)
ChancP	*Chancery Proceedings in the reign of Elizabeth*, 3 vols., 1827–32.
Chauncy	Chauncy, *Hist. Antiquities of Herts*, 2 vols., 1826.
Cl	*Calendar of Close Rolls*. (In progress.)
Crawford	*Crawford Charters*, 1895.
Cocks	Deed in possession of A. H. Cocks, Esq.
Cur	*Curia Regis Rolls*. (In progress.)
Cur(P)	*Three Rolls of the King's Court* (Pipe Roll Soc.), 1891.
,,	*A Roll of the King's Court* (ib.), 1900.
D	*Letters and State Papers Domestic*, 12 vols., 1856–72.
DB	Domesday Book (with refs. to VCH ed. for Bucks).
Desb	Langley, *History of the Hundred of Desborough*, 1797.
Dugd	Dugdale, *Monasticon*, 6 vols. in 8, 1817–30.
Dunst	*Dunstable Cartulary* (Harl. 1885).
EDG	Wright, *English Dialect Grammar*, 1905.
Eland	Deeds in the possession of G. Eland, Esq.
EMidl	East Midland.
EModE	Early Modern English.
Encl	Leadam, *Domesday of Enclosures* (Royal Hist. Soc.), 1897.
EPN	*Chief Elements in English Place-Names*, 1923.
Eyns	*Eynsham Cartulary* (Oxf. Hist. Soc.), 2 vols., 1907–8.
FA	*Feudal Aids*, 6 vols., 1899–1920.
Fees	*Book of Fees*, 2 vols., 1922–3.

FF	Feet of Fines.
FF(P)	*Feet of Fines* (Pipe Roll Soc.), 1894, 1896, 1898, 1900.
Fine	*Calendar of Fine Rolls.* (In progress.)
FineR	*Excerpta e rotulis finium*, 2 vols., 1835–6.
Fines	*Fines, sive Pedes Finium*, ed. J. Hunter, 2 vols., 1835–44.
For	Pleas of the Forest.
Forssner	*Continental-Germanic Personal Names in England*, 1914.
Förstemann	*Altdeutsches Namenbuch, Personennamen* (PN), *Ortsnamen* (ON), 2 vols. in 3, 1901–16.
Foster	Deeds in the possession of the Rev. Canon C. W. Foster.
Fr	Calendar of documents preserved in France, 1899.
Godr	*Libellus de vita S. Godrici* (Surtees Soc.), 1847.
Godst	*English Register of Godstow Nunnery* (Early Eng. Text Soc.), 1905.
Gross	*Rotuli Roberti Grosseteste* (Lincoln. Rec. Soc.), 1913.
HarlCh	Harleian Charters in the British Museum.
Harman	*Ex inf.* A. Harman, Esq.
Herts Sess	*Hertford County Records, Notes from the Sessions Rolls*, 2 vols., 1905.
HMC	*Historical Manuscripts Commission.*
HMN, HMS	*An inventory of the historical monuments in Buckinghamshire*, 2 vols. (North, South), 1912–13.
Inq aqd	*Inquisitiones ad quod damnum* (Record Commission), 1803.
Ipm	*Calendar of Inquisitions post mortem.* (In progress.)
IpmR	*Inquisitiones post mortem* (Record Commission), 4 vols., 1806–28.
IPN	*Introduction to the Survey of English PN*, 1923.
J	T. Jefferys, *Map of Buckinghamshire*, 1766.
KCD	Kemble, *Codex Diplomaticus Aevi Saxonici*, 6 vols., 1839–48.
Kenil	Kenilworth Cartulary (Harl. 3650).
Lathbury	Lathbury, R. H., *History of Denham*, 1904.
L	George Lipscomb, *History and antiquities of the county of Buckingham*, 4 vols., 1847.
Lib	*Calendar of Liberate Rolls.*
Linc	Lincoln Episcopal Registers.
LDD	*Lincoln Diocese Documents* (Early English Text Society), 1914.
LP	*Letters and Papers Foreign and Domestic.* (In progress.)
LS	*Subsidy collected in the Diocese of Lincoln* (Oxford Hist. Soc.), 1909.
LVD	*Liber Vitae Dunelmensis* (Surtees Soc.), 1841.
Lysons	D. and S. Lysons, *Magna Britannia*, vol. i. 1806.
Marst	North Marston Deeds *pen.* Magdalen Coll. Oxford, transcribed by W. D. Macray.
Mert	Merton College Deeds, transcribed by W. H. Stevenson.
Misc	*Calendar of Inquisitions Miscellaneous*, 2 vols., 1916.
Miss	Missenden Cartulary (Harl. 3688).
NED	*New English Dictionary.*
New	Transcript of New College deeds made in 1640.

NI	*Nonarum Inquisitiones*, 1807.
NLC	*Newington Longueville Charters* (Oxfordshire Rec. Soc.), 1922.
Nostell	Nostell Cartulary (Cott. Vesp. E. xix).
Nth Surv	Northamptonshire Survey (VCH Nth, vol. 1).
O	Earliest ed. of 1 in. O.S. map, c. 1825.
OET	Sweet, *Oldest English Texts* (Early Eng. Text Soc.), 1885.
OFr	Old French.
Ogilby	Ogilby, *Itinerarium Anglicanum*, 1675.
Ord	Ordericus Vitalis, *Historia Ecclesiastica*, 5 vols., 1838–55.
Orig	*Originalia Rolls*, 2 vols., 1805–10.
O.S.	Ordnance Survey.
Oseney	Oseney Charters in the Bodleian Library.
(p)	Place-name form derived from personal name.
P	Pipe Roll (Pipe Roll Society's eds., in progress).
P	Pipe Rolls (unpublished).
Pat	*Calendar of Patent Rolls*. (In progress.)
PR	*Great Rolls of the Pipe* (Record Commission) (1844).
QW	*Placita de quo Warranto*, 1818.
RBE	*Red Book of the Exchequer*, 3 vols., 1896.
Reading	Reading Cartulary (Harl. 1708).
Rec	Records of Buckinghamshire. (In progress.)
Redin	Redin, M., *Uncompounded Personal Names in Old English*, 1919.
Reg Roff	*Registrum Roffense*, ed. Thorpe, 1769.
RH	*Rotuli Hundredorum*, 2 vols., 1812–18.
Ritter	Vermischte Beiträge zur Englischen Sprachgeschichte, 1922.
Rot Dom	*Rotuli de Dominabus* (Pipe Roll Soc.), 1913.
Rutland	*MSS of the Duke of Rutland* (Hist. MSS. Commission), 4 vols., 1905.
St Alb	*Chronica monasterii S. Albani* (Rolls Series), 3 vols., 1863–76.
St Frides	*Cartulary of the Monastery of St Frideswide* (Oxf. Hist. Soc.), 2 vols., 1895–6.
Saints	*Die Heiligen Englands*, ed. Liebermann, 1889.
Searle	Searle, *Onomasticon Anglo-Saxonicum*, 1897.
Tax	*Taxatio Ecclesiastica*, 1802.
Terr	Terriers, derived from the Oxf. Archd. Papers, Bucks (Bodleian).
Thornb	Thornborough Deeds *pen.* Magdalen Coll. Oxford, transcribed by W. D. Macray.
Thorpe	Thorpe, *Diplomatarium Anglicum aevi Saxonici*, 1865.
VCH	*Victoria County History of Buckinghamshire*, 2 vols., 1905–8.
VCH	Unpublished material for the same.
Vern	*Letters and Papers of the Verney Family* (Camden Soc.), 1852.
VE	*Valor Ecclesiasticus*, 6 vols., 1810–34.
WellsL	*Liber antiquus temp. Hugonis Wells* (ed. Gibbons), 1888.
WellsR	*Rotuli Hugonis de Welles* (Lincoln Rec. Soc. 3 vols.), 1912–14.

Westb Deeds	A list of Ancient Deeds relating to Westbury, Brackley etc., now at Magdalen College, Oxford, privately printed by the Rev. R. Usher.
Wigorn	Worcester Episcopal Registers.
Winton	Winchester Episcopal Registers.
WM	Wm. of Malmesbury, *De gestis regum Anglorum*, 2 vols., 1887–9.
WMP	id. *De gestis pontificum Anglorum* (Rolls Series), 2 vols., 1887–9.
Wyc	Borough of High Wycombe (Hist. MSS. Comm. Report v, App. i, 554–565).
>	Developes to.
<	Developes from.

Reference is made to the parish register of any particular parish by giving the name of the parish in full, *e.g.* Edgcott 1626, indicates a form found in the Edgcott Parish Registers *s.a.* 1626.

Reference is made to the various county place-name books already published (*v.* summary bibliography in *Chief Elements of English Place-names*) by using the abbreviation PN followed by the recognised abbreviation for the county, *e.g.* PN Gl for Baddeley's *Place-names of Gloucestershire*.

For the phonetic symbols used in the transcription of the local pronunciation of place-names, *v. Chief Elements of English Place-names*.

NOTES

(i) After the name of every parish will be found the reference to the sheet and square of the 1-in. O.S. map (Popular edition) on which it may be found. The area covered by those sheets is shown in the Key-map included in this volume. Thus, **Gayhurst** 84 G 1.

(ii) Where a place-name is only found on the 6-in. O.S. map this is indicated by putting '6″' after it in brackets, *e.g.* **Woodham** (6″).

(iii) The local pronunciation of the place-name is given, wherever it is of interest, in phonetic script within squared brackets, *e.g.* **Medmenham** [mednəm].

(iv) In explaining the various place-names summary reference is made to the detailed account of such elements as are found in it and are explained in the *Chief Elements of English Place-names* by printing those elements in clarendon type, *e.g.* **Gayhurst** *v.* **gat, hyrst**.

(v) In the case of all forms for which reference has been made to unprinted authorities, that fact is indicated by printing the reference to the authority in italic instead of ordinary type, *e.g. Ass* 1262 denotes a form derived from MS authority in contrast to FA 1284 which denotes one taken from a printed text.

(vi) Where two dates are given, *e.g.* 979 (12th), the first is the date at which the document purports to have been composed, the second is that of the date of the copy which has come down to us.

(vii) Where a letter in an early place-name form is placed within brackets, forms with and without that letter are found, *e.g. Bunstow*(*e*) means that forms *Bunstow* and *Bunstowe* are alike found.

(viii) All OE words are quoted in their West-Saxon form unless otherwise stated.

ADDENDA

p. 19. LINFORD. Professor Ekwall calls attention to the grave doubts as to the justification for rendering OE *hlynn* as 'stream, pool.' The only certain use of *hlynn* in OE is as the equivalent of Lat. *torrens*. The suggestion in the text should probably therefore be abandoned. There is however an OE *hlin*, found once in the Riddles (no. 56), as the name of wood derived from an unknown tree. It is assumed by Kluge and by Falk and Torp in their etymological dictionaries (s.v. *lehne*, *løn*) that this is the English cognate of ON *hlynnr*, Dan. *løn*, Sw. *lönn*, 'maple,' and that the true OE form is *hlyn*, the *i* being a late spelling for *y*. Linford may therefore be OE *hlynford*, 'maple-tree ford.' Topographical enquiry neither proves nor disproves this suggestion.

p. 49. TURWESTON. Professor Ekwall is inclined to throw over the solitary, if repeated, evidence for an *l* in this name found in the Assize Roll of 1227, and would prefer to take the first element to be an unrecorded Anglo-Scandinavian name representing an East Scandinavian one found as *Thoruaster* in Old Swedish (Lundgren-Brate, *Personnamn*, 267). This suggestion leaves intact the explanation offered above of the curious shifting of accent in this place-name.

p. 60. BUCKINGHAM. In checking the forms for this name the editors noted that while the Parker text has *Buccingahamme*, the D-text has *Buccingahámme*, with an accent marking the *a* as a long vowel. Such a form is an impossible one but the fact that it could be written suggests that the true form in both cases may be the perfectly possible *háme* rather than *hamme*. This would agree with the *ham* found in the *Saints*-document which is remarkable for the excellence of its place-name forms and with the whole of the later evidence. On *a priori* grounds an *-ingham* name is more likely to go back to OE *-ingaham* than *-ingahamm* and the unique forms of the Chronicle may be due to early consciousness of the nature of the site.

p. 87. BURCOTT. Professor Ekwall calls attention to the existence in OE of *burcote* (*v.* Bosworth-Toller, *Supplement*) glossing Lat. *cubile* and found once in a continuous passage in the plural with the meaning 'bed-chambers.' It is conceivable that the modern Burcott, in one or more instances, goes back to this compound of OE *būr*, used to denote a collection of sleeping-rooms forming a simple type of lodging. On the other hand if *burhcotu* is the correct early form its meaning may be either 'defensible cottages' or 'cottages by the *burh*,' though there is no evidence remaining for such a *burh* near Burcott in Wing.

BUCKINGHAMSHIRE

Buccingahamscir 1016 D (c. 1050) ASC, 1016 E (c. 1200) ASC
Bucinghamscir 1010 E (c. 1200) ASC
Bucingahamscir 1010 E (c. 1200) ASC

For the origin of the county name *v.* Introduction xi.

BUCKINGHAMSHIRE RIVER-NAMES

The forms of the river-names of Buckinghamshire so far as they are found in early documents are as follows. Their interpretation is reserved for the present as they can only satisfactorily be dealt with as a whole.

LOVAT, R.

Louente a. 1200 Gervase of Canterbury, 1262 *Ass*
Lovente 1306 Abbr
Lavente 1276 RH

The alternative name *Ouzel*, a diminutive of Ouse, is of quite modern origin.

MISBOURNE, R.

Misseburne 1407 HMC xv. App. vii. 130, 1427 ib.
Mysseburne 1412 ib.
Messeborne 1475 ib.

OUSE, R.

Vse 1227 *Ass*
Huse 1227 *Ass*, 1252 Misc
Use 1247 *Ass*

RAY, R.

(ut bi) *geht* 848 BCS 452
Giht 983 (c. 1200) Abingd
Ychte 1185 P
Yhyst 1298 VCH ii. 132

The original river-name possibly survives in Yeat Fm (*infra*). The new name Ray is explained in EPN s.v. æt.

In addition to these we may note that the Wye on which Wycombe stands may be a genuine old river-name though no early independent occurrence of it has been noted. *v.* Wycombe *infra*. On the other hand the Chess is certainly a back-formation from Chesham itself.

There was a lost *aqua de Bune* mentioned in the Assize Roll of 1242 when a certain Johannes filius Galfridi was found dead in Claydon fields having fallen from his cart into the water of *Bune* and been drowned. This is first mentioned in a charter of 995 (*Hist. Abingdon*, I. 395) as *Bunon* (acc. sg.) in the bounds of Ardley (O). The stream rises in the hills on the left bank of the Cherwell and is later known as Claydon Brook. The identification is made certain by the name *Bun*way Hill in Addington North Field in a Terrier of 1577. From Hill Farm in Addington a foot-path runs down to and crosses Claydon Brook. In 1266 (Misc) we have mention of a Robert atte *Reye* in East Claydon, which looks as if Claydon Brook, earlier Bune Water, nearly gave us another Ray river.

Other general names in the county are Chiltern, once applied to a whole district as well as to the range of hills, as in *Chiltern-sætna* in the tribal hidage (BCS 297) and Bernwood the name of a large forest area in the west of the county. For the early forms of these names *v.* Chiltern Hundreds and Bernwood Fm *infra*.

The Icknield Way crosses the county diagonally. It is first mentioned as *Icenhylte* in 903 (BCS 603). Other forms are

Ykenildestret 1227 *FF*
Ekenyld 1340 NI
Ykenyldewey 1348 CL

In 17th cent. terriers it appears as *Aconill*, *Ecknell*, *Icknell*, *Acknell* Way while *Acknell* and *Hackney* are common pronunciations of the road name to this day. No suggestion can be offered as to its etymology.

THE BUCKINGHAMSHIRE HUNDREDS

At the time of the compilation of Domesday the whole of the county was divided into eighteen Hundreds and the place-names in this volume have been dealt with Hundred by Hundred, proceeding roughly from North to South of the county, ac-

cording to the Domesday scheme[1]. In later days these Hundreds were grouped in triple Hundreds: Bunsty, Seckloe and Moulsoe Hundreds as Newport Hundred, Stotfold, Lamua and Rowley Hundreds as Buckingham Hundred, Yardley, Cottesloe and Mursley Hundreds as Cottesloe Hundred, Ashendon, Ixhill and Waddesdon Hundreds as Ashendon Hundred, Aylesbury, Stone and Risborough Hundreds as the Three Hundreds of Aylesbury, Desborough, Burnham and Stoke Hundreds as the Chiltern Hundreds.

I. BUNSTY HUNDRED

Bonestou 1086 DB, 1175 P
Bunestou 1175 P
Bunstow(e) 1178 P, 1255 *For*, 1284 FA
Bunestow(a) 1182, 1189 P, 1241, 1247 *Ass*
Bonestowe 1227, 1241 *Ass*

The site of the Hundred meeting-place may be identified with Bunsty Farm in Gayhurst, close to the main road from Newport Pagnell to Northampton. It stands on high ground, near the southern border of the Hundred. For the etymology of the name *v.* Bunsty *infra*.

Cold Brayfield

COLD BRAYFIELD 84 E 4

Bragenfeld 967 (12th) BCS 1209
Braufeld c. 1175 *Drayton Charters* (twice)
Brahefeld c. 1175 *Drayton Charters*
Bragefeld 1184 P (p)
Brainfeud c. 1218 WellsL
Bramfeld 1237–40 Fees 1452, 1276 RH
Brafeud 1242 Fees 873
Braunfeld 1247 *Ass*, 1280, 1325 Pat, 1340 NI
Branfeld 1247 *Ass*
Braumfeld by Turveye 1279 Ipm
Branfelde juxta Lavendene 1284 FA
Braunfeld by Turveye 1376 Cl

[1] A map of the Hundreds is included in this volume.

Professor Ekwall points out that this name must be identical with that of Brafield-on-the-Green (Nth), ten miles away on the other side of Yardley Forest, and that the first form here given might equally well refer to that place. Early forms of the Northants p.n. are DB *Brache(s)feld*, *Bragefelde*, Hy ii (1339) Ch *Bragefelde*, 1332 ib. *Braunfeld*, 1284 FA *Braunfeld*, 1316 ib. *Braifeld* and these fully confirm the suggestion. This would point to the use of the name *Bragenfeld* to denote a wide area of country, probably a forest area of which Yardley Chase is the chief survivor. No personal name is known which would explain the first element and Professor Ekwall suggests that it may possibly contain the old British name for this forest area, for it is just in such areas that the old Celtic names survive, and he points out that we may have a second example of this element in the *Bragenmonna broc* (BCS 1107) in the boundaries of Cotheridge (Wo), which has survived in Bransford (Wo). For the later phonetic development whereby the *n* or *m* is lost and *aum* becomes [a·m] > [eim], Ekwall notes the parallels of Stoford (So) from *Stanford*, Havant (Ha) from *Hamanfunta*, and Cambridge (C) from *Cauntbrigge*. See p. 127 *note*.

Lipscomb (iv. 47) says it might not improbably have obtained its name of *Cold* from its bleak and exposed situation. The epithet seems first to have been applied in the 16th cent. (*VCH*), presumably to distinguish it from the Brayfield over the border in Nth. *v.* feld.

Gayhurst

GAYHURST 84 G 1 [geiə·st]

Gateherst 1086 DB
Gaherst Radulfi de Niueres 1167 P
Gaherst 1184 P (p), 1189 P, 1229 Ch
Gahirst 1227 *Ass* (p), WellsR
Gayhirst 1227 *Ass*
Gaihurste 1227 WellsR
Gathurst 1237 Fees 1452, 1255 *For* (p)
Gahurst 1242 Fees 873, Gross, 1262 *Ass* (p), 1276 RH, 1284 FA, 1291 Tax, 1346 FA, 1389 Pat
Gayhurst 1242 Fees 895, 1321 *Bodl* 23
Goherst 1242 Gross

Gothurst(e) 1290 Ipm, 1302, 1316 FA, 1340 NI, 1350 Ipm, 1360 IpmR, 1369 Cl, AD iv, Pat, 1378 Cl, Pat, 1431 IpmR, 1513, 1526 LP
Gayehurst 1301 Inq aqd, 1535 VE
Gothirst 1360 Pat
Gahyrst 1400 Pat
Goteherst 1436, 1458 Pat
Gotehirst 1440 IpmR, 1468 Pat
Gottehurst 1452–72 *Linc*
Gotehurst 1496 Ipm, 1503 Pat, 1535 VE, 1526 LS, 1584 BM
Geyhurst 1526 LP
Gothurst or, as it is now commonly called 'Gayhurst.' Lysons 1806

'Goats' wood' *v.* gat, hyrst. The very early loss of *t* is remarkable, but has its parallel in Witham (Ess), ASC 913 *Witham*, but commonly *Wyham* after the Conquest (*v.* forms in Zachrisson, *AN Influence*, 88–9). In Gotham (Nt), where the *t* has been preserved, there is evidence of its temporary loss in the 12th cent. (*Gaham*, D and C Durham 2 iii Ebor 10). Side by side with forms with loss of medial *t* there would seem to have been others in which the *t* was preserved. The French form, without medial *t*, has survived to modern times, the Norman *a*, which was not changed to *o*, having been substituted for the early ME dark *a*, which would have, and also in this name sometimes did, become ME long open *o*, later shortened in the first element of the compound. This form seems to have passed completely out of use.

BUNSTY FARM

Bunestowe 1241 *Ass*
Bonisty 1276 RH

'Buna's place' *v.* stow. For the name *Buna* *v.* Redin 87. Such compounds of stow with a personal name not known as a saint's name are uncommon.

HOO WOOD

le Ho 1276 RH

'Wood on the hoh or spur of land,' projecting towards the Ouse.

STOCKING WOOD (6")

Stocking 1223 Pat

v. stocking.

Hanslope

HANSLOPE 83 G 13 [hænsləp]

Hammescle 1086 DB

(H)anslepe 1086 DB (p)

Hamslap(e) 1086 DB (p), 1189 P, 1208 Fees 20, 1211, 1212 Fines, 1217 Pat, 1227 *Ass*, WellsR, 1237 Fees 1452, 1241, 1247 *Ass*, 1255 *For*, 1262 *Ass*, 1281 Ipm, 1292 Ch, Pat, 1306 Cl, 1316 FA, 1317 Pat, 1398 Ipm

Hamesclapa P 1159

Hamesclaye 1201 Fines

Hameslap(e) 1175 P, 1217 Pat, 1246 Gross, 1304 Ipm

Haunslape 1227 *Ass*

Hampslep 1231 *FF*

Hamslepe 1235 Fees 469 (p), 1241 *Ass*

Hamslop 1247 *Ass*

Hamsesclap 1250 Fees 1224

Hampslap(e) 1302 FA, 1315 Cl, 1326 Pat, 1327 Fine, 1344 Pat, 1346 FA, 1371 Cl, 1423 AD ii, 1434, 1447 Pat

Hamslapp 1257 Ipm

Hameslappe 1262 *Ass*

Haunslep 1262 *Ass*

Hampeslape 1333 Cl

Hampslak 1370 Cl

Hanneslape 1415 Pat, 1535 VE

Hanslep 1480 IpmR, 1509 LP

Hanslope 1488 AD v, 1509 LP

Hanslape 1496 Pat, 1509 LP

Auncelope, *Anslope* 1532 LP

Hans(e)loppe 1566 AD vi, Eliz ChancP

Hanslapp 1626 Vern.

The second element is clearly slæpe. The main part of the village is on the flat, with a road leading straight up the hill to the church from the village (Harman). The first would seem to be a pers. name. The forms suggest the name *Hāma*, familiar in OE heroic poetry, known to be usual in the 8th and 9th cents.,

and compounded in the place-name Havant (Hants), OE *æt Haman funtan*, in which case the full form of the OE name was *Hāmanslǣpe*.

The later forms show either development of epenthetic *p* between *m* and *s* or assimilation of labial *m* to the dental *s*.

BALNEY (Upper, Lower, and Badger's) (6″) [bɑni]

Balneie 1281, 1316 Ipm

Ballan-hæg or *-hege*, 'Balla's enclosure or hedge,' *v.* (ge)hæg, hege. The site would seem to forbid our taking the suffix to be the more usual eg, ieg even in its widest interpretation and the meaning given agrees well with its description as a 'park' in 1281. *Balla would seem to be a pet-form of a name in *Beald-*, *v.* IPN 172–3. Cf. Ballinger *infra*.

BULLINGTON END

Bullenden End 1663 *VCH*

Probably 'bulls' valley,' *v.* bula, denu.

HUNGATE END

Herngate Ende 1616 Rec. xi. 210

v. hyrne. Possibly the 'nook' or 'corner' is the definite spur of land on which the hamlet stands.

LINCOLN LODGE

The property of the corporation of Lincoln, in whose hands the advowson of the church rested from 1546 to 1860 (*VCH*).

STOCKING GREEN

Stokking' 1254 *FF*

v. stocking.

TATHALL END [tætəl]

Totenhale 1227, 1241 *Ass*

Tothale 1255 *For* (p), 1302 FA (p), 1336 Cl, 1350 IpmR

Tottehale 1256 Pat (p)

Totehal(e) 1276 RH, c. 1300 Misc

Tothalle 1313 Inq aqd

Tatnalle 1535 VE

Totnall 1539 LP
Tottall End 1616 Rec. xi. 210
Tattle End 1766 J

OE *Totan-heale*, *v.* healh. The first element is a personal name *Tota*, *v.* Redin 70. There are two 8th cent. examples of this name, of which a still earlier example occurs in Tooting (Sr). With loss of intervocalic *t*, the same name has produced Toynton (L). The vowel has undergone late unrounding. *v.* Introd. xxiii.

Haversham

HAVERSHAM 84 H 1 [hɑˑʃəm]

æt Hæfæresham 1012 (12th) Thorpe 553
Havresham 1086 DB
Haueresham 1176 P
Haver(e)sham is found down to 1450, with a variant *Hever(e)-sham* in 1235 (Fees 461, 465)
Harsham 1542 LP
Haversham vulgo *Hasome* 1675 Ogilby

'Hæfer's homestead' *v.* ham. The pers. name *Hæfer* is not on record in OE but may be assumed on the basis of this name and such others as Averingdown *infra*, Havering (Ess) and various Germanic parallels (cf. Ekwall PN *-ing* 44–5).

Lathbury

LATHBURY 84 G/H 2

Late(s)berie 1086 DB
Lateberia Johannis 1167 P
Lateburia al. *Lateberia* 1185 Rot Dom
Lattesbri 1199 Cur (p)
Latebyria 1223 Bract
Latebiry 1225 Pat, 1227 Bract, 1235 Fees 468, 1247 *Ass*
Late(s)bire 1227 *Ass*
Latebur(e) 1232 Bract, 1235 Fees 464, 1241 *Ass*
Lattebiry 1232 Bract
Lathbury 1241 *Ass*, 1490 Ipm
Latthebyre 1241 *Ass*
Lathebir 1255 *For*

Lattebyr 1262 *Ass*
Latthebury 1276 Ipm, 1326, 1344 Pat, 1352, 1357 Cl
Lasceburi 1282 Ipm
Lathebiri 1284 FA
Lathebury 1302 FA, 1316 Fine, 1325 AD i, 1373 Cl
Lath(e)bery 1367 Pat
Lathesbury 1368 Orig
Laithebury 1373 Cl

This is possibly a compound of the ordinary word *lath* and *bury* (*v.* burh), the reference being to some feature of the structure of the *burh*. The variant forms of the name would agree well with this suggested etymology, for the word *lath* itself has forms *latte* and *latthe* in ME, the relationship of which to one another is a matter of difficulty. *v.* NED s.v.

ERNESDON WOOD (lost)

Ernesdene 1207 Fines
Ernisden 1229 Ch
Yernysden 1535 VE

'Eagle's valley' *v.* earn, denu. For the phonetic development cf. *Herneshulle* in Maids' Moreton (1236 *FF*), *Yernesell* (1607) Terr. and *Elmerscroft* (1670), *Yelmerscroft* (1674) in Marsh Gibbon Terriers.

Lavendon

LAVENDON 84 E 3 [laˑndən]

Lawe(n)dene, Lavendene 1086 DB
Lawendon 1185 P
Lavenden(e) 1201 FineR, c. 1218 WellsL
Lavendone 1232 WellsL

Forms *Lavenden* and *Lavendon* prevail down to 1490, with a great preponderance of *-den* forms.

Laundone 1232 WellsR
Launden(e) 1241 *Ass*, 1281 Ipm, 1315, 1394, 1488 Pat, 1525 LP
Lawnden 1509 LP
Lavenden al. *Launden* Lavendon 1639

'Lafa's valley' *v.* denu. One English example of this personal name is recorded (Redin 51) and it is found also in Lavenham

(Sf). It is in origin a short form of a compound name ending in *lāf*, such as *Deorlāf* or *Wulflāf*.

ADDERSLEY (lost)

Adirsey 1535 VE
Aldersey 1766 J

This is spoken of as *Hatheresey* in *Rec. of Bucks.* ii. 218 and it is said that it is now Addersley near Eakley Lanes. The name is probably OE *Ēadheres ēg*, 'Eadhere's island,' *v.* eg. The later forms seem to be corrupt.

SNELSON

Snellestone(e) 1272 Ipm, 1284 FA, 1307 Pat, 1325 Cl, 1354 Ipm
Snelston 1513 AD i
Snelson 1826 B

'Snell's farm.' The name *Snell* (Redin 25) may be either of English or Scandinavian origin. In the 12th cent., the name *Snel* was borne by a serf of Shaftesbury abbey, doubtless a man of English descent (Harl. MS 61). The same name forms the first element of Snelsmore (Berks), where, again, it is more likely to be English than Scandinavian. Snelston (Db) and Snelson (Ch) which are formally identical with the present name may contain either the English *Snel*, or the ON *Sniallr* in an Anglicised form.

SNIP WOOD

Snypwode 1328 Cl

Probably '*snipe*-wood' though it stands on rather high ground to take its name from that bird. If it is the ordinary word *snip* that word goes back some 200 years earlier than the examples given in the NED and there is the possible further difficulty that the early forms of that word are spelled *snippe*.

TINICK (Fm)

Tynnokeswade (sic) 1227 Dugd. vi. 888
Tenokfeld 1543 LP
Ten Oak Field 1573 L. iv. 212
Tinnock fielde c. 1690 *Terr*

This would seem to be 'ten-oak(s)-wood' or 'field,' with early raising of *e* to *i* before following *n*. Cf. Tinhead (W) for *Tenhide*.

UPHOE (Manor)

Upho 1234 Ch, 1469 IpmR

'Upper spur of land' *v.* **hoh**. It stands on a well-marked spur of land.

Newton Blossomville

NEWTON BLOSSOMVILLE 84 E 4

Niwetone 1175 P
Neutona 1178 P
Newetone 1189 P
Newentone 1202 Fines

Down to 1400, *Neweenton* forms, with inflexional *-en*, are twice as numerous as the *Neuton* or *Newton* ones. After that we have

Newnton 1424 IpmR, 1536 LS, 1680 *Terr*
Newton 1513 LP
Neweenton 1524 LP

Robert de Blosseville is party to a fine in Newton B. in 1202[1] and his name is first attached to the manor in 1251 (Gross). Thereafter it appears as

Blostmevill(e) 1311 Cl, 1340 NI
Blosseville 1316 Pat, 1375 AD vi
Blosmeville 1358 Pat, 1391, 1424 IpmR
Blossomvyle 1397 AD v
Blosinveyll 1513 LP
Blosmaville 1524 LP
Blossomville 1526 LS
Blosefyld 1584 *Archd*

'New farm' *v.* **niwe, tun**.

1 Earlier association with the manor is suggested in *VCH*. Gilbert de Blossevile held two hides and a virgate in Lavendon in DB and this manor may be identified with Newton B. Lavendon is now separated from Newton by Cold Brayfield but the latter parish was assessed under Lavendon in DB and later.

COSTER PITS (Fm)

Coster ffeilde 1605 *Terr*

The first element is probably ME *costard*, 'apple.' Cf. Shenley Terrier, c. 1680 *Custard field*, c. 1700 *Coster field*.

Olney

OLNEY 84 E/F 2 [ouni]

Ollanege (dat.) 979 (12th) KCD 621
Olnei 1086 DB
Olnea 1175, 1189 P
Ouneya 1207 FineR
Ouneia 1208 Fines
Auneye 1227 *Ass*
Oleneye 1233 Lib
Olneye 1237–40 Fees 1452
After 1262 (*Ass*) the regular spelling is *Olney*(*e*), except for
Oulney 1658 Chicheley, 1766 J

'Olla's island' *v.* eg. Olney is almost surrounded by water. That there was an OE pers. name **Olla* is almost certain from the 10th cent. form of this name, which has preserved a double *l* of which there is no other trace. Such gemination frequently appears in hypocoristic personal names. It is possible that **Olla* may have been a short form of *Ōslāf*, but the name may well be very ancient, and its origin consequently lost.

OLNEY HYDE

la Hide 1343 Cl
v. hid.

Ravenstone

RAVENSTONE 84 F 1 [rɔˑnstən]

Raveneston 1086 DB
Raueneston(*e*), *Raueneston'* 1167 P, 1206 PR
Rauenestun 1253 Ch, c. 1260 *Bodl* 3
Rauenstone 1304 *Bodl* 19

with forms in *Raven*(*e*)*ston* down to

Raunston 1379 *Bodl* 36, 1465 ib. 37, 1471 Pat, 1509 LP, 1526 LS

Ranstone 1693 *Stoke Gold. Terr*
Ravenstone also *Raunston* 1568 Ravenstone

'Hrafn's farm,' the name being probably of Scand. origin, though the existence of names like Raveningham (Nf) makes it possible that we should carry the name back further and believe that it may also be from OE **Hræfn*. For the sound-development cf. Ranskill (Nt).

PARKFIELD (Fm)

This must take its name from the 'great park' in Ravenstone mentioned in *Bodl* 7 in 1270.

Stoke Goldington

STOKE GOLDINGTON 84 F 1

Stoches 1086 DB
Stoch Petri de gold' 1167 P
Stoke c. 1215 WellsR
Stokes 1235 Fees 461, 1251 Ch
Stok 1241 *Ass*
Stoke Goldington 1262 *Ass*

Peter of Goldington (co. Bedford) was an important tenant of the Honour of Peverel of Nottingham, to which the greater part of this place belonged. The association of his name with the place is at least as early as 1167.

EAKLEY LANES [iˑəkli]

Yckeleia c. 1165 (12th cent.) *Cart Ant* P 37[1]
Ykelee 1212 RBE
Ykele c. 1215 WellsR
Yckele 1229 *FF*
Ikelegha 1236 Bract
Ikelee 1241 *Ass*
Iocle 1242 Fees 873
Ykkele 1262 Ipm
Ykelei 1265 Misc
Ekley al. *Ikeley* 1616 Ipm (*VCH*)
Eakly 1693 *Terr*

[1] The first letter is blurred in the *Cart. Ant.* enrolment, and may be read either as I or Y. It was read as Y by Dugdale in the 17th cent., when the roll was no doubt more legible.

This would seem to be from OE *Iccan-leah*, 'Icca's clearing,' with the same personal name as is found in Itchenor (Sx), *Iccannore* (BCS 64, a spurious charter), Ickworth (Sf) and in Ickford *infra*.

Alternatively the personal name might be *Ica* as in *Icangæt* (BCS 240, a spurious charter), *Icancumb* (ib.), but as the latter appears as *Iccacumb* in BCS 1135 one cannot lay much stress on it. *Ick-* for *Itch-* is to be accounted for by early syncope of the vowel between *c* and *n*.

The lengthening of the vowel is difficult to account for. *Lanes* is a feudal addition, one of the two manors in the old parish of Eakley having been long in the possession of a family named *Lane* (Lysons 634).

HARLEY FIELD (Farm) (6″)

Harley 1607 *Terr*

'Boundary clearing.' It lies on the border of Gayhurst Par. and the elements are probably **har** and **leah**.

STOKE PARK WOOD

'Wood called Stoke Park' 1496 Ipm.

Self-explanatory.

Castle Thorpe

CASTLE THORPE 83 H 13

Castelthorpe 1252 Gross, 1401, 1447 IpmR
Throp 1255 *For*
Castelthrope 1486 Pat
Thrupp 1616 Rec. xi. 208

'The village (OE þorp) by the castle' of Hanslope, the head of the barony of that name.

Tyringham with Filgrave

TYRINGHAM 84 G 2 [tiriŋəm]

Te(d)lingham 1086 DB
Tringeham 1130 PR (p)
Tiringham 1184 P (p)

Tiringeham 1185 P (p), 1189 ib., 1237 Fees 1452
Tyringeham(a) c. 1215 WellsR (p), 1242 Fees 889
Tyringham 1227, 1241, 1247 *Ass*, 1284 FA, 1288 Ipm, 13th AD ii, iii, vi
Teryngham 1288 Ipm, 1323 Cl, 1406 IpmR, 1485 Pat, 1492 AD ii
Tirincham 13th AD vi
Tyrringham 1517 Encl
Terringham 1526 LS

The name appears once as *Tyrington* (1252 Gross).

'The ham of Tir's people,' *Tīr* being a pet-form of one of the OE names in *Tīr-*. The vowel has been shortened in the trisyllable. For the DB form, *v.* IPN 106. For the 1130 form *v.* Introd. xxvi. This early development of initial *tr* is strongly against any defence of the *d* in the DB form on the score that the p.n. might be derived from an OE pers. name in *Tīd-*.

* FILGRAVE 84 F 1

Firigraue c. 1218 WellsL
Filegrave 1240 Gross, 1247, 1262 *Ass*, *Inferior and Superior* 1284 FA
Fylegrave 1240 Gross, 1242 *Ass*, 1328 Pat
Fillegrave 1242 Fees 873, 1320–42 *Linc*
Phillegrave 1242 Fees 893, 1320–42 *Linc*
Philegraue 1247, 1262 *Ass*
Filgrave Magna, *Parva* 1316 FA, 1491 Ipm
Felgrave 1405 Pat, 1526 LP

This is probably from OE *Fyglan-græf*, 'Fygla's **græf**,' *v.* **græf**. The pers. name **Fygla* is found in Fyling (Y), Fillingham (L) and Figheldean (W). Already in DB the *g* of *Fygla* has disappeared in two out of the three forms for Fillingham. For the *r*, *v.* IPN 106. Originally divided into Lower and Upper Filgrave, alternatively known as Great and Little.

Warrington

WARRINGTON 84 E 3

Wardintone c. 1175 *Drayton Charters*
Wardington 1294 Ch, 1604 D

Wardynton 1326 Pat, 1353 Cl
Wardyngton 1343 Ch, 1350 Ipm, 1375 AD iii, 1391 IpmR, 1403 AD v
Waryngton 1474 Pat, 1545 LP

'Wearda's farm' *v.* **-ingtun.** This pers. name is not found independently in OE nor have we any compounds in *Weard-*, though names of this type are common in other Germanic languages. A pers. name *Wearda* may however be assumed from the p.n. *Weardan dun* (BCS 789) and *Weardan hyll* (ib. 663) and Wardington (O).

Like the name *Lafa* which occurs in Lavendon, *Wearda* when used as a personal name probably represents the shortening of a compound by using its second element. **Wearda*, that is, may be a short form of such a name as Leof*weard*, Æthel*weard*, or Wulf*weard*. The loss of *d* must be due to assimilation.

Weston Underwood

WESTON UNDERWOOD

Westone 1086 DB
Weston by Laundene 1281 Ipm
Weston by Olneye 1344 Pat
Westone Underwode 1363 Cl

West, probably in relation to Olney, *Underwood* in relation to Yardley Chase.

II. SECKLOE HUNDRED

Sigelai 1086 DB
Seggeslawa 1182 P, 1247, 1262 *Ass*, 1276 RH
Seggelawa 1189 P
Segelawa 1195 P, 1262 *Ass*
Seggelawe 1232 Fees 135
Segghelawe 1241 *Ass*
Segelowe 1284, 1302 FA
Seglowe 1316, 1346 FA

The second element is **hlaw**. The first may be a personal name *Secgg(a)* or, more probably, it is the OE *secg*, 'warrior,'

in the gen. pl. *secga*. Intrusive *s* is common in such forms as *Seggeslawa*. 'Warriors' hill' might well be the name for a Hundred meeting-place. The change from *g* [dʒ] to *k* is difficult and the gap of three hundred years in the forms unfortunate.

The actual site of the meeting-place has not hitherto been identified but in a Loughton Terrier we have *Secloe feilde* (1639) and *Seclo* (1693), while in Bradwell Terriers we have thrice mention in the 17th cent. of *Seckley field*. Etymologically this name may well be identical with that of the Hundred, and a place on the border of Bradwell and Loughton parishes would be central for the whole Hundred. If this is correct, the exact site may be on Bradwell Common, where cross-roads meet, at the highest point.

Bletchley

BLETCHLEY 95 B 2

Blechelai 1152–8 NLC
Blacchelai 1155 ib.
Blecelaie 1160–5 ib.
Blechelee 1212 Fines, 1310 NLC
Bletchele 1227 *Ass*, 1380 Pat
Blechesleye 1328 Cl

There were two manors in Bletchley, Church B. and Old or West B. manor (Lysons 51). These are called respectively *Overbleccheleye* (1325 Cl) and *Westbleccheslee* (1328 Cl).

'Blæcca's clearing' *v.* **leah**. The name *Blæcca* was borne by a 7th cent. *prefectus* of Lincoln. It forms the first element in Bletchingley (Sr) and Blatchington (Sx). The strong form **Blæc*, not found independently, occurs in Bletchingdon (O) and, perhaps, in Bletsoe (Beds).

Bradwell

BRADWELL 84 J 1 [brædəl]

Bradewelle 1086 DB, 1152–8, 1160–5 NLC, 1199 Fines
Brodewelle 1086 DB
Bradewulla 1155 NLC

The form *Bradewelle* prevails till 1378 with an occasional *Bradwell*. After that the latter form is the regular one.

'Broad spring' *v.* **brad, wielle**.

Calverton

CALVERTON 83 J 13 [kælvətən]

Calvretone 1086 DB
Caluerton 1227 *Ass*
Calvertone 1284 FA

OE *cealfra-tūn*, 'calves' farm' *v.* **cealf, tun**. The Nt place of this name is called [kɔ·vətən] or [kɑ·vətən], but no pronunciation except the spelling one has been traced for this one. In 1227 (*Ass*) there is mention of a *Caluercote*, apparently in Calverton.

BLACON BARN [bleikən]

Blaken field 1639 *Terr* (*VCH*)
Blacon ffielde 1680 *Calverton Terr*

This may represent OE *blacan*, weak dat. sg. of **blæc**, with later lengthening of the vowel in the open syllable, but the forms are too late for any certainty.

STONY STRATFORD WEST

Stani Stratford 1202 Fines
Strafford 1223, 1257 Ch
Stratfordia 1231 Bract

Forms in *Strat-* occur regularly to 1300. The first *Stret-* form is in

Stony Stretteford 1290 Ch

and from then down to 1400 they are twice as frequent as those in *Strat-*. In the 15th and 16th cents. *Stret-* forms are a good deal more common than *Strat-* ones. The form *Stony* is first found in 1257 (Ch) and is the regular one henceforward.

Stonyng Stretford 1491 Ipm

'The stony ford where (Watling) street crosses the Ouse' *v.* **stræt**. To become passable there must have been incredible material put down to afford a firm foundation...most probably the bed of the river was filled with stones, the depth at crossing now being some ten or a dozen feet (Harman).

WEALD (Upper, Middle and Lower) [wi·l]

Wald(e) 1199 Abbr, 1241 *Ass*, 13th AD iv (p), 1324 Cl

Waude 1241 *Ass* (p), 1324 Cl (p)
la Welde 1291 Ch (p), 1329 Cl (p)
atte Welde 1353 Cl (p)
the Weild 1626 Vern
Weale 1766 J, c. 1825 O, 1826 B

'Forest-land' *v.* **weald**. By position it must have been included in Whaddon Chase, forming an integral part of it, on the escarpment descending to the valley of the Ouse (Harman). The southern form *weld* from OE *weald* has ousted the earlier *wald*, which may be either the Anglian form which developed to *wold* or OE *weald* with the short diphthong preserved (Introd. xxiii). Upper Weald is called *Over* Weald in all the early maps.

Water Eaton

WATER EATON 95 B 2

Etone 1086 DB, 1232 Fees 1351, 1247 *Ass*, 1469 BM
Ettone 1185 Rot Dom, 1284 FA
Wattar Yeton 1534 LP
'River-farm' *v.* **ea**, **tun**.

WATERHALL

La Waterhall 1273 Ipm
So called from its situation on the Ouzel.

Great and Little Linford

LINFORD (Great and Little)[1] 84 H 1

(*a*) *Linforde* 1086 DB, 1175 P, 1224 Bract, 1225 Abingd, 1227 *Ass*, 1232–42 Fees *passim*, 1238 Gross, 1247, 1262 *Ass*, 1291 Tax
Lindeford 1175 P (p)
Lynford 1284 FA, Ch, 1392 AD ii, 1494 AD ii, 1496 Ipm, 1561 BM
Limford 1291 Tax
Lymford 1316 Ch, 1326 Abbr, 1535 VE
Mechel Lyngford 1396 Pat
Lidforth 1542 LP, *Lydforth* 1561 BM
Lyndford 1560 BM
Lenford 1561 BM

[1] Great Linford is in Seckloe, Little Linford in Bunsty Hundred.

(*b*) *Lufforde*, *Lunforde* 1220–34 WellsR
Lunforde 1227, 1241 *Ass*
Parua is first applied in 1224 (Bract) and *Magna* in 1227 (*Ass*).

OE *hlynn-ford*, 'ford by the stream or pool,' *v.* hlynn. There are spacious ponds amounting to small lakes both at Great and Little Linford (Harman). The *Lin-*, *Lyn-* forms are the regular EMidl forms, those in *Lun-* are Southern. The *Lym-* forms show partial assimilation of *nf* to *mf*, those in *ndf*, a common development of epenthetic *d*, those in *Lid-*, *Lyd-* simplification of the consonant group *ndf*. See Addenda.

* MARSH (Fm) (6″)
Merchs 1310 BM
le Marsh 1311 Inq aqd
(*Tykeford cum*) *Maresco* 1316 FA
v. mersc. Cf. Lat. *mariscus*, 'marsh.'

Loughton

LOUGHTON 95 A 1 [lautən]
Lochintone 1086 DB
Lufton 1152–8 NLC
Lugton(*a*) 1155 NLC, 1186 P
Locoton 1160–5 NLC
Luctune 1199 NLC
Lughton(*e*) 1219 WellsR (*Parva*), 1237–40 Fees 1451, 1325, 1362 Cl, 1367 Pat, 1376 Cl
Luwetune 1235 NLC
Luhtone 1241 *Ass*
Luffton 1242 Fees 892
Luchton 1242 Fees 872, 1245 Gross, 1262 *Ass*
Lauton c. 1275 *Bodl* 48
Lucton 1284 FA (*Magna*)
Loghton 1300 Ipm, 1316 FA
Louton 1284, 1302 FA
Loughton(*e*) 1300–20 *Linc*, 1346 FA, 1352 Ipm, 1378 Cl, 1493 Ipm
Lowton 1512 LP

OE *Luhingtūn*, 'Luha's farm.' Cf. *Luhantreow* in Crawford

Charters 49 (10th cent. MS). The name *Luha* occurs once, at the beginning of the 10th cent. The variant forms are largely due to the difficulty of the medial spirant [χ], which at one stage showed signs of developing to *f*. Cf. Broughton, Woughton *infra*. There were two parishes, Great and Little, but these were united in 1409 (*VCH*). *v*. **ingtun**.

Newport Pagnell

NEWPORT PAGNELL 84 H 2 [njuˑpət pænəl]

Neuport 1086 DB

v. **niwe, port**. It was already a borough in DB.

Under Hy ii (*AddCh* 47423–4) Godwin of *Neuport* or *Niwporte* attests charters of Gervase *Pagnell* and the borough is called *Neuport Paynelle* in 1220 (Bracton). It was part of the Barony of Dudley, which belonged to the Paynel family. *Paynel* or *Pain(n)el* is the common form of the second part of the name in the 13th and 14th cents., *Panell* first appears in 1367 (IpmR) and *Pannell* in Eliz (ChancP). The form *Pagnell* is from the Latinised form of the name, *Paganellus*.

BURY FIELD

Buryfeld 1454 AD vi, 1457 AD ii

Byryfeld 1470 AD ii

Bury Field is still unenclosed meadow land. The burgage holders in the borough had rights of pasture in this land, which was part of the lord's demesne (*VCH*). *bury* therefore denotes 'manor' here. *v*. **burh**.

CALDECOTE

Caldecote 1086 DB

Caudecote 1250 Fees 1215, 1272 Ipm

Calcote 1526 LP

'Cold cottages' *v*. **ceald, cot**. Lies on the top of rising ground, in an exposed situation.

KICKLE'S FARM

Gyckeley 1276 RH

Yclele 1279 Ipm

Gikkele rectius *Yickele* 1284 FA

Yckeleye 1302 FA
Yekele 1316 FA
Ikkele 1346 FA, 1350 Pat
The Hickles 1766 J

This is a difficult name but the first element may be a lost OE pers. name *Gicel(a)*, connected with OE *gicel* 'icicle.' The corresponding ON *Iǫkull* is used freely both as a first name and as a nickname. Professor Ekwall suggests alternatively an OE **Gīecla*, a diminutive from *gēac*, and Professor Zachrisson a pers. name **Gicca* from **Gīsica*, a diminutive of a name in *Gīsl*. The second is **leah**. The modern form is pseudo-comic as well as pseudo-manorial. For the dropping of the initial [j] cf. Ixworth (Sf), Easington (Nb), Ickwell (Mx), Ipswich (Sf).

PORTFIELDS (Fm)

le Portyfeld 1291 Ipm

v. **port**, **feld**. 'Town-(open)-field.' Cf. Portmeadow in Oxford.

Newton Longville

NEWTON LONGVILLE 95 C 1

Neutone 1086 DB
Newentona 1152–8 NLC

Down to the end of the 14th cent. forms in *Neu-*, *New-* are slightly more frequent than those in *Newen-*. After that *New-* forms tend to prevail but we have

Newenton 1402 Pat
Newnton 1526 LS, 1607, 1693 and 1703 *Terr*

OE *nīwan tune* (dat.), 'new farm,' *v.* **niwe**, **tun** (Introd. xxvi). The feudal addition records the fact that Newton was granted c. 1152–8 to the church of St Faith of Longueville by Walter Giffard, Earl of Buckingham, who was lord of Longueville as well as Newton. It is first attached to the p.n. in 1241 (*Ass*) and appears in the forms *Longeville* and *Lungeville*. It becomes *Longfylde* in 1526 LS, 1607 *Terr*. *v.* Introd. xxv.

BANDLAND COTTAGE (6″)

No early form of this name has been noted but it must be

the same as that found in the following field-names: *Banlond* in Thornborough (c. 1240), *Banland* in Loughton (1639), in Stewkley (1680), *Bandland* in Wavendon (1674), Loughton and Milton Keynes (1693), *Banneland* in Stoke Goldington (1607), *Bannland* in Marsh Gibbon (1674). OE bean, as in Banstead (Sr) always appears as *ben-* in Bk field-names and therefore seems impossible here. It is tempting to associate it with the word *ban* and to think of the compound as denoting land under some kind of prohibition, but there is no other evidence for such a usage.

TICKFORD END

Ticheforde 1086 DB
Tikeforde 1200 Fines, 1220 WellsR, 1241 *Ass* (p), 1284 FA, 1324 *Bodl* 49
Thickford 1240 Gross
Tykeford 1300 Cl, 1310 BM, 1316 FA, 1378 Pat
Tikford 1383 *Bodl* 58
Tykford 1470 AD ii

A *Thickelege* is found in or near Tickford in 1200 (Fines).

The first element is probably ticcen, 'kid,' animals' names being often thus associated with fords. For the phonetic development we may compare Ticknall (Db), KCD 710, 1298 *Ticcenheal(l)e*. The *n* was early lost from the consonant group *knf*.

Shenley

SHENLEY (Brook End and Church End)[1]

Senelai 1086 DB
Schenlega 1182 P
Schenle 1198 Fines, 1229 WellsR, 1242 Fees 878, 1262 *Ass*, 1302 FA (*Magna*)
Sanle(ia) 12th Ord, 1189 P, 1276 RH
Senle(a) 1189 P, 1223 WellsR, 1284 FA (*Nethere*)
Ouer(e)schenle 1262 *Ass*
Syndele 1291 Tax, *Sindele* 1337 Pat
Shenle Maunsel 1303 Ch
Shenle al. *Shendeley* 1435 Pat
Shendeley 1535 VE
Shenley Mansell 1826 B

[1] Brook End is in Mursley (now Cottesloe) Hundred.

OE *scīenan-lēage* (dat.), 'bright clearing,' *v.* sciene, leah, cf. Shenley, Herts. At one stage there was a tendency to develop epenthetic *d*. Shenley Church End stands on higher ground and was hence called *Over* Shenley. It was also known as *Magna* Shenley. Shenley Brook End is alternatively distinguished as *Nether* or *Parva* or *Ma(u)nsell*, the association with the Mansell family going back to the 13th cent. (Fees 461).

SHENLEY BROOK END

The 'Joh. atte *Brok*' who is mentioned in 1360 (Ipm) presumably lived at Brook End.

WESTBURY (Fm)

Westberie 1284 FA
le Westbury 1284 Ipm

'West,' probably in relation to the settlement of Shenley itself, and if so, pointing to Brook End as the older settlement. *v.* burh.

Simpson

SIMPSON 95 A 2

Sevinstone 1086 DB
Siwinestone 1086 DB, 1227 *Ass*, 1231 WellsR, 1237 Fees 1451
Sywynestone 1241, 1262 *Ass*, 1324 Cl
Seweneston(e) 1302 FA, 1350 Ipm, 1429 Pat
Suenston 1434 Pat, 1485 Ipm (al. *Synston*)
Symston 1495 Pat, 1535 VE
Simston 1526 LS
Simpton 1626 Vern
Sympson 1674 *Terr*

OE *Sigewines-tūn*, 'Sigewine's farm,' *v.* tun. The name *Sigewine*, of which only four examples are recorded before the end of the 11th cent., survived at least a hundred years later in the forms *Siwin*, *Sewin*. OE names compounded with *Sige* ('victory') are not common in local nomenclature. Selmeston (Sx) comes from *Sigehelm*, Sewardstone Green (Ess) from *Sigeweard*, Syerscote (St) from *Sigeric*, Syresham (Nth) and Syerston (Nt) come from *Sigehere*, Simondshall (Gl) and Symondsbury (Do) from *Sigemund*.

Stantonbury

STANTONBURY 84 J 1

Stanton(e) 1086 DB
Staunton 1235 Fees 314
Staunton Barry 1300 Ipm

Down to 1538 forms in *Stan-* and *Staun-* are equally common, with forms *Ston(e)-* in 1290 Ipm, 1377 Cl, 1464 Pat. After that the form *Stanton* prevails.

For the meaning *v.* stan. The form *Stantonbury* is a late corruption, said to be due to the 17th cent. lord of the manor (Sir John Wittewrong) who changed the name from *Barry* to *Bury* in consequence of the unearthing of numerous human remains in the parish (VCH). The form *-bury* however is found as early as c. 1450 in the Lincoln Diocesan Registers.

In 1235 Radulfus *Barri* held a fee in Stanton, and his name is associated with the place from 1300 onwards, the form *Stanton Barry* being found as late as Lysons (1806), *v.* IPN 105.

Stoke Hammond

STOKE HAMMOND 95 C 2 [stouk hæmən]

Stoches 1086 DB
Stokes 1185 Rot Dom, 1198 Fines, 1235 Fees 462
Stokes Hamund 1242 Fees 883
Stoke Hamund 1247 *Ass*
Stoke Hamond 1346 FA
Stokehamon 1535 VE, Eliz ChancP

v. stoc. Derives its name from *Hamon* son of Mainfelin, a 12th cent. descendant of the DB holder of the manor. Introd. xxvi.

* CHADWELL

Chaddle Barn 1826 B

This is pretty certainly OE ceald-wielle, 'cold spring,' in view of Chadwell (Ess, Lei, W) which have the same history. Cf. *FF* 1244 *Chaldewelle* in Bow Brickhill.

TYRELL'S MANOR (6″)

Lipscombe (iv. 359) says that Stoke Hammond came in Hy viii's time, about 1515, to the Tyrrells.

Fenny Stratford

FENNY STRATFORD

Fenni Stratford 1252 Ch
Fenny Stretford 1338 Pat

Forms in *Strat-* have been noted seven times down to 1509 as against four *Stret*-forms to 1533. In 1493 Pat we have *Veny Stratford*. *v.* Introd. xxv.

Fenny Stratford lies on Watling Street (*v.* stræt) and is so called in contrast to Stony Stratford. Fenny or marshy ground still exists at the bottom of the ascent upon which the town lies high and dry (Harman).

Willen

WILLEN 84 J 2

Wyle 1189 P
Wily 1189 P
Wilie 1208 Fines, 1242 Fees 872
Wilies c. 1218 WellsL, 1235 WellsR
Wylien(e) 1235 Fees 463, 1343 Misc, E iii IpmR, 1357 Ipm
Wylyen(e) 1262 *Ass*, 1346 FA, 1349 Cl, Pat, 1356 Fine, 1490 Ipm
Wylie 1237 Fees 1451, 1327 Ch, 1340 NI, 1349 Pat
Wylies 1240 Gross, 1284 FA
Wilne 1316 FA
Wyllyn 1517 Encl
Willien 1766 J
Wyllien 1806 Lysons

The modern form represents OE (*æt þæm*) *wyligum*, '(at the) willows,' *v.* welig. Alternative forms from the nom. sg. and nom. pl. seem also to have been used in early days.

Wolverton

WOLVERTON 83 J 14

Wlverintone 1086 DB
Wulfrintone 1195 CurP
Wolfrington 12th Nth Surv., c. 1218 WellsL
Wulurinton 1227 *Ass*

Wulverton 1227 *Ass*, 1262 *Ass*
Wulvreton 1227 *Ass*
Woluerington 1227 *FF*
Wlfrinton c. 1220 Eyns
Wlfreton 1237 Fees 1451
Wulrington 1240 Gross
Wulfrington 1241 *Ass*, 1276 RH
Wolurington 1262 *Ass*
Wulurington 1262 *Ass*
Woluerton 1262 *Ass*
Wolvrinton 1297 Pat
Wolvertone 1302 FA

'Wulfhere-farm,' the first element being a common pers. name. *v.* ingtun. Other names derived from *Wulfhere* are Woolverstone (Sf), Wolvershill (Wa) and Wolferlow (He). The *Wolverton*-forms as distinct from the *Wolvrington*- ones appear so early that we should perhaps be right in assuming that there were early alternative forms of the name—*Wulfheretun* and *Wulfheringtun*—rather than that the former are a reduction of the latter. A similar case is Alverton (Nt), DB *Alvretun*, 1190 *Alvrington*.

STONEBRIDGEHOUSE (Fm) (6″)
Stanebrige 13th (*VCH*)
Self-explanatory.

Woolstone

WOOLSTONE (Great and Little) 84 J 2 [wulsən]
Ulsiestone, *Wlsiestone* 1086 DB
Wulfsieton 1186 P
Wolse(s)ton c. 1218 WellsL
Wulsistone c. 1220 WellsR
Parva Wolsistone 1231 WellsL, 1235 Fees 465, 1274 Ipm
Wulliston, *Parva Wulsinton* 1236 Gross
Wlsintone 1237 Fees 1451
Wlfistone 1247 *Ass*
Wls(e)ton 1251 Gross, 1292 Ipm
Wlsiston 1255 RH
Wolfeston 1273 Ipm

Wolston(e) 1284 FA (*Parva* and *Magna*), 1333 Cl, 1490 Ipm
Wolstone Coudray 1302 FA
Wollestone 1323 Cl
Wulston 1526 LS, 1535 VE
Wooston 1585 *Archd*

'Wulfsige's farm' *v.* tun. Similarly Woolstone (D). At one stage there seems to have been the possibility of the development of an alternative form as if from *Wulfsigingtun*, cf. Wolverton *supra*. Woolstone *Coudray* is another name for Little Woolstone. It was held by the Coudray family, temp. E i (FA i. 106). The name *Wulfsige*, very common before the Conquest, was still common in the 12th cent., usually in the form *Wulsi*. Wolseley (St), Woolsington (Nb), Wolsingham (Du) and Woolstone (D) are also derivatives of this name.

* **Woughton-on-the-Green**

WOUGHTON-ON-THE-GREEN 95 A 2 [wu·ftən]
Ulchetune 1086 DB
Wocheton' 1167 P
Wochetun' 1167 Chancellor's Roll
Woketon(e) 1182 P (p), 1199 Cur, 1225 Pat, 1227 *Ass*, 1232 WellsR, 1235 Fees 463, 1262 *Ass*, 1302 FA, 1333 Pat, 1352, 1361 Cl
Weketune 1199 Fines (four times)
Wketon' 1199 Cur
Wicheton 1200 Cur (p)
Wokitun 1200 Cur (p)
Wuketone 1221 WellsR, 1227 *Ass*, 1240 Gross, 1241, 1247, 1262 *Ass*
Wokenton 1227 *Ass* (p)
Wukinton 1237 Fees 1451
Wocotone 1284 FA
Wokton 1318 Pat
Woughton 1459 IpmR, 1526 LS
Woketon al. *Woghton* 1480–96 *Linc*
Wafton al. *Woveton* 1700 Chauncy

In addition to these forms the *VCH* notes that in the 17th

cent. the place was called Woughton al. Wokington-on-the Green.

The interpretation of the first element in this name is difficult and the matter is not made easier by the fact that the DB form is almost certainly corrupt. If it were not for the *Wek-*, *Wik-* and *Wuk-* forms one might take the first element to be the pers. name *Wocc* found in *Wocces geat* (BCS 594) and in Woking (Sr) but these point to some different name. Perhaps the best name is the *Wehha* found in the Northumbrian genealogies (OET 171). This must have arisen from earlier *Weohha* by smoothing. That form in West Saxon would have yielded *Wuhha* under the influence of the initial *w* and these forms would account for the development of the vowel of the different early forms of Woughton. We should perhaps have expected from the ME forms an OE name with *c* or *cc* rather than *hh* but the development of OE *hh* to *k* has its parallel in Beckenham (K), 973 *Beohha hamm* (BCS 1295) and Cockfield (Sf), 10th cent. *Cohhanfeld* (KCD 685). Later *kt* > [*χt*] > *ft*. 'On the Green' because the village has grown up round a large central green.

For the appearance of an unnecessary *l* in a Bucks DB spelling, cf. *Olvonge* for Oving and *Oltone* for Wotton *infra*.

III. MOULSOE HUNDRED

Molesoueslau, *Moslei(e)*[1] 1086 DB
Moisselai[1], *Moslai*[1], *Moleslou* ib.
Mulesho 1241, 1247 *Ass*
Molesho 1241 *Ass*
Mulsho 1247 *Ass*, 1346 FA
Muleshowe 1262 *Ass*
Molleshowe 1262 *Ass*
Molishoe 1265 Misc
Moleso 1284 FA

The meeting-place of the Hundred was presumably in Moulsoe parish, but the exact site is unknown. The first DB form seems to be the gen. sg. of the name Moulsoe, i.e. *Muleshohes*, followed by **hlaw**, and this would point to the full name

[1] These forms, as pointed out in Rec. ix. 107, by Mr A. M. Davies, are clearly due to confusion with Mursley Hundred *infra*.

of the Hundred meeting-place being 'Moulsoe's hill.' Cf. *Bingameshou*, i.e. Bingham's *hoh*, as the full name of the Wapentake of Bingham (Nt). The other DB forms are corrupt. The position of Moulsoe village not far from the centre of the Hundred and on a conspicuous eminence made it a good meeting-place.

Astwood

ASTWOOD 84 F 4 [æstəd]

Estwode 1151–4 Fr
Estwude 1227 *Ass*
Hastwude 1241 *Ass*
Astwode 1242 Fees 884
Estwode by Neuport Paynel 1341 Pat

Forms in *Est*- are frequent down to 1355, those in *Ast*- are found in 1316 (FA) and regularly from 1453 (AD i) onwards.

'East wood' *v.* **east, wudu**. The parish forms a projecting point on the eastern border of Buckinghamshire

ASTWOOD BURY

'*the manor of Bury*' 1488 Ipm
v. **burh**.

DOVE HOUSE

'Formerly a dovecot attached to Astwoodbury House' (HMN 58).

Bow Brickhill

BOW BRICKHILL 95 B 3 [bou brikəl]

Brichell(a)e 1086 DB
Brichille 1152–8, 1160–5 NLC
Brikella 1155 NLC
Bolle Brichulle 1198 Fines
Bollebrikehulle 1237–40 Fees 1451, 1259 Gross

After this the first part of the name, down to 1348, is written *Bolle*, nearly always as part of an actual compound, except for *Bule*- in 1221 (WellsR) and *Belle*- in 1247 (*Ass*), 1284 FA, 1310 Orig. The second part of the name has the suffix **hyll** as *hella*

(1221 WellsR), *hille* four times down to 1257 and *hulle* thirteen times down to 1348. After that date the forms are

Bolnebrykhull 1363–98 *Linc*
Bolbrykhull 1394 Pat
Bowebrykhyll 1472–80 *Linc*
Bobrykehill 1526 LS
Bolebrykehill, *Bowbrikehill* 1535 VE
Boobrickhill 1542 LP

Professor Ekwall suggests that the first element in this name is British *brik*, the source of the Welsh *brig*, 'top, summit.' The word is now used chiefly of a 'tree-top,' but there seems reason to believe that the meaning was formerly more general. Cf. Evans' Welsh Dictionary. If this is correct, the compound belongs to a type which is further illustrated in Brill and Chetwode *infra*.

The first element is probably the ME pers. name *Bolle* (OE *Bolla* or ON *Bolli*), this Brickhill being distinguished from the others by the name of its one-time tenant. (Cf. Ab Kettleby, Lei, which probably has a similar history.)

CALDECOTTE [kælkət]

Caldecote 1247 *Ass*

and so uniformly except *Suthcaldecotes* in 1310 (Orig).

'Cold cottages' *v.* **cald, cot**. Faces north and is very exposed (Harman). The modern spelling is entirely artificial.

Great Brickhill

GREAT BRICKHILL 95 C 3 [brikəl]

Brichella 1086 DB

The history of the forms of *Brickhill* in this name is much the same as for Brickhill. It is first distinguished as *Magna* in 1247 (*Ass*).

DUNCOMBE WOOD takes its name from the Duncombe family who came into possession of the manor of Great Brickhill in the 16th cent. (L. iv. 59).

SMEWNES GRANGE (lost)

Smewenes melne 1251 *FF*
Smewynes 1330 Pat
Smewnes 1535 VE, 1541 LP

The pers. name *Smewin* is found in DB and may lie behind this p.n. Professor Ekwall suggests that it may be from an OE pers. name *Smēa-wine*, with the same first element that is found in the OE word *smēa-þoncol*, 'wise-thoughted.' Such a compound meaning 'sagacious friend' seems a very likely one.

Little Brickhill

LITTLE BRICKHILL 95 B 2 [brikəl]

Brichella 1086 DB
Parva Brichulle 1198 Fines

hull-forms are much the commonest down to 1452, only two *hill*-forms having been noted. After that date *hill*-forms prevail. In a few forms we find metathesis of the *r*, thus

Birkehill 1461 Pat
Birkhill Parva 1611 BM

but this does not seem to survive locally.

BATTLEHILLS (6″)

Battels Eliz ChancP

This is probably a manorial name derived from the family of *Bataille*; cf. Battleshield (PN Nb), but in this case we have no knowledge of such a family holding land in Brickhill.

Broughton

BROUGHTON 84 J 3 [brɔ·tən]

Brotone 1086 DB
Broctone 1237 Fees 145, Hy iii BM, 13th AD ii
Brouton 1241 *Ass*, 1284 FA
Brousthon' 1242 Fees 872
Bruhtone 1284 FA
Broughton' iuxta Neuport Paynel 1300–20 *Linc*
Broughtone 1316 FA
Broughton juxta Middelton Caynes 1351 Cl

Broughton juxta Mulsho 1419 IpmR

'Brook-farm' *v.* **broc, tun.**

Chichele

* CHICHELEY 84 G 3 [ʧitʃili], [ʧetʃli]

Cicelai 1086 DB
Chichelei 1151–4 Fr
Chichele 1197 Fines, 1241, 1262 *Ass*, 1349, 1458 Pat
Chichesle 1227 *Ass*
Checheleghe 1237 Fees 1451, 1288 Ipm
Chikel 1241 *Ass*
Chechel(e) 1242 Fees 884, 1262 *Ass*, 13th AD i, 1311 Ch, 1327 Pat, E iii *Bodl* 52
Chicheleg 1247 Gross
Checheleam Checheleie 1262 *Ass*
Checchele(ye) 1273 Ipm, 1331 Pat, 1490 Ipm
Chuchele 1284 FA
Chechelegh al. *Chucheleye* 1288 Ipm
Chichele 1318 Pat
Chicheley al. *Chegeley* 1524 LP
Chechylley 1526 LS

The second element is **leah**. The first would seem to be a pers. name. It is probably the name (or one allied to it) which appears in Latinised form as *Cichus* in the signature to certain Kentish Charters, probably all by one man (*v.* Redin 28), though that may be the name with unpalatalised final consonant, as in the pers. name which seems to lie behind Chicksand (Beds). On the other hand we have this same name with palatalised vowel, as in Chicheley, in Chichacott (D), DB *Chicecote*. Hence 'Cicca's clearing.' The *Chuch-* forms are probably due to the influence of *ch* on the preceding *i*.

THICKTHORN (Fm)

Thyckethorne 1311 Ch
Thykethornes 1311 Inq aqd

'Thick thorn-bushes.' There is a Thickthorn Wood close by and cf. *Thickthorn* in Stoke Goldington Terr. (1607).

Clifton Reynes

CLIFTON REYNES 84 F 3

Clystone, *Cliftone*, *Clistone* 1086 DB

The manor was held by Ralph de *Reynes* in 1302 (FA i 104) and is called *Clyfton Reynes* in 1383 (Cl)

Clifton by Olneye 1344 Ipm

So called from its position on comparatively high ground above the Ouse, looking across to Olney.

North Crawley

NORTH CRAWLEY al. Great Crawley and LITTLE CRAWLEY 84 G and H 4

Crauelai 1086 DB
Craule 1151–4 Fr, 1210 Fines, 1231 *FF*, 1241, 1247 *Ass*, 1284 FA, 13th AD ii, 1351 Ch, 1386 AD ii, 1404 IpmR
Crawele 1197 Fines (*Magna*), 1247 *Ass*, 1388 AD ii (*North*)
Crawle 1202 Fines (*Parua*), 1393 AD ii (*Great*)
Croule(*ia*) c. 1218 WellsR, 1247 *Ass*, 1284 FA, 1313 Cl
Crowle 1284 FA, 1425 IpmR, 1434, 1459 Pat
Crawley 1432 IpmR, 1455 LDD, 1490 Ipm, 1535 VE
Crowley 1460 IpmR, 1520 LP, 1574 *Foster*
Croley 1542 BM

'Crow-clearing' *v*. **crawe**, **leah**. There has been considerable hesitation in the development of this name. Some forms show preservation of the original *a*-vowel which had been shortened in the first element of the compound and this is the form that ultimately developed to modern *Crawley*. Others, probably under the influence of the independent word, show the usual change of that word from *crawe* to *crowe*. These forms have not been traced beyond the 16th cent.

HORNCASTLE

In 1262 Simon de *Horncastel* made default in Yardley Hundred (*Ass*) and in the same year, his place of origin being now spelled *Hornecastre*, he was party to a Fine in Edlesborough (*FF*). He or his family must ultimately have come from the more famous Horncastle in Lincolnshire and have actually

applied the name to their new home, or more probably, this should really be taken as a manorial name with the possessive *s* of *Horncastle's* (Farm) omitted. In any case the name cannot have originated locally for in Buckinghamshire the form would have been *Hornchester* rather than *Horncastre*. *v.* ceaster.

Emberton

EMBERTON 84 F 2 [emətən]

Ambritone, *Ambretone* 1086 DB
Embertone c. 1215 WellsR, 1237 Fees 1451, 1247 *Ass*
Emberdestone 1227 *Ass* (p)
Aumbertun 1247 *Ass*
Emberton al. *Emmerton* c. 1450 *Linc*
Emerton 1484 IpmR, 1502, 1594 Pat, 1626 Vern

OE *Ēanberht(es)-tūn*, 'Eanberht's farm.' *nb* > *mb* > *m* by assimilation. Amerton (St) has the same origin. The surname *Em(m)erton* is one of the commonest in the North Bucks registers.

HOLLINGTON WOOD

Hollingdon field 1639 *Terr*
Hollingdonslade 1694 ib.

OE *holegn-dun*, 'holly-hill' or *holan-dune* (dat.), 'hollow hill,' or *holan dene*, 'hollow valley,' with common later confusion of suffix. *v.* holegn, holh, dun, denu. For *slade* *v.* slæd.

MULDUCKS (6″)

Mulhediche 1241 *Ass*

The second element in this name seems to be dic and the modern form to be corrupt. The first element is quite uncertain. Possibly it may be the OE adj. *mylcen*, 'milken,' the epithet being applied to a ditch whose waters were milky in appearance. *mylcen-dic* might well appear as above in ME. Professor Zachrisson suggests that the *h*[1] may be inorganic and the compound really be *myln-dic*, 'mill-ditch,' a term in very common use.

[1] The *h* might even be a miscopying of a justice's clerk for *n*.

Hardmead

HARDMEAD 84 G 4 [hɑ·mi·d]

Horelmede, *Herulfmede*, *Herouldmede* 1086 DB
Harwemeda c. 1180 *Drayton Charters*
Harewemede 1194 Cur, 1195 Abbr, 1227 *Ass*, 1235 Fees 463
Haremade 1202 Fines, 1227 *Ass*, 1242 Fees 872
Harlemede 1223 WellsR
Haremede 1223 Bract, 1227 *Ass*, 1237 Fees 1451, 1291 Tax, 1311 Ch, 1366 Pat
Harmede 1241, 1247 *Ass*, 1291 Tax, 1302 FA, 1520 LP
Hardmede 1284 FA, 1318 Ch, 1323 Pat, 1385 Cl

Probably the 'mead' of *Heoruwulf* or of *Herewulf*, though the alternative DB form would point equally well to *Hereweald*. Otherwise that form must be explained as due to early development of epenthetic *d*. *v*. **mæd**. *er* early became *ar*, *w* in the unstressed syllable was lost, and an epenthetic *d* (not maintained later, at least in pronunciation) developed between *r* and *m*.

Milton Keynes

MILTON KEYNES

Mideltone, *Middeltone* 1086 DB
Middelton 1227 *Ass*, *Middeltone Kaynes FF*
Milton Keynes 1422 IpmR
Milton al. *Middleton Keynes* 1693 *Terr*

'Middle farm,' probably in relation to Broughton and Walton. *v*. **middel**, **tun**. Hugh de *Cahaignes* held land in Bk in 1166 (RBE) and Hugo de *Cayenes* is mentioned in 1227 (*FF*) as vouching to warranty in Milton.

Moulsoe

MOULSOE 84 H 3 [mʌlsou]

Moleshou 1086 DB, 1160–5 NLC, 1176 P
Molesho 1152–8 NLC, c. 1202 ib., 1235 Fees 558, 1247 *Ass*, 1284 FA
Mulesho 1189 P, 1227 *Ass*, 1233 WellsR, 1235 Fees 462, 1247, 1262 *Ass*
Muleshou 1189 P, 1232 Fees 1358

Mullesho 1242 Fees 880, 1319 BM
Mulsho 1325 Cl, 1344 BM, 1373 Cl
Mulso 1435, 1477 Pat, 1490 Ipm, 1806 Lysons
Mulsoo 1526 LS
Moulsoe c. 1550 *Linc*
Mulshoe 1766 J

'Mul's spur of land' *v.* hoh. 'The village stands on a conspicuous eminence declining towards the east' (L. iv. 250). The name *Mūl* is found also in Moulsford (Berks), Moulsham (Ess), Molesworth (Hu). There are two early examples of its independent use, one of them being the name of the brother of king Cædwalla of Wessex who was killed in 687. In the place-name Moulsoe the vowel has been shortened before the consonant group.

Petsoe

PETSOE (Manor) 84 F 3
Petrosho 1151–4 Fr
Pottesho 1197 Fines, 1242 Fees 872, 1279 Ipm, 1285 QW, 1316 FA, 1349 Ipm, 1376 Cl
Petteshowe 1238 Gross
Petisho 1284 FA
Petesho 1302 FA
Pettesso 1327 BM
Peteshoo 1520 LP

The first form, which stands unconfirmed, is probably corrupt, and the OE form was probably *Peotes-hōhe* (dat.), 'Peot's spur of land,' in which *Peot* may possibly be a shortened form of a compound-name in *Peoht-* such as *Peohthelm* or *Peohthun*. The form *Piot* is on record in OE in the 8th cent.

EKENEY-CUM-PETSOE (lost)
Hekenhey 1242 Fees 884
Ekeneia 1246 Gross
Hekeney 1252 Gross, 1262 *Ass*
Egeney 1291 Ipm, 1411 Pat
Ekeney 1291 Ipm, 1302 Fa, 1323 Cl, 1346 FA, 1397, 1413 IpmR, 1520 LP
Okney 1362–98 *Linc*

Ekney 1535 VE
Okeney c. 1450 *Linc*, 1526 LS
Okeney al. *Ekeney* 1806 Lysons
Eckney Wood 1826 B

Professors Ekwall and Zachrisson agree in suggesting that the first element here is the OE adj. **æcen**, an alternative and more regular form of **acen**. The suffix is *eg* and the whole name probably denotes an island grown over with oaks. The dat. form *æcnan ege* would have unpalatalised *c*. The *o*-forms would then have to be explained as due to an alternative form of the name with the adj. *ācen*, ME *oken*, or as due to late and conscious etymologising by those who suspected that the name had something to do with ME *oke*, 'oak.'

Sherington

SHERINGTON 84 G 2 [ʃə·tən], [ʧə·tən]

(*a*) *Serintone* 1086 DB
S(c)herintone 1185 Rot Dom, 1227 *Ass*
S(c)heryngton 1355, 1474 Pat, 1492 Ipm, 1509 LP, 1533 LDD

(*b*) *Syrenton* 1151–4 Fr
Schirintone 1179, 1189 P, 1237 Fees 1451, 1247, 1262 *Ass*
Sc(h)iriton R i *P*
Syrintone 1227 *Ass*, 1230 WellsR
Shiringtona 1232 Bract, 1241, 1262 *Ass*, 1303 Cl, 1361, 1376 IpmR, 1378 Pat
Chirintona 1232 Bract
Syrington 1241 *Ass*
Syrincton 1242 Fees 896
Cyrington 1262 *Ass*
Shirenton 1262 *Ass*
Shirrington 1312 Orig

(*c*) *Srinton* 1151–4 Fr, 1250 Misc
Srynton 1295 Ipm
S(c)hrington(e) 1278 Ipm, 1316 FA, 1320 Fine, 1346 FA, 1360 Fine, 1374 Cl, 1403 IpmR

Scringtone 1302 FA
Shryngton 1367, 1374, 1380 Pat
Churton or *Cherryngton* 1524 LP

OE *Scīringtūn*, 'Scira's farm,' *v.* ingtun. There has been a tendency from early times to lower the *i* (which must already have been shortened in the trisyllable) to *e*, cf. Sheringham (Nf). The forms under (*c*) can only be explained as due to a tendency to shift the stress from the first to the second syllable. *v.* Introd. xxvi.

Walton

WALTON 95 A 3

Waldone c. 1218 WellsR, c. 1225 ib.
Walton(e) c. 1225 WellsR, 1284 FA
Walton Marescalli 1237 Fees 1451

v. **weala, tun**. This is probably the derivation though the forms in Hugo de Wells suggest the possibility of **weald, tun**.

PERRY BARN and LANE (6″)

Periforlong 1237 *FF*

The same 'pear-tree' (*v.* **pirige**) is probably referred to in all these names.

WOODLEY'S FARM. It is possible that the Will. de *Wodlie* mentioned in 1241 (*Ass*) may have come from here. *v.* **wudu, leah**.

Wavendon

WAVENDON 95 A 3 [wɔndən], [wɔˑndən], [wɑˑndən]

(*gemæru*) *wafanduninga* 969 BCS 1229
Wavendone, *Wawendene* 1086 DB
Wauendene 1185, 1189 P
Wauendon 1186, 1189 P

The form *Wauendon*, except for sporadic forms in -*den*(*e*), prevails till

Wavyngden 1300 Ipm
Wavyn(g)don 1300–20 *Linc*, 1340, 1341 Pat, 1369, 1375 Cl, 1512 LP
Wavindon 1333 Ipm
Wavendene 1346 FA
Wavynden 1390 Pat

Waunden 1405–20 *Linc*, 1482 AD v, 1535 VE
Wondon 1509 Vern

This clearly contains the same pers. name that is found in Wandon End (Herts), c. 1300 BM *Wauendene*, and that pers. name must be the OE cognate of the name *Waba* which Piper gives in the *Libri Confraternitatum* 363. Hence, 'Wafa's hill.'

IV. STODFOLD HUNDRED

Stodfald 1086 DB, R i *P*, 1284 FA
Stofald, *Stodfalt* 1086 DB
Stodfold 1227, 1247 *Ass*, 1255 *For*, 1262 *Ass*, 1302 FA
Stotfald 1241 *Ass*
Stotfold 1262 *Ass*, 1316 FA

The name is the OE **stodfald**. The site of the Hundred meeting-place was in Lamport 'in a ground anciently known by the name of Stock or Stofield.' (Willis, *Hist. of Buckingham*, 280.)

Akeley

AKELEY 94 A 10

Achelei 1086 DB
Akileia 1152–8 NLC
Akeleia 1155 NLC, 1176 P
Akelay 1179 P
Achelay 1179 P
Acleya 1217 Bract
Aklye 1220 Fees 312
Acle 1220 Pat, 1221 Bract, 1228, 1230 Ch, 1235 Fees 461, 1247 *Ass*, 1302, 1316, 1346 FA, 1396 Pat
Ackle 1228 Ch
Aklee 1234–41 NLC
Akeleya 1245–62 NLC
Akele 1270 Pat
Acle by Bukyngham 1375 Pat, *subtus Whittilwod* 1399 ImpR
Okelee 1411 Pat
Ekeley 1577 AD vi
Akeley or *Oakeley* 1755 BW[1]

[1] It may be of interest in this difficult name to give the complete set of forms derived from the institutions to the living in the Lincoln Registers.

Probably *Acan-leah*, 'Aca's clearing,' *v.* **leah**. The name *Āca* may be inferred from *Acantun* (BCS 1289) = Acton (Sf) and from Occleston (Ch), DB *Aculuestune*. The early forms are inconsistent with derivation from *āc-leah*, which would have become *Ackley* or *Oakley* in modern times. It is clear however that some of the forms have not been uninfluenced by the ready association with that more common type of name, which is found in the not very distant Oakley *infra*.

AKELEYWOOD

'wood of *Ackle*' 1228 Ch

Self-explanatory.

STOCKHOLT (Fm) [stɔkəl]

Stocholt 1229 Cl, 1242 Ch, 1255 *For*
Stokholt 1235 Pat, 1282 Ipm
Stockwell feild 1639 *Terr*

'Stump-wood' *v.* **stocc, holt** (Introd. xxvi).

Biddlesden

BIDDLESDEN 83 J 8 [bitəlzdən]

(*a*) *Bechesdene*, *Betesdene* 1086 DB
Beth(e)lesdena c. 1145 *HarlCh* 84 H 18, 1199 *HarlCh* 85 C 25
Betlesden(a) c. 1145 *HarlCh* 84 H 45, Hy ii *HarlCh* C 22–4, 1221, 1387 Pat
Betelesden c. 1160 *HarlCh* 84 D 1, 1394 Pat
Beddlesden 1575 BM

(*b*) *Buttlesden(a)* Hy ii Dugdale, *Cartae Antiquae* (Facs[1]), 1244 Fees 1149, 1274 Fine
Butlesden 1231 *FF*, 1234, 1237 Cl, 1242 Fees 870, 1255 *For*, 1310, 1341 Cl, 1374, 1392 Pat, 1522 LP
Buthlesden 1256 BM
Butelesden 1337 Cl

They run *Aclee* (1300–20), *Oclee* (1320–42), *Okele* (1347–62), *Occle* (ib.), *Ocle*, *Acle* (1363–98), *Acle* (1405–20), *Accle* (1431–6) and *Akeley* after this.

[1] MS volume in the possession of Lord Winchelsea.

(c) *Bittlesden* 1224 Pat, 1274 Fine, 1755 BW
Bitlesden 1231, 1232 Cl, 1294 Pat, 1369, 1385, 1394 Pat
Bithlisden 1242 Fees 935
Byt(t)lesden 1255 *For*, 1272 BM, 1331 Pat
Bit(t)elesden 1338, 1376 Cl
Bittilsden 1534 LDD
Bidleston 1766 J

The first element in this name is a pers. name *Byttel*. This would account for the various forms of the stem-vowel (*v*. Introd. xxiv). No such name is on record but there is an OE *Byttic* which is another diminutive formation from the same name *Butt(a)*, which lies behind Butley (Sf), Buttington (Gl), Buttinghill Hundred (Sx). This name is cognate with ON *Butti* and it is possible that the OHG *Buzili*, which Förstemann, PN (331) takes to be a *Bōt-* name, should really be taken as a *But-* one. The later *d* has often led to voicing of the earlier *t* to *d*. The *th* forms are to be explained as due to the frequent confusion of *thl* and *dl*. v. IPN 110 n. 3.

EVERSHAW (Fm)

Evresel 1086 DB
Euersache Hy ii BM
Eureshæ 1199 *HarlCh* 85 C 25 (p)
Heuersæ c. 1200 *HarlCh* 85 C 24 (p)
Euersag c. 1200 *HarlCh* 85 C 22 (p)
Evershage 1200 Cur
Euershawe 1227 *FF*

OE *eofor-sceaga*, 'boar-wood or -thicket,' *v*. **eofor, sceaga**.

GORRELL (Fm) (6")

Gorhal' 1232 Cl, 1291 Tax
Gorehale 1241 *Ass*
Gorehall 1535 VE

OE *gor-heale* (dat.), 'dirty corner of land,' *v*. **gor, healh**.

WHITFIELD WOOD

boscus de Wytefeld 1255 *For*

'White open land,' *v*. **hwit, feld**. Named from Whitfield (Nth), across the border.

Foscott

FOSCOTT 94 A 11

Foxescote 1086 DB
Foxcote 1197 Fines
Foscote 1486 BM, 1526 LS
Foscotte 1535 VE

'Fox-cottage(s),' presumably so-called because fox-infested. *v.* **cot(e)**, cf. Foscote (Nth) and Foscott (D). No stress need be laid on DB *s*, cf. Gawcott *infra*.

Leckhampstead

LECKHAMPSTEAD 94 A 11

Lechamstede 1086 DB, 1152–8, 1160–8 NLC, 1186 P, 1206 Fines, 1227 WellsR, 1235 Fees 462, 1262 *Ass*
Lecamstede 1227 *Ass*, 1333 Pat, 1338 Ipm
Magna, Parva Lechamstede 1242 Fees 895
Lekhamstede 1304 Cl, 1495 Ipm
Lekehamsted(e) 1307, 1308 Ch, 1517 Encl, 1766 J
Leykhamstede 1323 Pat, 1340 NI
Leycamstede 1512 LP
Lykehamstede 1517 Encl
Lekehampsted 1525 AD vi

OE *lēac-hām-stede*, 'leek-homestead,' *v.* **hamstede**. This form is actually found for Leckhampstead (Berks). A similar compound with *ham* is found in Leckhampton (Gl). *leac* possibly has the wider sense which it has in the OE compound *leac-tun*, 'kitchen-garden.' The name of the river *Leck* on which it stands must be a back-formation. *Great* Leckhampstead was the name of a manor in the north part of the parish in distinction from Little L.

LIMES END

Lymeswodes 1542 LP
Lymesend 1607 *VCH*

This is the manor of Little Leckhampstead which Wm. de *Leames* held in 1284 (FA i. 79). His successor in 1316 was Alan de *Leume* (ib. 100).

NAST END (lost)

A manor first mentioned by this name in 1606 (Ipm) and not mentioned again after 1811 (*VCH*). Doubtless *at then est end* gave rise to *Nast End* (*v.* æt) in contrast to Middle, South, and Limes End, which survive.

* Lillingstone Dayrell and Lovell

LILLINGSTONE DAYRELL 83 J 10 and LOVELL 83 J 11

Lelinchestune 1086 DB
Lil(l)ing(e)stan 1086 DB, 1154–8, 1155, 1160–5 NLC, 1189 P, 1220 Fees 318, 1235 ib. 449, 1227, 1241 *Ass*, 1255 *For*, 1249 Ch
Litlingestan Daireli 1166 P
Lutlingestan Daireli 1166 P (Chancellor's copy)
Lilling(e)ston 1194 Cur (p), 1241 Fees 881, 1242 Ch
Lingestan 1219 Fees 253, 1231 Bract
Lulling(e)ston 1235 Fees 461, 1302 FA, 1512 LP
Lollingeston 1235 Fees 451
Lillingestune 1237 Fees 1447
Lingeston 1242 Fees 881
Lilligestan 1247 *Ass*
Lillestone 1284 FA
Lillynstone Dayrel 1316 FA, *Lyllingston Dansy* 1352 Pat

OE *Lytlinga-stan*, 'stone of the people of *Lytel* or *Lytla*,' *v.* stan (the reference possibly being to a county boundary stone) and cf. Littleworth *infra*. *tl* was early assimilated to *ll*. Early confusion with tun has taken place in the second element. Before the Conquest the manor was undivided. Lillingstone Dayrell belonged to the *Dayrell* family who derived their name from *Airelle* between Bayeux and Caen.

Lillingstone Lovell was in Oxfordshire until 1844. It was known as *Magna L.* in distinction from L. Dayrell or *Parva* (1255 *For*). It was held by the Dansy family in the 13th cent. and by the Lovells in the 14th. In 1255 (*For*) there is mention of a *Wike Lullingstan*. This was presumably a dairy farm of one of the manors. *v.* wic.

CHAPEL GREEN

Takes its name from a chapel dedicated to St Thomas à Becket endowed in the 13th cent. by the Dayrell family.

Luffield

LUFFIELD (Abbey)[1] 83 H 9

Luffeld 1200 Cur, 1201 Abbr, c. 1218 WellsL, c. 1220 Eyns, 1224 Pat, 1230 Ch, 1285 Fine
Loffeld 1274 Ipm
Luffield 1341 AD i

'Lufa's open ground' *v.* feld. For *Lufa v.* Redin 51. This name is found with gemination as *Luffa* in Luffenham (R) and Luffenhall (Herts). It is possible that this may actually be the name contained in Luffield.

Maids' Moreton

MAIDS' MORETON 94 A 10

Mortone 1086 DB
Mourton by Buckingham 1281 Ipm
Murton 1325 BM
Moorton 1376 Cl, 1392 IpmR
Maidenes Morton 1480–96 *Linc*
Morton beside B. 1491 IpmR
Made Morton 1546 LP
Maydes Morton Eliz ChancP
Maid smorton (sic) 1584 *Archd*

'Farm on the mor or swampy ground.' *Maids'* from the tradition that the church was built in the 15th cent. by two maiden ladies of the Peyvre family (L. iii. 40).

COLLEGE (Fm) (6″)

The property of All Souls College.

HOLLOWAY SPINNEY (6″)

Holewey 1241 *FF*
Holloweway feild 1607 *Terr*

'Hollow road,' referring to the old track which runs on the east side of the spinney. *v.* holh, weg.

[1] The abbey stood in Nth but the parish is in Bk and Nth.

PAGE HILL

p'iteshull', *prattoshull* 1241 *FF*
Pratchell 1607 *Terr*

If these identifications are correct it is clear that the modern form is corrupt. The two old forms show that we have a compound of **hyll** and the old pers. name *Prat(t)* found in Ailmarus *Prat* in Lincs (*Bardney Cart.* 212 *b*). This must be a nickname connected with OE *prætt*, 'trick.'

WELLMORE

Wellmore feeld c. 1725 *Terr*

This must take its name from the *Radewell* in this field in the same Terrier, a name already found in 1241 (*FF*) and denoting 'red spring.' *v.* **read, wielle.**

Radclive

* RADCLIVE 94 B 10 [rætli]

Radeclive 1086 DB

This form remains the common one down to 1379, except for

Redeclive 1314 Ch

then we have

Radeclife 1362 *New* 4
Radeclef 1385 Pat
Raclyff 1526 LS
Ratcliff 1537 LP, 1590 *New* 32, 1755 BW
Ratclyffe 1542 LP
Ratley 1675 Ogilby
Radcliff c. 1825 O

OE *rēadan clife* (dat.), 'red cliff' above the Ouse. *v.* **read, clif.** For *d* > *t* before *c*, cf. Ratcliff (Mx). Final *f* is often lost, as in [jakli] for Aycliffe (Du). Cf. also *Ratley* in Speed's map for Ratcliffe (So). 'The soil all round the village has under certain aspects a distinctly reddish hue' (Harman).

CHACKMORE

Chalkemore 1229 Cl (p), E i BM
Chackemore 1241 *Ass*

Chakkemore 1247 *Ass*
Chakemor(e) 1255 *For*, 1284 FA, 1301 Ipm, 1379 Cl
Jackemore 1316 FA, 1317 Pat
Chakmore 1363 *New* 5 (Radclive), 1542 LP
Chackmore 1590 *New* 32 (Radclive)
Cheackmore 1639 *Terr*

The phonetic development and the fact that there is no chalk in the neighbourhood suggests that the two forms in *lk* are due to errors of transcription and stand for *kk*. Dismissing them, we clearly have the OE pers. name *Ceacca* found in *cæccam wæl* (sic) BCS 565 and in *Ceacca wyll* (KCD 1307). This last is in the bounds of Whitchurch (O) and clearly contains the same pers. name that is found in the name of the bordering parish of Checkendon (O) of which the ME forms vary between *Cheken-* and *Chaken-*. Hence 'Ceacca's **mor**.'

Shalstone

SHALSTONE 94 A 8 [ʃɔ·lstən]

Celdestane, *Celdestone* 1086 DB
Scaldestuna Hy i (1267) Ch
Shaldestun c. 1200 *HarlCh* 85 E 40
S(c)haldeston 1227 *Ass*, 1242 Fees 870, 1255 *For*, 1316 FA, 1317, 1377 Cl, 1391 Pat
Saldestone 1199 *HarlCh* 85 C 25, 1230 WellsR, 1237 Fees 1446, 1284 FA
Chaldeston(e) 1255 *For*, 1373 Pat, 1512, 1542 LP
Scheldestone, *Scaldeston'* 1291 Tax
Saldistone 1302 FA
S(c)halleston 1422 AD iv, 1766 J
Shaweston al. *Shalston* 1522–47 *Linc*
Shalson 1584 *Archd*
Shaulston 1680 *Terr*

It would seem that the first element in this name must be the same as that in Shelswell (O), just four miles away, of which most of the early forms similarly vary between *Scheld-* and *Schald-* with one form *Scildeswelle* in DB, apparently an error. A pers. name **Sceald* is not found elsewhere, but it seems more reasonable to assume it than to take *sceald* as a common noun

in the gen. case, the adj. *sceald* used substantivally to denote a 'shallow ford' or the like, for such genitival compounds are very rare and the early substantival use of *schald* is otherwise unknown.

Stowe

STOWE 94 A 9

Stou 1086 DB
Stowa 1255 *For*

v. **stow**. Perhaps originally named after some saint, whose name was later dropped. Cf. Stow-on-the-Wold, earlier Stow St Edward's.

BOYCOTT (Fm)

Boicote 1086 DB, 1255 *For*
Boichot 1199 *HarlCh* 85 C 25
Boycote 1255 *For*, 1268 *Ass*

'Boia's cottage(s).' *Boia* is a name of continental origin found in late OE, cf. the name of the *Boïi* on the continent. *v.* Forssner s.n. and *Crawford Charters* 130.

DADFORD 94 A 9 [dædfəd]

Dodeforde 1086 DB, c. 1200 *HarlCh* 85 C 24, 1255 *For*, 1284 FA, 1320 Ch, 1379 Cl
Doddeforde 1227, 1241 *Ass*, 1242 Fees 870, 1247 *Ass*
Dudeford c. 1200 *HarlCh* 85 C 24 (p)[1], 1291 Tax
Dadef' 1237 Fees 1446
Dodford 1540 LP

'Dodda's ford.' The mod. form shows dialectal unrounding of *o* to *a*. Introd. xxiii.

LAMPORT

Landport, *Lanport* 1086 DB
Lamport 1152–8, 1155, 1160–5 NLC, 1493 Ipm
Langeport 1227 *Ass*, 1237 Fees 1446, 1262 *Ass*, 1280 Ipm, 1350 Cl, 1372 Pat
Lancport, *Langport* 1255 *For*
Long(e)port 1325 Cl, 1420 IpmR

[1] On the seal attached to the charter.

OE (*se*) *langa port*, 'the long port or town.' It would seem early to have lost its status as such, to judge by its documentary record. The mod. form is due to an assimilation which had already begun to take place in the 12th cent. Cf. Langport (So), Lamport (Nth).

Water Stratford

WATER STRATFORD 94 B 9

Stradford 1086 DB
Straforde 1197 Fines, 1242 Gross
Stretford 1237 Fees 1446
Stratford 1255 *For*, 1284 FA
Weststratforde 1302 FA
Weststretford 1307 Ch
West Watrestretford 1383 Pat
Stratford ad Aquam 1542 LP

v. **stræt, ford**. This Stratford is the farthest west of the three in Bk, and lies on the Ouse. The *stræt* is the Roman road which ran from Dorchester on Thames, through Alcester to join Watling St. at or near Towcester. *v*. Introd. xxiii.

NEWBOTTLE (lost)

Neubotle 1199 *HarlCh* 85 C 25, 1200 ib. 85 C 22
Neubothle c. 1200 ib. 85 E 40, ib. 85 C 24
Newbottle Hill 1639 *Terr*

v. **niwe, botl**. This and *botl* in *Botolph* Claydon are interesting as the only examples of that distinctively Anglian element in the county and both are in the north of it.

* Turweston

* TURWESTON 94 A 7 [təˑstən], [tʌsən], [ta′westən], [təwes′tən]

Turveston(*e*) 1086 DB, 1218 Pat, 1252 Misc, 1284 FA, 1296 Cl, 1634 *Terr*
Turueston(*a*) c. 1200 Eyns, 1241 *Ass*, 1292 Ch, 1335 Cl, 1337, 1366 Pat, 1383 Cl, 1394 Pat
Toruestona c. 1200 Eyns
Turlestone 1227 *Ass* (bis)
Turwestone 1242 Gross, 1707 *Westbury*
Turreston' 1242 Fees 870

Thurueston 1262 *Ass*, 1291 Tax, 1320–42 *Linc*
Turviston(e) 1302 FA, 1344 BM
Turston 1732 *Westbury*

Probably 'Thurulf's farm,' the clue being furnished by the 1227 form. The normal development would have been to Thurlston, as in the Sf place of that name, but in this name an alternative form *Thurvestone* seems to have arisen through loss of *l* from the cons. group *rlv*. This developed regularly to *Thurston* with loss of *v* from the cons. group *rvst* but no trace of this form can now be found, and in its place we have a form *Turweston* which, except for a possible occurrence in 1242, is first found in 1707. It must have originated by some process of semi-vocalising of the *v*, combined with folk-etymologising in the attempt to explain a puzzling name. The process has gone so far as to lead to a present-day pronunciation with the stress on the second syllable. A somewhat similar process has led to the development of Coney Weston (Sf) from late OE *Konungestune*, DB *Cunegestuna*, 1291 Tax *Conegestone*, *Conewestone*, *v*. Ritter 85. The pers. name is of Scand. origin. The name survived, as representing ON *Þórolfr*, into the 12th cent. in the Danelaw. It is the source of the Thurlbys in Lincs, of Thulston (Db) and Thurlston (Sf). It was never in common use in the Buckinghamshire region, and to this may in part be due the violent changes which it has undergone in this present name. The change of initial *th* to *t* under French influence is natural for Turweston is less than a mile from Brackley, where the Beaumont earls of Leicester possessed a castle and held their court (cf. IPN 98). The name cannot have arisen before the last quarter of the 9th cent. and is probably considerably later. For *t* from *th*, cf. Turville *infra*. See Addenda.

Westbury

WESTBURY 94 A 8

Westberie 1086 DB
Westbiry Hy ii (1269) Ch
Westburg c. 1218 WellsL
Westburi 1302 FA

'West *burh*' *v*. burh. Probably so called because it is in the extreme west of the county.

WESTBURY WILD (6″)

le Welde c. 1290 Westb Deeds (27), 1300 ib. 42, 1317 ib. 56
le Wolde c. 1290 Westb Deeds (27), 1291 ib. 38
Westburywelde 1405 Eland ii

v. weald. There is still a wood here. For the fluctuating forms *v.* Introd. xxiii.

V. LAMUA HUNDRED

Lammva 1086 DB
Lammve 1086 DB
Lamva 1086 DB
la Muwe 1232 Fees 1257, 1302 FA
la Mue 1241, 1247 *Ass*
Muwe 1262 *Ass*
Lamuhe 1284 FA
la Mewe 1316 FA
Moue 1346 FA

The site of the Hundred meeting-place is traditionally in Park Meadow, in Steeple Claydon, on the north side of the road from Winslow and Middle Claydon (L. iii. 81). In Lipscomb's days some obscure indications of ditches or earthworks were still visible. Professor Ekwall suggests that the second element in the name is OE *mūga*, '*mow*, heap,' pointing to some artificial mound or other structure marking the meeting-place—a very apt solution. The first is the definite article, the name being Normanised in official use. Steeple Claydon stands on a well-marked hill and forms a good centre for the whole Hundred.

Addington

ADDINGTON 94 D 12

Edintone 1086 DB
Adinton(e) 1175 P, 1198 Fines, 1227, 1241, 1247 *Ass*, 1260 Ipm, 1262 *Ass*, 1284 FA, 1320 Ch
Aditon' 1242 Fees 871
Addinton 1242 Fees 895
Adington(e) 1247 *Ass*
Adyngton 1425 BM

'Æddi's farm' *v.* ingtun. *Æddi* is probably the same person who gave his name to the neighbouring parish of Adstock. Cf. also Addingrove *infra*. The name *Æddi* is recorded early, the best known bearer of the name being *Æddi* Stephanus, the biographer of St Wilfrid.

Adstock

ADSTOCK 94 C 11

Edestoche 1086 DB
Adestoca Hy ii Rutland (iv. 23)
Adestochia R i ib.
Hadestoke R i P, 1227, 1247, 1262 *Ass*, 1284 FA
Hadestache c. 1198 Cur(P)
Addestok(e) 1221 WellsR, 1227, 1241 *Ass*, 1252 Ch, 1375 Pat
Adestoke 1227 WellsR, 1229 Ch, 1242 Fees 871, 1248 Gross, 1249 Ipm, 1262 *Ass*, 1302, 1316, 1346 FA, 1305, 1337 Ipm
Hedestok' 1235 Fees 461, 1262 *Ass*
Addestocke 1241 *Ass*
Astocke 1584 *Archd*

'Aeddi's stocc.'

Charndon

CHARNDON 94 E 9 [tʃɑ·dən]

Credendone 1086 DB
Charendone 1227, 1247 *Ass*, 1242 *FF*
Chardon(e) 1255 *For*, 1316 FA, 1491 Ipm
Charindone 1255 *For*
Charledon 1269 Pat
Charndone 1316 FA
Chaundon 1761, 1766 Edgcott

Probably from OE *Cærdan-dun*, 'Cærda's hill,' *v.* dun. The pers. name *Cærda* is found in Welford in Berks in *Cerdan hleaw* al. *Cærdan hlæw* (BCS 963). The DB form would then be a bad spelling with *Cred-* for *Cerd-*. *Cærd-* would become ME *Chard-* and the first *d* was early lost from the full form *Chardendone*. The DB form is probably due to confusion with Long Crendon (*v. infra*).

Steeple Claydon

STEEPLE CLAYDON 94 D 10

Claindone 1086 DB
Cleindon 1200 Cur, c. 1215 WellsR
Clendon 1200 Cur, c. 1215 WellsR, 1219 Bract
Stepelclaendon c. 1218 WellsL
Stepel Cleydon c. 1220 WellsR, 1242 Fees 871, 1247 *Ass*, 1255 *For*, 1262 *Ass*, 1284 FA, 1357 Pat
Cleidon 1235 Fees 465
Claydon 1235 Fees 556
Stepelcleyndon 1275 Ipm
Stepul Cleydon 1286 AD i
Stepulclaydone 1356 FA, c. 1433 BM
Clayndon al. *Cleydon* 1297 Ipm
Cleyndon 1298 Fine
Cleydon 1299 Fine
Stupelcleydon 1315 Fine
Stuble Claydon 1541 LP

OE *clǣgigan dūne* (dat.), 'clayey hill,' the village standing on the Oxford Clay. For the persistent inflexional *n*, *v*. Introd. xxvi. The distinction between the three Claydons by naming one from its *steeple* or tower must go back to a time when their churches were more definitely distinguished by the height or some other feature of their towers than they are at present. For *Stupel v*. Introd. xxiii.

KINGSBRIDGE (Fm)

Kyngebruge Hale 1320 Ch
Kyngesbrugge (p) 1340 NI

Self-explanatory. The name may go back a long way as the manor of Steeple Claydon was held direct of the king (TRW).

REDLAND BRIDGE

la Redeland 1320 Ch

'Reed' or 'red land' *v*. **hreod read, land**. It is perhaps worthy of note that in BCS 883 there is reference to a 'red slough' (*readan slo*) not more than two or three miles away.

Edgcott

EDGCOTT 94 E/F 10

Achecote 1086 DB, 1152–8, 1155 NLC, c. 1215 WellsR, 1226 BM, 1237–40 Fees 1447, 1241 *Ass*, 1284 FA, 1314 Cl, 1317 Pat, 1355 Cl, 1373 IpmR, 1385 Pat, 1420 IpmR, 1461 ib.
Echecote 1162 P, 1235 BM, 1247 *Ass* (p), 1255 *For* (p)
Hecchecota Gaufridi 1167 P
Hachecota 1167 Chancellor's Roll
Acchecot 1241 *Ass*
Hachecote 1242 Fees 881
Agecote 1363–98 *Linc*, 1452–72 ib., 1535 VE
Hachecote 1415 AD iii
Eggecote 1493 Ipm
Eggecotte 1526 LS
Edgecote 1598 D

Probably a compound of OE *ǣcen*, 'oaken,' and **cot**, referring to the material of which the cottage(s) were made. Eachwick (Nb) earlier *Achewic*, *Echewic* may be similarly explained, rather than as in PNNb, though Ekwall suggests for this name (*Anglia Beiblatt* 32, 260) a hypothetical pers. name *Æca*. When the name was no longer understood it was readily associated with the common word 'edge.' There is a curious similarity to the forms of Agecroft (La), for which Ekwall gives *Achecroft* (1394), *Agecroft* (c. 1540), *Edgecroft* (1577), *Aggecroft* (16th cent.). Edgcott (Nth) has a different origin.

Marsh Gibbon

MARSH GIBBON 94 E 8

Merse 1086 DB, 1214 Abbr, 1229 Bract, 1241, 1247 *Ass*, 1284 FA
Gibbemers 1273 Ipm
Mersh Gibwyne 1292 Ipm
Mersshgibewyne 1323 Cl
Marsh Gibbyon, *Marsh Gubbyon* Eliz ChancP
Marsh Gibwen 1806 Lysons

v. **mersc**. The connexion with the Gibwen family goes back to the 12th cent. (RBE 317).

BLACK BREACH (lost)

Black Bretch 1674 *Terr*

v. brech under Bourton Brake *infra*. The name last appears in the first ed. of the 1″ O.S. map.

GUBBINS HOLE

Gubbons Hole 1670 *Terr*

Lipscombe (iii. 48) says that the place is called Gubbin's Holt, Hold or *vulgo* Hole, and that it preserves the name of the family which gave its distinctive name to the parish.

RHON HILL

Ranell 1670 *Terr*
Rannell 1674 ib.
Ranhill 1674 ib.

This would seem to be from OE *rān-hyll*, in which the first element is an OE word *rān*, only found in *rancumb* (BCS 724), *ranwyll* (ib. 894) and *randun* (ib. 390). This word would seem to be cognate with ON *reinn*, 'strip' and OHG *rain*, 'boundary strip or balk,' which is used in a series of similar compounds—*Raimpach* with *bach*, *Reinperc* with *berg*, *Reinbrunna* with *brunne*, *Reintal* with *thal*. This sense-interpretation is in striking agreement with the topography of its appearances in English so far as they are known. The three OE examples are all in lists of bounds, Rhon Hill is on the bounds of Marsh Gibbon parish and it is very probable that we have yet another example in Ran Dan Woods on the borders of Bromsgrove Parish for which unfortunately we have no early forms[1].

Padbury

PADBURY 94 C 11

Pateberie 1086 DB
Paddeberi (v.l. *Padebir̃*) *Hamonis* 1167 P
Padeberia 1185 Rot Dom, 1186 *P*, 1189 *P*
Padebire 1201 Fines
Paddesbur 1300–20 *Linc*
Paddebury 1363–98 *Linc*

[1] *ex inf.* Mr F. T. S. Houghton, F.S.A.

After this date forms in *-bury* are the commonest, then those in *-biry*.

Padburne Eliz ChancP

'Padda's burh.' There is one independent 7th cent. example of the name *Padda*.

Poundon

POUNDON 94 E 9

Paundon (p) 1255 *For*
Pondon 1291 Tax
Powendone 1316 FA

The paucity of forms and the corruptness of the first makes the etymology of this name very uncertain but it may be from OE *Pohhandun*, *Pohha* being a name which is actually on record in OE and occurs in the name of Poughley (Berks). If so, the *a* in the first form is a mistake. Professor Zachrisson suggests alternatively derivation from OE *pawa*, 'peacock,' possibly used as a pers. name. This would explain both the *a*- and the *o*-forms but the existence of such a name is very doubtful and the site forbids the idea of peacocks themselves.

Thornborough

THORNBOROUGH 94 B 11

Torneberge 1086 DB, 1175 P, 1227 *Ass*
Torneberga Hamonis 1167 P
Turneberg 1200 Cur, 1209 Abbr
Thornburn c. 1218 WellsL
Tornebyr' c. 1218 WellsL
Thorneberge 1227 *Ass*, 1242 Fees 871
T(h)orneburuwe 1235 Fees 462, 465
Torenbergh c. 1238 Fees 1447, 1241 *Ass*
Thorenberg 1241 *Ass*
Thornburgh 1247 *Ass*

From 1316 FA onwards *-burgh* forms prevail.

'Thorn-hill' *v.* þorn, beorg. As the village lies rather lower than the surrounding country, the reference is probably to the hill to the south-west of it. From the fact that the neighbouring parish is *Thorn*ton we may perhaps infer that when they were

named the whole district was thickly overgrown with thorn-scrub. One might have taken *beorg* as 'barrow' and associated it with the two large bowl barrows near the western side of the parish but these seem to be referred to in the Thornborough Deeds (no. 1244) as *les Lowes*.

COOMBS

Albonescumbes 1244 *Thornb* 111, c. 1260 ib. 75

'Alban's valleys' *v. cumb*. The *Alban* is probably derived from the Nigel de Aula S. Albani (i.e. of St Alban's Hall) who is mentioned more than once in the Thornborough Deeds (cf. no. 5) as possessing lands there. He must have belonged to St Alban's Hall in Oxford which was certainly in existence in 1305 and possibly earlier (*v.* Ingram, *Memorials of Oxford*, 1837).

HATCHETLEYS (lost)

Hachgate c. 1240 *Thornb* 101
Hatchetleys c. 1825 O

'Hatch-gate,' used of a wicket-gate or of a sluice-gate. *v.* NED s.v.

SHELSPIT (Fms)

Sheldesput 1246 *Thornb* 17

The first element is probably the same p.n. found in Shalstone *supra*. The site forbids any question of a 'shallow' here though the coincidence of a similar name *Scheldesput* in Cheddington (*Mert* 382) is to be noted. The 'pit' (*v.* **pytt**) is probably one of the gravel pits of which there are several in the neighbourhood.

THORNBOROUGH MILL (6")

Milnedoneslade 1247 *Ass*

'Mill-hill valley' *v.* **myln, dun, slæd**. The Mill lies in a small valley opening on to the Ouse and this is clearly the *slæd* of the early reference.

Twyford

TWYFORD 94 D 9

Tueverde, *Tuiforde* 1086 DB
Tuiford Radulfi de Felgeris 1167 P

Twyforde 1224 WellsR
Tviford 1227 *Ass*

'Double ford' (*v.* **twi-**), the reference being to the double ford by which the old road to Cowley crosses the two streams at Twyford Mill. Compare Twyford in Berks, Oxford, Northampton, Derby, and Bede's *ad Tuifyrdi*. The first DB form keeps the old locative ending, later modified under the influence of the common noun.

VI. ROWLEY HUNDRED

(*to ðæm*)*rugan hlawe* 949 (1200) BCS 883
Rovelai 1086 DB
Ruelea 1176 P
Rugelawe 1227 *Ass*
Ruelowe 1247 Fees 1403

Browne Willis (p. 2) states that the site of the Hundred meeting-place lay in certain grounds called Rowley Hill in Lenborough Lordship. This Rowley Hill is clearly the '*rugan hlawe*' (*v.* **ruh, hlaw**) mentioned in the bounds of Chetwode and Hillesden in BCS 883. One would like to determine the exact site but the bounds of that charter are not easy to trace. After leaving the 'rough hill' they go along a little stream (*riþig*) to Offa's pool and then up stream to 'Bylian pol' and so across the mead to the sike (*v.* **sic**) and up from the sike to Cowley. Now the present boundary of Hillesden parish runs down a little stream which rises from $\frac{1}{2}$ to $\frac{3}{4}$ of a mile S.W. of Lenborough and flows into a larger stream which still forms the boundary of the parish and follows that stream as it makes its way up towards Cowley. This would place the 'rough hill' somewhere just north of Stocking Wood. Half a mile north, just out of Hillesden parish, is a well-marked but unnamed hill higher than anything in the neighbourhood (401 ft.) and it is difficult not to believe that this is the actual meeting-place of the Hundred.

Barton Hartshorn

BARTON HARTSHORN 94 C 8

Berton(*e*) 1086 DB, 1189 P, c. 1210 BM, c. 1200 Eyns, 1241 *Ass*

Bertonia c. 1180 *Oseney* 153
Barton 1237–40 Fees 1447, 1284 FA
Barton by Chetewode 1392 Pat
Barton Hartshorn c. 1450 *Linc*
Barton and Herteshorne al. *Beggars Barton* 1541 LP

v. beretun. *Hartshorn* was perhaps the name of a separate hamlet, ultimately united to that of Barton. Why so-called it is difficult to say, but it may be noted that the name is found more than once in early records as the name of a messuage, and may refer to some adornment of the house. It is found as a p.n. in Hartshorne (Db).

Beachampton

BEACHAMPTON 94 A 12/13

Becentone 1086 DB
Bechentone 1086 DB, 1160–5 NLC
Bechamton 1152–8, 1155 NLC, 1223 Pat, 1235 Fees 462, 1247 Fees 1403, 1284 FA
Becchamton 1175 P
Becchamtuna 1175–84 *Oseney* 162
Bechantone 1181 NLC
Bechamptone c. 1215 WellsR, 1227 *Ass*, 1228 *FF*, c. 1238 Fees 1447
Bechehampton 1230 *FF*, 1240 Gross, 1241, 1247, 1262 *Ass*, 1252 Ipm, 1298 Cl, 1307 Ch, 1369 AD i, 1382 Pat, 1499 Pat
Bechehamton 1235 Fees 468
Becchampton 1242 Fees 871
Beauchampton 1399 IpmR, 1512 LP
Beachampton Eliz ChancP
Betchampton 1654 Hillesdon

OE *bece-hāmtun*, 'the hamtun on or by the stream,' or *bece-hǣmatun*, 'farm of the stream-dwellers,' *v.* hǣme, an interpretation which agrees very well with its situation, the houses being divided by a brook running between them. The vowel should have remained short (cf. the 1654 form) but association with the common *beech* was inevitable and has led to the modern long vowel. Beech trees are numerous here (Harman).

Buckingham

BUCKINGHAM 94 B 10

Buccingahamme (dat.) 918 (c. 925) ASC(A), 915 (c. 1000) ASC(D)
Buccyngaham c. 1000 Saints
Bochingeham 1086 DB
Bukingeham 1152–8 NLC
Bockyngham 1280 Ipm
Buckyngham 1508 AD vi

'The hamm of Bucc's people.' This *hamm* is almost surrounded by the Ouse. For the name *Bucc(a)* *v. Mod. Lang Rev.* xiv. 235–6. See Addenda.

BOURTON [buˑətən]

Burtone 1086 DB, 1152–8 NLC, 1179 P, 1241 *Ass*, 1326 Fine
Bortone 1086 DB, 1284 FA, 1320 Ch
Burcton' 1176 P
Bourton 1314 Cl, 1316 FA
Burton Blakeheg 1330 Fine
Boorton 1376 Cl
Buorton, *Buerton hold* 1517 Encl
Boreton 1535 VE, 1755 BW

v. **burhtun**. The *burh* which gave name to this place may well be the southernmost of the two built on either side of the river by Edward the Elder at the beginning of his attack on the Danelaw, in 918 according to the *Chronicle*, more probably in 913. If so the name means 'farm by the fort' rather than 'fortified enclosure.'

BOURTON BRAKE

The Breach c. 1825 O

The dialectal *breach*, 'land broken up by the plough,' used locally a few years ago (Harman), has unfortunately, here and elsewhere on the modern O.S. maps, been replaced by the word *brake*. Cf. *la Breche* in Chetwode (*FF* 1240).

* GAWCOTT

Chauescote 1086 DB
Gavecote 1255 RH, 1285 QW, 1331 Pat
Gauekcote 1284 FA

Gauecote 1316 FA
Galcote 1480 BM
Galcotte 1517 Encl
Gocot 1675 Ogilby

This name would seem to be a compound of OE *gafol*, 'tax, tribute, rent' and **cot**. Similar compounds with **ierþ**, **land**, **mǣd** are common in OE. It may be suggested that the original cottages at Gawcott were built on territory belonging to the borough of Buckingham, for Gawcott is still in the parish of Buckingham. If so, it is probable that their inhabitants paid their *gafol*, or rent, to the reeves of Buckingham, and that the name arose spontaneously to denote a group of cottages outside the borough, but united to it by the payment of rent there. Inorganic *s* is very common in DB[1].

LENBOROUGH [lembərə]

Ledingberge 1086 DB
Liþingeberg Hy ii (c. 1300) *Reading* 90 *b*, c. 1200 (c. 1300) ib. 91, 91 *b*, c. 1300 ib. 90 *b*
Lingeberg Hy ii (c. 1300) *Reading* 90 *b*, c. 1200 (c. 1300) 90 *b*
Lengeberg 1196 Cur
Lithingeberge 1201 Fines
Lethingeberg 1227 *Ass* (p), 1284 FA
Lidhingeburghe 1237–40 Fees 1447
Lechengberghe 1241 *Ass*
Ledingebure 1247 *Ass*
Lethinberge 1255 *For*
Ledyngberwe 1262 *Ass*
Lethyngboru 1280 Ipm
Leddingeberge 1284 FA
Lethingberge 1302, 1316 FA
Ledeburn 1311 Cl
Lethyngburgh 1331 Pat, 1346 FA, 1392 Pat
Lethenberg 1331 Cl
Lethingborne 1371 Cl

[1] Professor Ekwall would take this difficult name to be from OE *Gafancotu*, OE **Gafa* being a pers. name cognate with OHG *Gaba*. He would take the *alc* forms as inverted spellings which arose when *l* had become silent in the combination *alk*.

Lethingburgh 1373 IpmR
Lemburgh 1412 BM, 1493 Ipm (otherwise *Lenyngburgh*)

Professors Ekwall and Zachrisson agree in suggesting that we have here a folk-name in *-ingas*, derived from OE *hliþ*, 'hill, slope.' OE *Hliðinga-beorg* (*Hleoðunga-beorg*) would account for the ME forms. For such a name cf. the p.n. *Lythyngeshull* found in Kimble in the 13th cent. (AD ii). Hence, 'hill of the slope-dwellers.' *v.* Introd. xii. n. 1.

Chetwode

CHETWODE 94 C 8/9 [tʃitwud]
Cetwuda (dat.) 949 (12th) BCS 883
Ceteode 1086 DB
Chettewuda Roberti 1167 P (*Chetewuda Rodberti*, Chancellor's Roll)
Chetwud(e) 1223 Pat, 1227 *Ass*, 1229 Bract
Chetwode 1231 WellsR

and so to the end of the 13th cent. except for 1257 Pat *Shetwode.*

Chitewode 1465 Pat
Chitwood 1535 VE, 1604 Vern, 1668 HMN 86, 1766 J
Chickwood 1615 Ogilby

A compound of the same type as Brill, the first element being the British and the second the English word for a wood, *v.* IPN 26. Raising of *e* to *i* is specially common in association with palatal *ch.*

SIDNUMS
Syddenham 1535 VE
Siddingham 1826 B

OE *sīdan hamme* (dat.) descriptive of the broad hamm in the bend of the river here. The vowel is shortened in the trisyllable. There seems to be no justification for the pseudo-genitival *s* now found on the map.

Hillesden

HILLESDEN 94 C 10 [hilzdən]
Hildesdun 949 (12th) BCS 883, Hy ii (1313) Ch
Ulesdone, Ilesdone 1086 DB

Hildesdon 1184 P, R i BM, 1189 P, 1207 Fines, 1241, 1247 *Ass*, 1255 *For*, 1274, 1280 Ipm, 1284, 1302 FA, 1315 Pat
Hildesden(e) 1203 Fines, 1267 Ch
Ildesdone 1227 *Ass*
Hillesdon 1242 Fees 882, 1506 Pat, 1826 B
Hyllesdon 1490 Ipm
Hillersden 1755 BW

'Hild's hill' *v.* **dun**. *Hild* in OE is normally a feminine name, but it would seem that it might also be used as a shortened or pet-form for the numerous OE men's names compounded with *Hild-* as the first element. Cf. *Hild* and *Hilde* as the names of moneyers in Saxon times (Redin 7, 123), both of them presumably men, and the p.n. compound *Hildes hlæw* (KCD 621) now Hildslope Hundred (Berks). Cf. also Ilsley (Berks) and Hilsley (Gl). The genitival inflexion remained syllabic until the middle of the 18th cent. at least, but does not seem to have survived to the present day.

BRASSES SPINNEY (6″)

This is almost certainly for *Brasshead's* Spinney, *Brasshead* being a pers. name found in Hillesden in the 17th cent. (cf. Rec. xi. 137).

HILLESDENWOOD (Fm) (6″)

(nemus de) *Hillesden* 1230 Ch
(boscus de) *Hildesdan* 1255 *For*

v. **denu**. Self-explanatory. Cf. also *Hildesdene* brook (1230 Cl). Here, as in Waddesdon, Beachendon and Pitstone, we have different features in the same parish named after the same person.

Preston Bisset

PRESTON BISSET 94 C 9

Prestone 1086 DB
Prestinton 1162 P
Prestona Manasseri 1167 P
Preston Byset 1327 Ipm

'Priest' or 'priests' farm' *v.* **preost**. The *Manasser* of 1167 is Manasser Biset, *dapifer* to Henry II.

CASEMORE (Fm)

Casemore 1674 *Terr*

Probably 'Casa's *mor*.' The pers. name *Casa* may be inferred from *Casan þorn* (BCS 1005) and Casewick (L).

COWLEY

Cufanlea 949 (12th) BCS 883
Coueleia c. 1200 *AddCh* 9211
Cuuele c. 1200 (14th) *Miss* 131, 1301 Ch
Couele 1227, 1247, 1262 *Ass*, 1284 FA, 1336 Pat, 1341 Cl
Couelegha 1232 Bract, 1241 *Ass*
Kouele 1242 Fees 870
Couleye 1371 Cl
Coueley 1406, 1465 Pat

'Cufa's clearing' *v.* **leah**. For the pers. name *v.* Redin 90

Thornton

THORNTON 94 A 12

Ternitone 1086 DB
Thorintona Hy ii (1267) Ch, c. 1215 WellsR, 1247 *Ass*
Turintone 1163 P
Torentone 1166 P
Thornton(e) 1208 Fees 20, 1284 FA, 1338 Ipm, 1348 Pat
Torintune c. 1215 WellsR
Torenton 1237–40 Fees 1447, 1246 Ch
Thorington 1242 Fees 871
Tornton 1279 Ipm
Thorneton 1348 Pat, 1495 Ipm

'Thorn-bush farm,' *v.* **þorn**, **tun** and (for the DB form) **þyrne**. The varied medieval forms represent the valiant attempts of the clerks to deal with a word which always gave them special difficulty. See Thornborough *supra*.

HASELEY (lost)

Haseleie 1086 DB
Hasellye 1237–40 Fees 1447
Haselaya 1242 Fees 871

Haseleye 1242 Gross, 1364 *New* 5 (Radclive)

'Hazel-clearing' *v.* hæsel, leah. Haseley (O) has the same origin.

TYRRELCOTE (Fm)

Terricot c. 1825 O

The name is explained by the statement in Lipscomb (iii. 119) that Humphrey Tyrrell became lord of Thornton (c. 1500).

Tingewick

TINGEWICK 94 B 9 [tindʒik]

Tedinwiche 1086 DB
Tinsuicȝ 1088–1094 (*Arch. Journ.* IV. 249)
Tingwich' 1163 P
Tengewicha Abbatis 1167 P
Tengewichia 1167 Chancellor's Roll
Tinguic 1194 Cur
Tingwic c. 1198 Cur (P)
Tyngewik c. 1218 WellsL, 1262 *Ass*
Tingwich c. 1218 WellsL
Tingwik 1227 *Ass*, 1255 *For*
Tingewik 1227 *Ass*, 1237–40 Fees 1447, 1247 *Ass*
Tingwyk 1242 Fees 871
Tyngwyk 1262 *Ass*, 1296 AD iii
Tyngewyk 1276 Pat, 1284 FA, 1316 Pat, 1322 Misc
Tynchewyk 1281 Ipm, 1341 Cl (p), 1422 *New* 3

OE *Tīdinga-wīc*, 'dairy farm of the people of *Tīda*,' with very early loss of intervocalic *d* and the palatalised [ndʒ] for [ŋ] which is found from time to time in p.n. Local legend speaks of a river *Tinge* now built over. River-names in *-inge* are not uncommon but probably this is only a coincidence and *Tinge* may be assumed to be a back-formation from *Tingewick*. The name *Tīda*, short for such a compound name as *Tīdhelm* or *Tīdbeorht*, is well recorded. There was early opportunity for French influence to play on this name, for immediately after 1089 the manor was given to the Abbey of the Holy Trinity at Rouen.

For a full discussion of the loss of *d* due to AN influence, *v.* Zachrisson, *Two Instances of French Influence on English PN* 5 ff. and more briefly IPN 111.

To judge by the first and other of the early forms given above, there seems to have been a stage in the history of this name when it was likely to develop final *wich* rather than *wick*.

WOOD FARM

Cf. *boscus de Tingewik* 1227 *Ass*

Self-explanatory.

VII. MURSLEY HUNDRED

Mursalai, *Muselai* 1086 DB
Muresle 1195 Cur (p), 1238 Fees 1374, 1262 *Ass*, 1265 Misc, 1346 FA
Mureslegh 1232 Fees 1357
Murs(e)le 1247, 1262 *Ass*

The exact site of the Hundred meeting-place in Mursley is unknown. The village itself stands high, well in the centre of the Hundred. To the east of it lies the highest hill in the district, with three or four foot paths and old tracks leading up to it and this may well be the actual site. For the etymology *v. infra*.

Drayton Parslow

* DRAYTON PARSLOW 95 J 1 [pɑ·zlou]

Draitone, *Draintone* 1086 DB
Northdreitune c. 1230 (14th) *Miss* 119
Drayton Monacorum 1237–40 Fees 1450
Dreyton Passelewe 1268 Pat, 1283 Ipm
Drayton Passele(y) 1330, 1421 Pat
Drayton Passelowe 1421, 1422, 1501 Pat
Drayton Pasloo 1535 VE
Drayton Paslow 1526 LS

v. **dræg**. There can certainly be no question of a water-meaning for *dræg* here and the exact sense must remain undetermined. The *n* in the DB form is probably an error, cf. *Langrave* for Grove and *Pincelestorn* for Pitstone *supra*. 'North' in contrast to Drayton Beauchamp, 'Monacorum' because the monks of Woburn claimed certain rights of overlordship here. Already in DB the manor was held by Ralf *Passaquam*, the

second name being a translation of OFr *Passe l'ewe*. The vowel of the final syllable has been assimilated to that of the common *-low* suffix in p.n. For the *ars*, *v.* Introd. xxiii.

Dunton

DUNTON 95 E 1

Dodintona 1086 DB, 1242 Fees 878
Dudinton 1198 Fines, 1237–40 Fees 1450
Dodington(a) 1220 Bract, 1268, 1298 Ipm
Dudingtone 1221 WellsR
Doddintone 1284 FA
Dodyngton 1316 FA, 1320–42 (*juxta Whitechurche*) *Linc*, 1337, 1344 Cl, 1375, 1396, 1465 Pat
Dodynton 1333 Pat, 1345 Cl
Dadyngton 1344 Cl
Dodyngton al. *Donton*, *Dondyngton* 1465 Pat
Donyngton 1480–96 *Linc*
Donington al. *Dunton* 1522–47 *Linc*
Donington al. *Donton* ib.
Dunton al. *Duddington* c. 1550 *Linc*
Donton al. *Dinton* c. 1600 *Linc*
Dunton al. *Dinton* ib.
Donton, *Danton* 1609 Vern

'Farm of Doda or Duda' *v.* ingtun. The *a* in one or two of the forms is significant of the change from [*u*] to [ʌ] in the pronunciation. The forms from the Lincoln Registers show how complete was the confusion of forms between this place-name and the not very distant Dinton. *v. infra*.

Hoggeston

HOGGESTON 94 E 14 [hɔgstən]

Hochestone 1086 DB
Heggeston' 1199 Cur
Hoggeston 1200 Cur, 1201 Fines, 1226 WellsR, 1241, 1247 *Ass*

and so regularly except for

Hoguston 1341 Pat
Hoguston al. *Hoggeston* 1396 Pat

OE *Hogges-tūn*, 'Hogg's farm.' This pers. name is not found apart from p.n., as here and in Hoxton (Mx). Its existence is supported by the appearance of a weak form **Hocga*, which lies behind Hockliffe (Beds). It is apparently the ordinary word *hog* (OE *hogg*). It is possibly more than a coincidence that the next parish but one to the west is Hogshaw, cf. Introd. xx. The forms with *-uston* point to preservation of the syllabic force of the *e* till the end of the 14th cent. at least but no trace of such a pronunciation can be found now.

Great and Little Horwood

HORWOOD (Great and Little) 94 C 12 and 13 [hɔrud]

Horwudu 792 (c. 1250) BCS 264, 1152–8, 1160–5 NLC
Hereworde 1086 DB (sic)
Horrewde 1227 *Ass*
Horewode 1228 WellsR
Horwode 1301 Ch

These last are the regular forms down to 1502, with the exception of

Harewode 1242 Fees 881, 1461 IpmR
Herewode 1284 FA
Harwod 1509 LP
Horroda (sic) 1512 LP
Herwood 1535 VE
Harwood 1766 J, 1806 Lysons

'Filthy' or 'muddy wood' *v.* **horh**, **wudu**. The soil is clayey. The forms with *a*, from the 16th cent. onwards, point to a dialectal development similar to that found in Harpole (Nth), DB *Horpol*, but no trace of it can be found in the present local pronunciation.

GREENWAY FARM

'Possibly takes its name from the family of Greenway who held the manor of Singleborough in the 16th cent.' (*VCH*).

NORBURY COPPICE

The *-bury* is a Camp, 'an almost rectangular work...not shown on the O.S. maps' (HMN 178).

RODDIMORE (Fm)

Rodymore Hill 1756 *Terr*

Roddi- is here clearly OE *rudig*, ME *rody*, 'ruddy,' and the reference is to the colour of the soil. There are numerous gravel-pits in the neighbourhood. For this colour-application of *red* and *ruddy*, cf. the familiar old phrase '*red* gold.'

SINGLEBOROUGH [siŋkəlbʌrou]

Sincleberia 1086 DB
Singlebergh 1152–8, 1160–5 NLC, 1247 *Ass*
Singlesbergh 1155 NLC
Singelberge 1185 Rot Dom
Sinkelberg(h) 1231 Cl, 1247 *Ass*
Sincleburuwe 1235 Fees 467
Sinkelesbergh 1237–40 Fees 1450
Singelbur(gh) 1242 Fees 880, 1284 FA
Sengelbur 1242 Fees 880
Cincleberge 1262 Ipm
Synclesburwe al. *Cintleberwe* 1297 Ipm
Syncleborwe 1302 FA
Senclebergh 1326 Pat, Fine, Cl
Syncleburgh 1329 Cl
Senc(e)leberewe 1334 Cl, 1335 Ipm
Chingelbiry 1366 Pat
Sengleburgh 1377 Pat, 1378 Cl, 1398 Pat, 1401 Inq aqd
Seynt-le-burgh 1383 IpmR
Shyncleburgh 1461 IpmR
Shinglesborough 1510 LP
Synkleborow 1520 LP, *Sincleborow* Eliz ChancP

'Gravel hill' *v.* beorg. There is gravel in Singleborough. It is always being dug at Shelspit on its N.W. edge (Harman). This makes it certain that here we have the common word *shingle*, meaning small pebbles. For the variant forms *v.* shingle.

WARREN FARM

Scuccanhlau 792 (c. 1250) BCS 264
Shucklow 1766 J
Shucklow Warren 1826 B

'Goblin's barrow' *v.* **scucca, hlaw.** The 'barrow' or 'hill' is that round which the 500 ft. contour runs. For the idea of such haunted barrows we may compare the phrase in the OE gnomic verses, *draca sceal on hlæwe*, 'the dragon must (ever be) in the barrow.' In Shugborough (St) and Shuckburgh (Wa) *scucca* is combined with *beorh*.

SIX LORDS INN

The inn-name refers to the division of the Lordship of the manor of Singleborough into six parts in 1606 (*VCH*).

Mursley

MURSLEY 94 D 14 [məˑzli]

Muselai 1086 DB, *Musel'* 1199 Cur
Mureslai 1147–66 *AddCh* 47482
Murselai 1152–8 NLC
Merselai 1155 NLC
Meselaie 1160–5 NLC
Murslai c. 1180 (14th) *Miss* 119 *b*
Mureslea 1189 P, R i *P*
Meresle 1195 Cur(P), 1211 Fines, 1350 Ipm
Muresle 1200 Cur, 1201 Fines, 1241, 1242 *Ass*, 1341 Pat, 1350 Ipm
Mursle(e) 1252 Ipm, 1392 Pat
Murreslee 1369 Cl, AD i
Moresley 1526 LS
Murseley 1564 BM
Muresley 1766 J

The early forms of this name show clearly that the suffix is **leah**. The first element must be a lost pers. name *Myrsa*, which we find again in a form with assimilation of *rs* to *ss* in Missenden *infra*. In explanation of such a name two possibilities suggest themselves: (1) *Myrsa* may be from **Myrgsa*, earlier **Myrgisa*, a pers. name derived from the stem of OE *myrge*, 'merry,' (2) a derivative of the Germ. stem **murs* found in Germ. *morsch*, 'friable,' MHG *zermürsen*, 'to crush.' Beyond that we cannot go at present.

HYDE (lost)

la Hyde 1300 Ipm

v. hid. The name of this manor survived to the mid. 19th cent. in Hyde Meadow (Rec. i. 70).

SALDEN [sɔ·ldən]

Sceldene 1086 DB
Schaldene al. *Scaldena* 1175 P
Saudene 1203 Fines
Salden(e) 1224 Bract, 1241 *Ass*, 1284 FA, 13th AD ii, 1302 Pat, FA, 1331 Cl, 1351 AD
S(c)halden 1242 Fees 883
Saldene al. *Schalden* 1332 Ipm
Saldeyn 1402 Pat, 1437 IpmR
Saldeyn al. *Salden* 1440, 1462 Pat
Solden 1760 Addington
Saulden 1766 J

'Shallow valley' *v.* sceald, denu. The *s* for *sc* [ʃ] is due to AN influence. This is an example of that influence, which is noted in spellings by Zachrisson (IPN 113), being extended to pronunciation.

Nash

NASH 94 B 13

Esse 1231 Cl, 1302 FA
Asse c. 1275 (1400) St Alb
Essche 1346 FA
Asshe 1389 Pat
Nassche 1520 VCH ii. 141

v. æsc. 'At the ash-tree.' cf. Nashway Farm *infra*.

HOLYWELL (Fm) [hɔliul]

Halywell 1461 IpmR

Self-explanatory. *v.* halig.

NASH BRAKE

The Breach c. 1825 O

Cf. Bourton Brake *supra*.

* Stewkley

STEWKLEY 95 D 1

Stivelai 1086 DB, Hy i (c. 1230) *Kenil* 13, 1197 Fines
Stiuecle(ia) c. 1135 (c. 1230) ib. 33
Stiuecelea, *Stiueclai* 1182 P
Stiwelai 1196 FF (p)
Stiuelage c. 1198 Cur (p)
Stiuele(y) 1217 Bract, 1226 WellsR, 1238 Fees 464
Stiuecle 1227, 1241 *Ass*
Stivcleg 1235 Fees 556
Stiuekele 1242 Fees 892

and so with slight variants to

Steuecle 1290 Fine, Pat
Stieuekele 1290 Pat, *Stieuecle* Ch, 1320 Pat
Styuecle 1338 Cl
Stucle(y) 1394 IpmR, 1446 IpmR
Stukelee 1414 Pat, 1416 IpmR
Stukeley 1485 Ipm, BM

'Stump-clearing' *v.* styfic, leah. This is the most probable explanation, but as there is some evidence for a personal name *Styfic*, found in Stetchworth (Skeat, PNC 27) one cannot be quite sure.

DODLEYHILL (Fm)

Dudley Hill 1607 *Terr*
The leah of *Duda* or *Doda*.

LITTLECOTE [lidkət]

Litecota 1086 DB, 1155 NLC
Litecote 1152–8 NLC
Litlecot(e) 1189 P, 1284 FA, 1300 Ipm, 1345 Pat
Letlecote 1195 Cur
Lutlecote 1195 Cur, 1241 *Ass* (p)
Lyt(t)elcote 1386 IpmR, 1485 Ipm
Lidcote 1691 Thornton
Littlecote al. *Lidcote* 1720 L. iii. 329
Littlecote al. *Litcote* 1806 Lysons

Self-explanatory. Pronunciations of *little* with a *d* are fairly common dialectally (EDG 514).

Swanbourne

SWANBOURNE 94 D 13

Suanaburna 792 (c. 1250) BCS 264
Soeneberno, *Sueneberne*, *Sueneborne* 1086 DB
Suaneburne 1152–8 NLC
Swaneburne 1160–5 NLC, 1227 *Ass*, 1242 Fees 878 (*Superior*, *Inferior*)

The only other forms of note are

Swaneburg 1227 *Ass*
Suaynburn 1469 Pat
Swanbrough 1606 D

OE *swāna-burna*, 'peasants' stream,' *v.* swan. Alternatively it might be 'swans' stream' but 'the stream is merely a water-course passing by hedges with barely enough water for swans to frequent it, though at times it is larger' (Harman). The DB form *swen-* also makes swān more probable than *swan* for it would seem that the scribe has given us a form influenced by the Scandinavian cognate 'swain' (ON *sveinn*). For the suffix confusion *v.* burh.

Tattenhoe

TATTENHOE 95 B 1

Taddenho 1167 P (*Thadenho* Chancellor's copy)
Tatenho(u) 1179 P, 1215 WellsR, c. 1219 WellsL, 1227 *Ass*, 1232 Fees 1357
Thotenho 1227 *Ass*
Totenho 1227 *Ass* (p), 1247 ib., 1247 Fees 1404, 1302 FA
Toternho 1237–40 Fees 1450, 1346 FA
Totho 1262 *Ass*
Totherno 13th AD iv
Totenhoo 1400 Pat, 1509 LP
Totynhoe 1486 Pat
Totonho 1490 Ipm
Tottynho 1534 LP

'Tata's spur of land' *v.* hoh. This *hoh* has also given rise to *Howe* Park in this parish. The vowel is long in OE *Tāta* and

seems to have developed to ME open *o* before shortening took place. Then the vowel was shortened in the trisyllable and late unrounding has taken place. This explanation however only holds good if we believe that here, as in Totternho (Beds), Skeat's view (PN Beds) holds good that the *r* which appears in certain comparatively late forms is purely excrescent.

Whaddon

WHADDON 94 B 14 [wɔdən]

Wadone 1086 DB

Waddon 1152–8 NLC, 1175 P, 1241 Abbr, 1242 Fees 878, 1302 FA, 1333 Fine

Whaddon 1238 Fees 1374, 1242 Pat, 1286 AD i, 1299 Fine, 1316 FA

Whauddone 1284 FA

OE *hwǣte-dūn*, 'wheat-hill' (*v.* hwæte, dun) with assimilation of *td* to *dd*.

WHADDON CHASE

chace of Whaddon 13th AD iii

CODDIMOOR (Fm)

Codimor c. 1200 (16th) NLC

Codesmor c. 1200 AD ii, c. 1219 (16th) NLC

Cotesmor 1231 WellsR

Codemor 1291 Tax

Codimere Close 1547 L. iii. 506

OE *Codesmor* or *Codingmor*, 'Cod's mor.' For such a personal name we may compare Alanus fil. *Chod* in Lincolnshire (Stenton, *Danelaw Charters* 308).

SNELSHALL PRIORY (Site of) [snelsəl]

Snelleshal(e) 1226 Pat, 1227 *Ass* (p), 1228 Pat, 1230 *FF*, 1246 Ch

Snelleshall 1251 Gross

Snelsoo 1542 LP

'Snell's healh.' The pers. name *Snell* may be either OE or Scand. Cf. Snelson *supra*.

Winslow

WINSLOW 94 D 12/13 [winzlou]

et Wuineshauue (sic) 792 (c. 1250) BCS 264
Weneslai 1086 DB
Wineslawe Hy ii (1301) Ch, 1247 *Ass*
Wyneslowe 1247 *Ass*
Winslawe 1262 *Ass*
Wyncelawe 1346 Pat
Wynslowe 1492 AD i

OE *Wines-hlāw*, 'Wine's hill,' *v.* hlaw. The name *Wine*, earlier *Wini*, somewhat rare before the 10th cent., was common from thence to the conquest. The present is one of the earliest examples of its use. The latest example which has hitherto been observed occurs in the attestation of Asloc *filius Wine* to a 12th cent. grant to Castleacre Priory (Harl. 2110, 16*b*). In place-names the name is widely distributed. Winston (Sf), Winshill (St) and Winsley (Sa) are three examples. The name *Win(e)ca* contained in Winchendon (q.v.) may be a diminutive of *Wine* or its corresponding weak form *Wina*.

SHIPTON

S(c)hipton 1279 RH, 1330 Pat
Sipetonam 1301 Ch
'Sheep-farm' *v.* sceap, tun.

* VIII. COTTESLOE HUNDRED

Coteslau, *Coteslai* 1086 DB
Coteshala, *Corteshala* ib.
Coteslawa 1189 P, 1247 Fees 1404, 1247, 1262 *Ass*, 1265 Misc
Cotteslawe 1195 Cur, 1227, 1241 *Ass*
Coddeslawe 1241 *Ass*
Koteslawe 1262 *Ass*

The site of the Hundred meeting-place was probably identical with North rather than with South Cottesloe, and it stands high above the level of the country round, in the middle of the Hundred. The second set of forms in DB are due to confusion with Courteenhall (Nth). For the etymology *v.* Cottesloe *infra*.

Aston Abbots

ASTON ABBOTS 95 F 2

Estone 1086 DB, 1200 Cur, 1227 *Ass*, 1237–40 Fees 1450
Aston 1242 Fees 878, 1247 *Ass*
Aston Abbatis 1262 *Ass*

'East farm,' but why 'east' it is difficult to say, unless the name was fairly late in origin and arose from its being the most easterly farm of the Abbey of St Alban's, to whom it belonged in DB (TRE).

BURSTON

Bricstoch, *Brichstoch* 1086 DB
Briddesthorne c. 1215 (14th) *Miss* 111*b* (p), 1247 *Ass*, 1275 Ipm, 1284 FA, 1374 IpmR, 1375, 1379 Cl
Bridelestorn 1227 *Ass*
Bridelestir 1231 Bract
Bridelesthon 1242 Fees 877
Brydesthorne 1302 FA
Briddestorn 1330 Ipm
Byrdyston 1517 Encl
B(e)yrdesthorne 1539 LP
Birdsthorn 1563, 1609, 1723 *Aston*
Burston 1664 *Aston*

'Briddel's thornbush' *v.* þorn. The name *Briddel* is not on record in OE but is a regular diminutive formation from the well-established *Bridd* (Redin 18). Cf. Birdsall (Y), Burcott (O). The *l* is lost from the consonant-group *dlsth*, *sth* > *st*, and metathesis of the *r* has taken place. The first form is clearly a blunder. Apparently the form for Brigstock (Nth) has got into the Bucks return.

OXLEY'S FARM

Oxleaze Farm 1826 B

It looks as if the modern name were corrupt and that the name was really 'ox-pasture.' *v.* læs.

Creslow

CRESLOW 94 F 14 [krislə], [kristlə]

Cresselai 1086 DB
Kerselawe 1175 P, 1279, 1327, 1375 Pat
Kerselowe c. 1215 WellsR, 1302 FA, 1323, 1375 Pat
Kerslawe 1237–40 Fees 1450, 1239 Gross
Kereslowe 1242 Fees 877
Kerslawe 1278 Misc
Kyrselawe 1293 Misc, 1298 Pat
Kerslowe 1324 Cl
Cruislawe 1382 Pat
Kyrslawe 1389 Pat
Creslowe 1422 Pat
Carslowe 1485 Pat
Kyrslow 1526 LS
Kyrslewe 1535 VE
Crislow 1762 Swanbourn
Christlow 1780 Swanbourn, 1806 Lysons
Crestlow 1806 Lysons

Creslow stands at the head of a well-watered valley, with one or two pools in the neighbourhood of the village, the land being described as 'fine pasture.' It may be suggested therefore that the name is OE *cærsehlaw*, 'cress-hill.' Watercress grows abundantly in the brook which flows by Creslow pastures (Harman). *v.* cærse. The modern form is due to fresh late metathesis, and the common development of epenthetic *t* between *s* and *l*.

Cublington

CUBLINGTON 95 E/F 4

Coblincote 1086 DB
Cubelintone 1154 (1200) Eyns, 1227, 1247 *Ass*
Cublicumba 1178 P (p)?
Cublintone 1237–40 Fees 1450
Coblington 1238 Gross, 1284 Ipm, 1347 Ipm
Cubelington 1241 *Ass*
Cobelinton 1262 *Ass*, 1348 Ipm
Cobelentone 1265 Misc
Kobelington 1265 Pat

Coblintone 1284 FA
Cublyngtone 1302 FA, 1396 Pat
Coblyntone 1339 Pat
Coblyngton 1446 IpmR

A pers. name *Cub(b)a* is not on record in OE but is implied in the medieval forms of Cubley (Db). A mutated form **Cybba* must be the origin of Kibworth (Lei). Such a name may well have arisen as a pet-name, derived either from the name *Cufa* (*v.* Cowley *supra*), with the common gemination of consonant found in such names, or from the pers. name *Cuðbeorht*, with assimilation of *b* to *bb*. There is an OE name *Cuba* but this is simply another spelling of *Cufa*, *b* representing the bilabial continuant and not the stop *b* at all. It will not therefore help to explain this name. From a diminutive *Cubbel* must have come the p.n. *Cubbelingtun*, 'Cubbel's farm,' with an alternative form *Cubelingcot(u)*, 'Cubbel's cottages,' if the DB form is correct. It is possible that the form *Cublicumba* also refers to this place. There is mention of a *Holcombe* in 1680 (*Terr*). If, as is probable, Kipling Cotes (Y) contains a patronymic from an OE *Cybbel*[1], it supplies further evidence of the existence of an OE *Cubbel*. The pair of names *Cubbel*—*Cybbel* will then stand to each other in the same relation as *Cubba*—*Cybba*.

Grove

GROVE 95 E 3/4
Langrave 1086 DB
Grava 1222 WellsR, 1244 Gross
La Grave 1227 *FF*, 1247 *Ass*, 1284 FA, 1311 Cl
La Grave near Leycton Hy iii Ipm
La Grove by Mentemore 1346 Misc
Grove Neyrnuyt 1347 Ipm
Grave 1366 Pat
Groove Eliz ChancP

Self-explanatory. *v.* **graf(a)**. Defined as near Leighton Buzzard or from its tenure by the Neyrnuyt family, which goes back to the 13th cent. (*FF* 1256).

[1] The DB *Climbicote* cannot stand against the evidence of the later forms, esp. *Kybblingcotes* from the Percy Cartulary.

Hardwick

HARDWICK 94 C 14 [hɑ·dik]

Hardwich, *Hardvic*, *Harduich* 1086 DB
Herdewyc 1208 Fees 20
Herdewic 1220 WellsR
Herdwic 1227 *Ass*, 1235 Cl
Herdewik 1237–40 Fees 1450, 1284 FA
Hardewych Hy i (1330) Ch
Herdwyk 1262 *Ass*, 1358 AD iii
Herdwik Moeles 1281 Ipm
Herdwik by Aylesbyry 1297 Ipm
Hardewyk 1346 FA
Herdewyk 1349 Cl
Hurdewyk 1377 IpmR
Hardwyke 1435 IpmR
Hardweke 1605 *Terr*
v. heordewic. The early *a* form in DB is noteworthy.

FURZENHILL

Furcenhull 1255 RH

'Furze-covered hill' from an unrecorded OE adj. *fyrsen*. The passage in which the name is found refers to the road between *Furcenhull* and Collett, RH i. 45. There is a well-marked footpath which runs west from Furzenhill, joins Akeman St. near Waddesdon and then goes on to Collett.

Linslade

LINSLADE 95 E 3 [lintʃeid], [linsleid]

Hlincgelad 966 (12th) BCS 1189, 1012 KCD 721
Lincelada 1086 DB, 1237–40 Fees 1450, 1241 *Ass*, 1245 Gross, 1247, 1262 *Ass*, 1297 Ch, 1336 Cl, 1400 Pat
Linchelad(*e*) 1178 P (p)
Linslad 1245 Gross
Lynchlad 1251 Ch
Lynchelad' 1276 Ipm, 1302 FA, 1324 Fine, 1344 Pat, 1360 Fine, 1368 Cl, 1377 IpmR, 1385 ib., 1395, 1399, 1464 Pat, 1526 LS

Lyncelade 1277 Fine, 1284 FA, 1316 Pat
Linselade 1302 Ipm
Linchlade 1425 IpmR, 1806 Lysons
Lynchelade al. *Lyncelade* 1543 LP

The two elements of this name are clearly **hlinc** and **gelad** but the exact significance of the name is difficult to determine. The site described must clearly be that of the original village, where St Mary's Church and Manor Farm stand in a broad bend of the Ouzel.

Mr F. G. Gurney in an illuminating paper on the OE bounds of Linslade in *Bedfordshire Historical Rec. Society*, vol. v, part II, p. 174, shows that the 'lince' or 'linch' here is a steep natural lince of bank and sand-mounds, overgrown with trees, to the south of the Church, and he inclines to interpret the **gelad** as referring to the westernmost of the channels into which the Ouzel divides itself here, the one which now forms the county boundary, and he thinks that the whole compound describes this particular channel lying below the linch. This may be so, but alternatively it may be suggested that *gelad* refers to the foot-path which skirts the lince and makes its way past the church to Broadoak Farm. This path is probably much older than the present road to the west and represents the original means of progress up the valley of the Ouse. If so the name means 'linch-path.'

The variant pronunciations of the name are due to AN influence. *v.* IPN 100–1. Cf. Lintz Ford (PN Nb Du).

SOUTHCOTT [sə·kət]

Suthcotes 1240 *FF*
Sutchote, *Succote* 1284 FA
Suthcot(e) 1286 Ipm, 1338 Cl
Southcote by Leighton Buzzard 1310 Misc
Southcotes 1373 Orig
Surcote 1826 B

'South cottage(s),' in relation to Linslade. The curious local pronunciation may have been influenced by the neighbouring *Burcott*, but cf. Circourt (Berks) which has the same history.

TIDDINGFORD HILL (lost from map but survives locally) [tidnfut], [tinfut]

Yttingaford 966 (c. 1200) BCS 1189, 900 A (10th) ASC
Tyttyngford Beds. Rec. Soc. v. 176

This identification is made by Mr F. G. Gurney in the paper mentioned above. He shows that the ford was one which carried the road called *þiodweg* in a Chalgrave charter (BCS 659), still known locally as '*The Ede way*[1],' now largely fallen into decay, across the Ouzel west of Grovebury farm and up the hill on the other side towards Wing. That hill is locally named as above[2] and we clearly have here another case of the prefixing of the final *t* of *æt*, *v.* æt. The *Yttingas* is a folk-name which must be associated with the pers. name found in *yttinges hlawe* in Berks of BCS 777. This last is now Titlar Hall in Lower Appleton and shows the same development of initial *t*.

Mentmore

MENTMORE 95 F 3

Mentemore 1086 DB

This is the regular form except for

Mantemore 1247 *Ass*, 1276 RH
Mintemore 1334 Cl
Mentymore 1396 IpmR

'Mænta's mor.' The pers. name *Mænta* is not on record in OE but Ekwall (PN *-ing*) shows that it must be postulated for Minting (L) and that it is the English cognate of OHG *Mantio*. *æ* > *e* > *i* before the nasal.

LEDBURN [lebə'n]

Leteburn 1288 Orig, 1299, 1382 Ipm
Ledburn 1416 IpmR, 1447 AD vi
Ledbourn 1488 Ipm

[1] Mr Gurney makes this identification but has overlooked the interesting way in which OE *þiodweg* > *thedewey* and then is curiously misunderstood as 'Th' edeway.'

[2] Since the above paper was written Mr Gurney informs me that he has found *Tyttyngford hyll* in a deed of 1511 and *Tidenford* in the Tithe Award of 1836.

Leborne 1626 Vern
Leburne 1641 HMN 196
Lyburne Green 1766 J

Professor Zachrisson suggests that the first element in this name may be OE (*ge*)*lǣt*(*e*). As the little stream on which Ledburn stands flows past cross-roads at the village we may take it that (*ge*)*læt*(*e*) here has its recognised sense of 'cross-roads.' For this use of the word, cf. Radlett, Herts < *rād*-(*ge*)*lǣtę*. *t* is later voiced to *d* before *b* and *db* assimilated to *bb*.

REDBOROUGH (Fm)

Ridborowe ffeilde 1607 *Grove Terr*

Forms scanty, but it may be 'cleared hill.' *v.* **ridde, beorg.**

ROWDEN (Fm)

Royesden 1372 Cl
Roughden 1766 J

OE *rūgan dene* (dat.), 'rough valley,' *v.* **ruh, denu.** The 1372 is probably corrupt.

Soulbury

SOULBURY 95 D 2 [sʌlbəri]

Soleberie 1086 DB
Sulheberi 1151–4 Fr
Soleburn' 1155 Fr
Sulebire 1198 Fines, 1220 Fees 313, 1231 Gross, 1241 *Ass*
Sulebyr 1208 BM
Solebur 1235 Fees 460, 1288 Ipm
Solebroc 1227 *Ass* (?)
Sollebir 1235 Fees 555, 1274 Abbr
Solesbur' 1242 Fees 877, 1337 Pat
Solebir 1262 *Ass*
Soleburie 1284 FA
Sullesbyri 1288 Ipm
Sulesbur' 1291 Tax, 1337 Pat
Sullesbirii 13th AD i
Solebury 1302 FA, 1315 Ch, 1346 Pat
Sulbury 1305 Pat, 1512 AD vi, 1535 VE, Eliz ChancP, 1628 Vern

Solbury 1316 FA
Sulbery 1393 Pat, 1481 IpmR, 1526 LS, 1602 AD v
Soulbury 1755 Swanbourne

'Sula's burh.' The pers. name *Sūla* is not found independently in OE but it may be assumed from Sulham (Sx, Berks), Souldrop (Beds), Souldern (O) and from *Sulangraf* (BCS 691), *sulanford*, *sulanbroc* (BCS 1282). In origin it may be cognate with ON *Súla* (Lind, *Personbinamn* s.n.), cf. ODan *Suli*, a nickname related to ON *sūla*, 'pillar,' found in Sulby (Nth), and OE *syl*, 'pillar,' from the same stem. The vowel was shortened before the cons. group and this pron. is preserved locally though obscured by the present faulty spelling.

BRAGENHAM [brægnəm]

Brageham 1178 P, 1241 *Ass*, 1302 FA
Bracham 13th *Dunst*
Brakenham 1241 *Ass*, 13th *Dunst*
Bragenham 1284 FA, 1393 Pat, 1512 AD vi
Bragnam 1481 IpmR, 1766 J, c. 1825 O
Braggeham 1500 Pat

One can only offer a solution of this difficult name on the assumption that our true guide is the *Brakenham* form. In this case it may be that the first element is that found in Bracknell (Berks), *Braccanheal* BCS 778, and Brackley (Nth), DB *Brachelie*. That element is not itself easy of explanation but that it is a pers. name is made almost certain by the p.n. Bracklesham (Sx), *Brakelesham* BCS 807 (late copy), which clearly contains a dimin. *Braccol* derived from it. These names are probably to be associated with OHG *bracco*, 'greyhound.' If that is the true history of the name we may compare for its phonological development the history of Dagenham (Ess), 692 BCS *Dæccanham*, 1262 FF *Daginham*, 1274 Cl *Dagenham*, 1286 FF id., 1287 FF *Dageham*, 1289 Abbr *Dagenham*, 1350 BM *Dakenham*, 1428 FA *Dagenham*[1], and in Eggington (Beds), earlier *Ekendon*. Professor Ekwall has supplied the further parallels of Eggergarth (La), *Ekergart*, c. 1240, *Egergarh* 1212 and Waggoner's Wells (Sr), earlier *Wakener's Wells*. In all these cases *k* has been voiced to *g*, usually before *n*.

[1] Forms due to the kindness of Mr P. H. Reaney.

CHELMSCOTT

Chaumundiscate 1195 Cur(P)
Chaumundesfunt 1200 Cur
Chaimundescot 1200 Cur
Chalmundescote 1203 Fines
Chelmundechote 1251 Gross
Chelemundecote 1265 Misc
Chelmincote 1273 RH
Chelmecote 1282 Ipm
Chelmundescote al. *Chelmescote* 1284 Ipm
Chelmondescote 1332 Ch
Chelmescote 1347 Ipm
Chelmundescote 1434 IpmR
Chelmyscote 1446 IpmR
Chelmscote 1500 Pat
Chelmscourt c. 1825 O

'Ceolmund's cottage(s).' The persistent *a* of the first four forms is curious, but occurs elsewhere in early forms of place-names undoubtedly derived from personal names in *Ceol-*. Cf. *Calmundelei*, the Domesday form of Cholmondeley (Ch). *v.* **cot**. Cf. Chelmscote (Wa), Cholmondeston (Ch).

HOLLINGDON

Holendone 1086 DB
Holedene 1086 DB, 1163 P
Holendene 1241 *Ass* (p), 1262 *Ass*, 1353 Cl (p)
Holindon 1247 *Ass*
Hollenden 1418 L. iii. 463
Holynden 1500 Pat, 1517 Encl
Hollington, *Dark* and *Upper* 1766 J, 1826 B

OE *holan dene* (dat.), 'hollow valley,' or *holegn denu*, 'holly valley,' *v.* **hol(h)**, **denu**, **holegn**.

LISCOMBE

Liscumbe 1273 RH
Lysco(u)mbe 1284 FA, 1302 FA, 1393 Pat, 1375 Cl, 1394 IpmR
Lisco(u)mbe 1285 QW, 1382 Cl
Lyncecombe 1346 FA
Lyscum 1766 J

The first part is possibly a lost pers. name *Lissa* found also in Liston (Ess), *Lissingtun* BCS 1289, *Listuna* DB, and Lissington (L) and a lost *Lissingley* in Lissington (DB *Lesintone*, Danelaw Ch *Lissincton*). This must be a pet-form from an OE name in *Hlīs-*. Such is not actually found but cf. those in *Hrōð-*, *Sige-* with similar meaning. For this difficult name Ekwall notes the possible parallels of *Liscombe* (BCS 738) in a late copy of a Dorset charter and Liss (Ha). The form in *Lynce-* is probably due to the neighbouring *Linslade*.

WINSCOTT (Fm)

Wainscoat Farm 1826 B

If Bryant's form is correct, this may mean 'farm(house) in which there is *wainscot*-work' but there is not enough to go upon.

Weedon

WEEDON 94 G 14

Weodune 1066 (12th) KCD 824
Wedone 1220 Fees 313, 1262 *Ass*, 1295 Ipm, 1302 FA, 1318 AD ii, 1328 Pat
Weduna 1231 Bract, 13th AD iv
Wedon by Aylesbury 1328 Misc
Weodone 1346 FA, 1376 *New*
Wedon-in-the-Vale 1363 AD iii, Cl

This hill name is also found in Weedon (Nth), *Weodun* in BCS 792, 812. There is in OE a word *wīg*, *wēoh* meaning 'idol,' probably also 'temple,' found also in the compound *wēofod*, 'altar.' The root-idea in the word is 'sacred,' 'holy,' as in Goth. *weihs*, and Professor Ekwall suggests that these Weedons are hills with some ancient heathen religious associations. Cf. also *Cusanweoh* (BCS 72) and Willey (Sr), *Weoleage* (BCS 627). The corresponding ON *vé*, 'temple,' is fairly common in p.n. both simple and compound. The OS *wīh* is found in a few p.n. (*v.* Förstemann ON s.n.).

WEEDON HILL

Wedonhull 1328 Misc, 1363 AD iii, Cl
Wodenhull 1328 Cl

Wedonehel 1337 Misc

Self-explanatory.

Whitchurch

WHITCHURCH 94 F 13

Wicherce 1086 DB
Hwitchirche 1185 Rot Dom
Witchirche c. 1200 *AddCh* 6026
Hucherche c. 1200 ib.

Possibly 'stone' rather than 'white' church. Bede (iii. 4) says that *Candida Casa* was so called because built of stone.

BOLEBEC CASTLE (site of) (6″)

So called from the family of Bolebec, into whose possession the manor came in the 12th cent. (L. iii. 508).

Wing

WING 95 E 2

æt Weowungum 1012 (12th) Thorpe 553
Witehunge 1086 DB
Wienge 1181 NLC
Wengia 1200 Fines
Wungia 1200 Cur
Wongia 1209 Abbr
Wiungua Hy ii BM
Wenghe 1208 BM
Weng(e) c. 1215 WellsR, c. 1218 WellsL, 1227 *Ass*, 1235 Fees 463, 1245 Gross, 1247 *Ass*, 1255 Ch, 1262 *Ass*, 1275 Pat, 1284 FA, 13th AD i, 1316 FA, Pat, 1324 Cl, 1362 Pat, 1367 Ipm, 1382 Pat, 1400 IpmR
Weynge 1302 FA
Guionga 1317 Pat
Wyeng(e) 1325, 1380 Cl, 1397 Pat
Wyng(e) 1349 Pat, 1512 LP

The OE form is the dat. pl. of **Wiðungas*, a folk-name in the plur., the *w* in the form given above being a common error of transcription due to confusion between the similar letters *wen* and *thorn*. The origin of the name is unknown but *v.* Ekwall, PN *-ing* 67–8 and Zachrisson, *Some English PN Etymo-*

logies 6. The loss of medial *th* led to the coming together of two vowels, a fact which long influenced the forms and presumably the pronunciation also. These people must also have given their name to the neighbouring Wingrave. *v. infra.*

ASCOTT

Estcota 1220 Bract (p), 13th AD iii
Ascote 1262 *Ass*, 1482 IpmR

'East cottages,' so called in contrast to lost 'west cottage(s)' mentioned in *Biwestcothulle* (AD vi C 4827).

BURCOTT

Burcota 1219–21 Bract
Burcotes 1316 Pat

OE *burh-cotu*, 'fortified cottages,' the same name is found in Bierton *infra* and in Sa and So. See Addenda.

COTTESLOE, North and South

Coteslawe 1284 FA
Cotslow 1766 J
Cotslowe 1826 B

The OE name *Cotta* is well-established and there must have been a corresponding strong form *Cott* found here and in Cottesmore (R), Cottesbrook (Nth), Cottesbach (Lei), Cossall (Nt). It is curiously confined in its distribution.

CRAFTON LODGE

Croustone 1086 DB
Croftone 1200 Fines, 1200 Cur, 1237–40 Fees 1450, 1247, 1262 *Ass*, 1284 FA, 1286 Ipm, 1302 FA, 1304 Ipm, 1317 Pat, 1367 AD vi, 1372, 1380 Cl, 1435 AD iv, 1479 AD vi, 1488 Ipm, 1545 AD vi
Croftun 1200 Cur
Croxton 1200 Cur
Croston 1304 Cl

OE croh-tun, 'saffron-farm.' *s* for *h* is common in DB, while the *f* is a common development from OE *h*. The vowel has been unrounded in modern times. *v.* Introd. xxiii.

LITTLEWORTH

Litlengeworth 1227 *Ass*

'Enclosure of Lytel's people,' OE *Lytelinga-worþ*. The same patronymic form is found in Lillingstone *supra*, Litlington (C), Littleton (Mx) and Lidlington (Beds). This name *Lytel(a)* is probably a diminutive of those names in *Lut-* noted under Ludgershall *infra*. *v.* **worþ**.

NETHERWELD (lost)

There were manors of Nether and Upper or Over Weld. The earliest clear reference to this that has been noted is in the name of 'Henry de *la Welde* near Wyeng' (1325 Cl). *v.* **weald**. The same Henry is apparently referred to as Henry de *Walda* in 1316 (Pat). *v.* Introd. xxiii.

Wingrave

WINGRAVE 95 G 2 [wingruv]

Withungrave 1086 DB
Witungrave 1086 DB
Wiengraua 1175 P, 1198 Fines, Cur
Wengrava R i P, 1198 Fines, 1201 Cur, 1220 Fees 313, 1223 WellsR, 1241 *Ass*, 1283 Ipm, 1284 FA, 1292 Ch, 1328 Misc, Cl, 1346 AD vi, 1364 Cl, 1372 Pat, 1375 Cl, 1382 IpmR, 1385 Pat, 1399 AD iii
Wingrave 1198 Cur
Wenggraue c. 1220 *Bodl Berks* 16
Wengraue 1227 *Ass*, *FF*
Weyngrave 1241 *Ass* (p), 1302 FA
Wingraue 1262 *Ass*
Wyngrave 1291 Ch, 1301 Ipm, 1355, 1379 Cl, 1418 IpmR, 1500 BM, 1509 LP
Wayngrave 1346 Cl
Wingrove 1365 IpmR (and still locally)

OE *Wiþunga-grāf(a)*, 'grove or thicket of the Withungas.' *v.* Wing *supra* and **graf(a)**.

HELSTHORPE (Fm) [elstrəp]

Helpestorp(e) 1086 DB, 1237–40 Fees 1451

Helpestrope 1086 DB, 1227 *Ass*, 1237–40 Fees 1451, 1262 *Ass*, 1284 FA, 1367 AD vi
Hilpestorpe 1223 WellsR (p)
Helperthorpe 1225 Bract
Helperestrope 1225 Bract
Helpetorp 1241 *Ass*
Helpesthorp(e) 1328 Cl, 1346 FA, 1365 Fine, 1367 Pat
Helpstrop 1360 Pat, 1479 AD vi
Helpesthrop(e) 1363 AD iii, Cl, 1364 Pat
Helpisthorp 1364 Pat
Elstrap 1766 J

'Helphere's village' *v.* þorp. The name **Helphere* is not actually found in OE but other compounds in *Help-* are known and the compound name has given rise to a patronymic form in Helpringham (L). *v.* Ekwall, PN *-ing* 141. On the other hand the only evidence for an *er* in this name comes from Bracton's Note Book. This is not strictly an original source but consists of copies from Plea Rolls, and its *Helper-* forms may be due to a misreading. If so, the origin of the name is OE *Help*. *Helpe*, presumably the weak form of this stem, was used as a personal name in the 12th cent.

MERCER'S HOUSE (6″)

Bury Manor in Wingrave was given to the Mercers' Company as part of the endowment of St Paul's School by Dean Colet and this gave rise to Mercers' Farm, now Mercer's House (*VCH*).

NUP END

Dryvers Knopp 1546 AD vi

OE cnæpp, with rounding of the *æ* to *o* = [ɔ] under the influence of the labial *p*, or an adaptation of ME *knoppe*, 'rounded protuberance.' Nup End stands on just such a site to the north-west of Wingrave. The modern form shows partial unrounding.

ROWSHAM [rɑuʃəm]

Rullesham R i *P*, 1227 *FF*, 1363 *New* 44 (Weedon)
Rolesham 1198 Fines, 1284, 1302 FA, 1375 Cl

Rollesham 1198 Cur, 1227 *Ass*, 1235 Fees 536, 1241, 1247, 1262 *Ass*, 1266 Pat, 1285 Abbr, 1315 Ch, 1346 Cl
Rulesham 1242 Fees 877
Roulesham 1301 Ipm, 1346 FA, 1476 AD iii
Rolvesham 1363 AD iii, 1363 Cl
Rulsam 1465 Pat
Rulsham 1465 IpmR
Rowsham 1518 AD iii
Rowlsham 1538 LP
Rowsome 1640 *Foster*

OE *Hrōðwulfes-hām*, 'Hrothwulf's ham.' The history is the same as that of Rousham (O), except that the full form of the latter was preserved much longer than that of the present name. See the forms in Alexander (PN O). Rolleston (St) also contains OE *Hrōðwulf*.

IX. YARDLEY HUNDRED

Erlai 1086 DB
Aerlega 1182 P
Erlea 1184 P
Erleie R i P
Erle 1195 Cur, 1227, 1241, 1247 *Ass*, 1284, 1302 FA
Herlegh 1232 Fees 1357
Ersle 1247 *Ass*
Erlegh 1262 *Ass*
Erlee 1262 *Ass*
Erele 1316 FA

The site of the Hundred meeting-place is now marked by Yardley Farm in Pitstone. For the etymology *v.* that name *infra*.

Cheddington

CHEDDINGTON 95 G 4
Cetedone 1086 DB
Cetendone 1086 DB
Cetedene 1086 DB
Chettend' Hy i (13th) *Nostell* 112
Chetendon ib., c. 1200 *AddCh* 6026, 1220 Fees 303, 1227 *Ass*, 1237–40 Fees 1451, 1241, 1247 *Ass*, c. 1250 *Mert* 397, 1284 FA

Chedendon c. 1165 (13th) *Nostell* 111 *b*, 1203 Fines, 1247, 1262 *Ass*
Chedindone 1167 RBE, 1219 WellsR
Chettendon c. 1190 (13th) *Nostell* 111 *b*
Chetind' c. 1195 (13th) *Nostell* 112 *b*
Chetendun c. 1225 *Mert* 395, c. 1240 ib. 393
Chettindon 1227 *Ass*
Chetingdone 1229 WellsR, 1284 FA, 1314 Cl, 1367 AD vi, 1469 IpmR
Chetindon 1242 Fees 877, c. 1250 *Mert* 413, 1277 Orig, 1278 Fine, 1284 Ipm, 1286 AD vi
Chetyngdon 1291 Ch, 1337 Pat, 1344 Ipm, 1407 AD vi
Chedyndon 1339 Pat, 1373 Cl, 1392 *Mert* 2990
Chetyndone 1340 NI, 1349 AD vi
Chedyngton 1365 Fine, 1378 Cl, 1407 AD vi, 1489 *Mert* 1881, 1535 VE, 1545 AD vi
Chedyngdon 1383 Cl, 1386 Pat, 1407 AD vi, 1429 *Mert* 3005
Chedingden 1511 *Mert* 1374
Chedynton 1529 *Mert* 3118
Chetyngton 1535 VE
Shedyngton 1535 VE
Chetington 1526 LS
Chiddyngton 1537 LP

OE *Cettan-dun*, 'Cetta's hill.' For the name *Cett*(*a*) cf. Chettisham (C) and *Cettan treo* (BCS 210). This name may be a variant pet-form of *Cedda*, with unvoicing of the medial consonant as suggested by Zachrisson, *Two instances of Fr. influence on English PN* 10, n. 2. The later hesitation between *t* and *d* is probably an example of French spelling influence, ultimately affecting pronunciation, as noted by Zachrisson in the same paper pp. 8, 9.

Cholesbury

CHOLESBURY 106 A 4

Chelewoldesbye 1227 *FF*
Cherewoldeberi 1230 WellsR
Chelweldesbyr' 1262 *Ass*
Chelewoldesbyr' 1262 *Ass*
Chelvaldisbyry 1285 QW

Chilwaldesbury 1330 Fine, 1331 Ipm
Chelwaldesbury 1363 Cl
Chelwoldesbury 1363 AD iii, 1364 Pat, 1377 IpmR
Chelwardisbery 1385 Pat
Chelwardesbury 1417 Pat
Chollisbury 1526 LS

'Ceolweald's **burh**,' the reference being to a plateau-camp, locally known as 'the Bury.' Cf. VCH ii. 22–3 and HMN 106.

PARROT'S FARM

The farm takes its name from the family of *Perot*. Thos. Perot held a tenement in Cholesbury called *Coldelowe* in 1330 (Fine).

Drayton Beauchamp

DRAYTON BEAUCHAMP 95 J 3

Draitone 1086 DB

The Beauchamp family are first mentioned in connexion with it in 1221 (WellsR) and the name is first suffixed in

Drayton Belcamp 1238 Gross

The pronunciation is indicated in

Drayton Becham 1526 LS

v. **dræg**. There is no river-bend to be cut off here, but the sense 'place where timber is dragged' is not improbable for Drayton lies at the foot of well-wooded hills.

PAINESEND

This was in the tenure of John Payne in the 16th cent. (*VCH*).

SHIRE LANE (6″)

Shyreway 1607 *Terr*

A lane running along the boundary of Herts and Bucks.

Edlesborough

EDLESBOROUGH 95 F 5 [edʒbərə]

Eddinberge 1086 DB
Edulf(u)esberga 1175, 1185 P
Edulueberga 1178 P

Aedulf(u)esberga 1181, 1185, 1189 P
Adulfesberga 1185 P
Eduluesburg 1197 FF(P), 1227 *Ass*
Eduluesbur(i) c. 1200 (c. 1230) *Wardon*, 1262 *Ass*
Eduluesberge 1203 Fine, 1227, 1247 *Ass*
Eduluesbir 1212 Fine
Edolueberg(h) c. 1215 WellsR, 1331 Ch
Edulveberge 1219 WellsR
Edelesbergh 1227, 1247 *Ass*
Edelvesberg' 1229 Cl
Edolvesberg(h) 1232 Fees 1357, 1241, 1247, 1262 *Ass*
Eduluesburghe 1237–40 Fees 1451
Eddelesburgh 1241 *Ass*
Edulsberg 1241 *Ass*
Edelesbur(i) 1242 Fees 876, 1253, 1268, 1294 Pat
Edelfesburg 1247 *Ass*
Edeluesbir 1247 *Ass*
Edleberg(h) 1262 *Ass*, 1526 LS
Edelesburg(h) 1262 *Ass*, 1305 Pat, 1348 Cl, 1367 Pat
Edlesbur' 1262 *Ass*
Edullesbouruh 1270 Ipm
Edlesberg 1281, 1323 Pat
Edulvesburwe 1284 FA
Edelesborewe 1287 Ipm
Edelesburwe 1291 Ch
Edlesbeorg 13th AD iii
Edelisberue 13th AD i
Edolvesbur 13th AD i
Edesbergh 1302 FA
Edlesburgh 1316 Cl, 1337 Pat, 1344 Ipm
Edesburgh 1327 Pat, 1365 Pat, 1369 Cl, 1480 Pat
Edysborogh 1535 VE
Edesborough 1626 Vern
Edgeborough 1665 Herts Sess
Edgborough 1716 Wing

'Eadwulf's **beorg**.' In interpreting *beorg* we may note Lipscomb's statement (iii. 349) that 'the Church stands on an eminence which has the appearance of having been either an

ancient barrow or perhaps a Roman summer encampment.' For *Eadwulf* > *Edle*, cf. Edlingham (Nb). Later the *l* was lost from the consonant-group *dlsb* and *ds* has become *dg* in the local pronunciation by a common development fully discussed by Zachrisson, *Studier i Modern Språkvetenskap*, viii. 123–34. The name *Eadwulf* was common before the Conquest and remained in use until the 13th cent. In place-names it occurs in Edlingham (Nb), Adlington (Ch, La), Edlaston (Db) and, in the Anglo-Scandinavian form *Yadulf*, in Yaddlethorpe (L).

BUTLER'S FARM

Botylers 1393 IpmR

This is the land held in 1302 (FA) by Philip le *Boteler*.

DAGNALL

Dagehale 1192 (c. 1300) *Bardney Cart.* 233 *b*, 1235 Cl, 1241 *Ass*, 1300 Pat
Dagenhale 1196 FF(P), 1202 Fines, 1227, 1247 *Ass*, 1309 Ch, 1328, 1339, 1372 Cl
Dagenale 1196 FF(P), 1241 *Ass*
Daggenhale 1227 *Ass*, 1328 Fine
Daggehale 1322 Pat
Dagnale 1480 IpmR, 1493 Ipm
Dagnall 1539 LP

OE *Dagganheale* (dat.), 'Dagga's healh.' The pers. n. **Dagga* is not found in OE but is a regular formation for a pet-name for the numerous OE names in *Dæg-* (cf. IPN 174). It is found also in Dagworth (Sf), DB *Dagaworde* and has given rise to a diminutive **Daggel* which must lie behind Daglingworth (Gl), rather than the name *Dægel*, suggested by Baddeley (PNGl), for that should have given *Dayl-*. The group Dagnall, Northall, Ringshall and Hudnall in this parish is interesting. They all contain the suffix *healh* and lie in nooks in the slopes of the Chilterns.

HUDNALL (lost)

Hudenhal 1227 *Ass*
Hodenhale 1299 Abbr, 1309 Ch, 1348 Cl, 1367 Pat, 1376 Cl
Hudnale 1480 IpmR
Hudnoll Eliz ChancP

OE *Hūdanheale* (dat.), 'Huda's healh.' The name *Hūda* was borne by a *minister* of King Æthelwulf of Wessex, who became Ealdorman of Surrey and was killed in battle with the Danes in 853. The same name forms the first element in Huddington (Wo).

NORTHALL

Northale 1241 *Ass*, 1305, 1339, 1342 Pat, 1372 Cl
Northhale 13th AD iii
Northall 1345 Cl
Northalle 1480 Pat

'North healh.' 'North' either because it is the northernmost of the four *healh* sites in this parish, or in contrast to *South* End, near it.

RINGSHALL (Fm)[1]

Ringeshale 1235 *FF*, 1262 *Ass*
Ringsal 1766 J
Ringsall c. 1825 O

'Hring's healh.' The name *Hring* is not actually found in OE but compounds with *Hring-* though rare, are adequately recorded. *Hringuine* occurs in a genuine Kentish charter of 762. In place-names, *Hring* forms the first element in Ringshall and Ringsfield (Sf) and *Ringesdone*, DB, in Rippingale (L). The same uncompounded name is found in German and ON. *v*. *Hringa* in Förstemann (PN) and *Hringr* in Lind, *Norsk-Isländska Dopnamn*.

Hawridge

HAWRIDGE 106 B 5 [hɔridʒ]

Hoquerug' 1191–4 *HarlCh* 57 C 3
Aucrug H iii BM
Hauekrigge 1227 *Ass*
Haurugge 1231 Bract, c. 1270, 1338 Misc, 1346 FA
Haurigge 1233 WellsR, 1247 *Ass*, 1402 Pat, 1526 LS
Hawerugh' 1235 Fees 463
Haurig 1235 Gross

[1] Ringshall is partly in Herts.

Hockerig 1241 *Ass*
Hauweregge 1242 Gross
Haueregg 1284 Ipm
Haberugge 1284 FA
Hawerugge 1300 Ipm, 1398 Pat
Hawerigg 1300 Ipm
Hawridge 1561 BM
Horidge 1627 Vern
Harridge 1664 Herts Sess
Worrage c. 1825 O

'Hawk-ridge' *v.* **heafoc, hrycg.** The etymology is beyond question but the very early loss of the *k* is noteworthy. No parallel can be cited.

GEARY'S WOOD

Probably takes its name from the family of Jasper Geary, who held tenements in Hawridge in the early 17th cent. (*VCH*).

Ivinghoe

IVINGHOE 95 G 4

Evinghehou 1086 DB
Hiuingho 1195 Cur(P)
Iuingeho 1195 Cur(P), 1199 Fines
Ivingho 1227 Ch
Ivengho 1241 *Ass*, 1255 *For*
Ivingo 1303 Cl
Ivanhoe 1665 Herts Sess

OE *Ifinga-hō(g)e* (dat.), 'the **hoh** of Ifa's people.' For *Ifa* as an OE name *v.* Forssner 169. The same name is found in Ivington (He) and its strong form in Iveston and Ivesley (Du). The place stands at the base of a considerable spur of land jutting out from the main range of the Chilterns (Harman). For the DB form *v.* IPN 113 (top) and cf. the DB form for Tingewick. The curious way in which Scott, who is always thought (and probably rightly so) deliberately to have altered *Ivinghoe* to *Ivanhoe*, actually hit upon one identical with a form found in documentary evidence in the 17th cent. (not then published) is worthy of note. The coincidence is the more remarkable seeing that *an* for *ing* is without parallel in other p.n.

IVINGHOE ASTON

Estone 1086 DB
Est Aston 1299 Cl, Ipm, 1315 Pat
Aston 1387 IpmR
Ivyngho Aston 1491 Ipm

'East farm.' Not markedly to the east of Ivinghoe village but lying on the east side of the parish. 'East' Aston, presumably because it is the easternmost of the four Buckinghamshire Astons.

THE COOMBE (6″)

Cumba c. 1286 (1299) *Winton*
v. cumb.

DUNCOMBE TERRACE (6″)

Takes its name from the Duncombe family who in the 16th cent. lived at Barley End in this parish (*VCH*).

ELSAGE (Fm) (6″)

Elneshegge 1392 *Mert* 2999
Olneshegge 1392 *Mert* 2990
Elvyshegg 1429 *Mert* 3005, 1448 ib. 3004
Eluyshegge 1489 *Mert* 1881
Ellyshege 1508 *Mert* 1882
Elshege 1539 *Mert* 1875
Elshage 1547 *Mert* 2964
Elsage 1591 *Mert* 1878

The first two forms would seem to be corrupt and the OE form of the name to have been *Ælfeshecg*, 'Aelf's hedge,' though one would have expected this to come out as *Alsage*, rather than *Elsage* (*v.* Introd. xxiii).

HORTON

Hortone 1086 DB
Horton juxta Ivingho 1464 IpmR

v. horh, tun. 'Muddy farm.' It lies close to the river.

SEABROOK

Sebroc 1227 *Ass*
Seibroc 1227 *FF*

Seybroc 1241 *Ass*, 1250 Fees 1212 (p)
Seybroke c. 1250 *Mert* 397, 1291 Ch, 1292 Ipm, 1346 FA, 1348 Ipm, 1355 Pat, 1399 IpmR
Saybroke 1284 FA
Seibroke 1334 Ipm
Seabrook 1625 Cheddington

A personal name **Sǣga* (< **Sǣiga*) is suggested both by the forms above and by the early spellings of Seaton (Rutland) DB *Seieton* 1187 P *Saieton*. Names compounded with *Sǣ-* are common. The diminutive suffix *-iga* occurs in the 'heroic' personal name Wudiga, contracted in *Widsith* to Wudga. A similar contraction seems to have taken place here.

Alternatively Professor Ekwall would take the first element to be an OE *sǣge*, 'slowly moving' (cf. MLG *sege*, 'dripping, blear-eyed,' ON *seigr*, 'tough,' lit. 'dripping slowly') found in the compound *on-sǣge*, 'assailing.' The brook now forms part of the Grand Junction Canal, but judging by the lie of the land it can never have had much of a fall.

Marsworth

MARSWORTH 95 H 4 [mɑ·zəθ]
(*æt*) *Mæssanwyrð* 1012 (12th) Thorpe 553
Missevorde 1086 DB
Messewurda 1163 P
Messewrda Hy i (1267) Ch
Massewrth 1199 Cur
Messeworth 1200 Cur, 1215 WellsR, c. 1218 WellsL, 1227, 1262 *Ass*, 1284, 1316, 1346 FA, 1377 Ipm
Messewurth 1200 Cur, 1262 *Ass*, 1276 RH
Masseworth 1201 Cur, 1301 Ipm, 1312 Pat, 1328 Ch, 1335 Fine, 1363 AD iii, 1367 Cl, 1526 LS
Massewurth 1201 Cur
Messewrth 1227 *Ass*, 1242 Fees 877
Maseworth 1301 Ipm
Mosseworth 1338 Cl
Masworth 1364 Pat, 1490 Ipm, 1582 AD vi
Mesworth 1546 LP
Mersworth 1766 J

'Mæssa's enclosure' *v.* **worþ**. For the pers. name **Mæssa*, *v.* IPN 173 and cf. Massingham (Nf), Messingham (L). The *r* of the modern form is an attempt to show the characteristic long *a* of the dialectal pronunciation. *v.* Introd. xxiii.

Pitstone

PITSTONE 95 H 4

Pincenestorne 1086 DB
Pincelestorne 1086 DB
Pilketorn' 1195 Cur(P)
Pichelesyorne 1220 Fees 313
Pichelestorn 1227, 1241 *Ass*, 1243 Gross, 1286 Ch
Pichestorn 1227 *Ass*
Pychestorn 1235 Fees 461
Pychelestorn 1235 Fees 465
Pychenestorn 1235 Fees 555
Picheles þorne 1237–40 Fees 1450
Pichelesthorne 1247 *Ass*, 1306 Fine, 1307 AD v, 1316 FA
Pychelesthorne 1262 *Ass*, 1339 Pat, 1593 BM
Puchelesthorne 1284 FA
Pichelesturne 1285 Ch
Pychelstorne 1396 Pat
Pittleshorn 1526 LS
Pytcheleythorne 1536 LP
Pychesthorne 1593 BM
Pidlesthorne 1641 *Mert* 2966
Pittlestone 1743 Hughenden
Pittelsthorne 1766 ib.
Pightlesthorne or *Pitstone* c. 1825 O
Pightlesthorn 1826 B

'Picel's thornbush.' The name *Pīcel* is found in the form *Püchil* in LVD and seems to be a diminutive of the rare OE name *Pīc*. Since 1500 the phonetic development has probably been affected by association with the common dial. pightle which itself has an alternative form *pichel* (NED s.v.). It is to be noted that the same pers. name appears in a stream in Pitstone called *Pichelesburne* c. 1400 (*St Alb* iii. 326). The DB form is probably corrupt (*v.* Introd. xx).

BARLEY END

Bereleie 1241 *Ass* (p)
Berle(e) 1291, 1293 Ch
Barleyend 1520 AD vi

'Barley-clearing' *v.* **bere, leah.**

DUNCOMBE FARM

v. Duncombe Terrace *supra.*

WARD'S HURST

Wardhurst 1333 *FF* (*VCH*)

'Watch' or 'outlook hill.' *v.* **weard, hyrst.** The spot commands an extensive view to the north and north-east. The modern form is corrupt and has been extended to the neighbouring *Ward's Coombe.*

YARDLEY (Fm) (6")

Erle 1227 *Ass*, 1284 FA, 1339 Pat
Yardley 1826 B

(For further forms *v.* Hundred name.)

Possibly *Eorlan-lēah* becoming *Erlele* and then *Erle*. Hence 'Eorla's clearing,' **Eorla* being a shortened form of one of the OE names in *Eorla-*. Ekwall would take this and Arley (La 2) and (Wa) and Early (Berks) to be OE *ere-lēah*, 'clearing for ploughing.' For initial *y* cf. Ernesdon *supra*. The *d* is late and epenthetic.

Slapton

SLAPTON 95 F 4

Slapetone 1086 DB
Slaptone 1223 WellsR, 1237–40 Fees 1451, 1241 *Ass*, 1284 FA

'Farm on the *slape*' *v.* **slæp.** The village lies on a slight slope. Lipscomb's statement (iii. 449) that Slapton 'occasionally suffers from excess of humidity and partial inundation: the soil is a deep stiff clay' makes the existence of a *slape* highly probable. Cf. Slapton (Nth).

WHADDON

Wadone 1086 DB
Waddon' c. 1200 *AddCh* 6026, 1372 Cl
Whaddunam 1231 Bract
Whaddon 1706 *Terr*

'Wheat-hill' *v.* **hwæte, dun** and cf. Whaddon *infra*.

X. ASHENDON HUNDRED

Essedene 1086 DB
Essendon(e) R i *P*, 1195 Cur(P), 1238 Fees 1373, 1247, 1262 *Ass*
Essendun 1195 Cur(P)
Assendon 1227 *Ass*
Esshendon 1241 *Ass*

The prominent hill on which Ashendon stands made an appropriate meeting-place for the Hundred.

Ashendon

ASHENDON 94 H 10

Assedune 1086 DB
Assedone 1086 DB
Essendon c. 1218 WellsL, 1242 Fees 880, 1284 FA
Essesdon 1235 Fees 467, 1237–40 ib. 1448 (*Marescalli*)
Essenden 1242 Fees 882
Essedon 1247 *Ass*
Ayssendone 1255 *For*
Esshendone 1316 FA
Esseden 1325 Cl
A(s)shedon 1327, 1341, 1361 Cl, 1398 IpmR
Assheden 1327, 1348 Cl
Esshes(e)done 1335 Ipm, 1346 FA
Ass(e)nyndon 1361 Cl, 1379, 1397 AD vi
Ashingdon 1391 IpmR
Eschendon 1424 IpmR
Es(s)henden 1461 IpmR, 1465 Pat
Asshyngdon 1546 LP

OE *æscen-dūn*, 'ashen-hill,' i.e. 'grown over with ashes.' Cf. Ashdown Forest (Sx) with the same history and *v.* Lipscomb (i. 6) 'Ashendon...is conjectured to have derived its name from the nature of the wood with which this district abounded.' There are a good many old ash trees here, though they are being gradually displaced by elm (Harman). *Marescalli* because it was held of the Earl Marshal.

HILL (Fm)

(Wm. atte) *Hulle* 1340 NI

Self-explanatory.

POLLICOTT (Upper and Lower)

Policote 1152–8, 1155, 1160–5 NLC, 1290 Cl, 1262 *Ass* (*Magna*), 1397 AD vi (*Parva*)
Policote Marescalli 1237–40 Fees 1448
Pulicote 1241 *Ass* (p), 1242 Fees 880
Polekote Cressy 1242 Fees 881
Policote Bokecot 1255 RH
Polycote Walence, *P. Boketot* 1302 FA
Pollicott 1639 *Terr*

There is some evidence for an OE name *Poll* or *Pōl.* Polesworth (Wa) is *Polleswyrð* in *Saints* (c. 1000), Polesden (Sr) is *Pollesden* (1428 FA), and it is possible that the same name may be found in Polling (Ha), left unexplained by Ekwall (PN *-ing* 67). There is also a *polesleage* in KCD 641 (W), unidentified, but this may be the common word *pōl*, 'pool.' It may be suggested therefore that the original form of this name was *Polingcot*(*u*), i.e. Pol's cottage(s), with *-ing-* used in the same way as in certain -ingtun- names, the *ing* being later reduced to *i.*

Upper and Lower P. were once distinguished as Great and Little. The former was held of the Earl Marshal by Hugo de Cressy (Fees 881), the latter by Thomas Buketot of the same overlord (ib. 880). *Valence* from the family name of the Earl Marshal.

WATBRIDGE (Fm)

This bridge must take its name from the brook it spans or at least from the name of the man from whom the brook is

called, for the stream is the *Wottesbroc* dealt with under Waddesdon *infra*.

Chearsley

* CHEARSLEY 94 J 11 [tʃi·əzli]

Cerdeslai Cerleslai 1086 DB
Cherdesle(e) Hy ii (1313) Ch, 1235 Fees 461, 1241, 1262 *Ass*, 1296 Cl, 1314 FA, 1332 Cl, 1360 Ipm
Cherdsle 1204 Fines (p)
Cherdele 1227 *Ass*, 1255 *For*, 1270 Pat
Chardesleye 1296 Ipm, 1326 Cl, 1505 Pat, 1535 VE, 1542 LP
Chardesle(e) 1302 FA, 1332 Cl, 1339 Pat (*Valence*), 1359 Cl
Chaddesle 1330 Ipm
Cherdesley 1335, 1339 Pat, 1397 AD vi
Charesley 1526 LS, *Cherysley* ib.

'Ceolred's clearing' *v.* leah. Names *Cered*, *Cyred* and *Kyred* are found in BCS 537, 541 and 677 respectively. Searle (s.n.) suggests with great probability that these and the name *Cerred* found in DB are forms of OE *Cēolrǣd*, and this would account for the forms of Chearsley. The *l* in one of the DB forms is probably an error due to anticipation of the coming *l* but it is just possible that it may be a last trace of the *l* of the full form *Ceolræd*. The name should have become [tʃa·zli] but a spelling pronunciation now prevails.

The assimilation of *lr* to *rr* which ultimately produced forms like *Cered*, *Ceored*, is evidenced in this name in the first half of the 9th cent. In 845 *Ceolred* bishop of Leicester attests, as *Ceored*, a contemporary charter of Beorhtwulf King of the Mercians (Harmer, *English Historical Documents*, III). It is at least a curious coincidence that this charter relates to Wootton Underwood, four miles from Chearsley. The Mercian kings had no Chancery. The charter in question, written for a local thegn, was doubtless written locally and is evidence that such a form as *Ceored* might have arisen in the immediate neighbourhood of Chearsley as early as 845.

Grendon Underwood

GRENDON UNDERWOOD 94 F 10 [grindən]

Grennedone 1086 DB

Grenedone 1197 P(R)
Grendon 1231 Ch
Gryndon 1626 Vern

'Green hill.' Cf. Lipscomb (i. 252), 'the place is supposed to derive its name from the verdure of a little hill near the village: and its vicinity to the forest of Bernwood...and in ancient evidences it is sometimes called 'under Bernwood.' *v.* **grene, dun.**

FINEMEREHILL HOUSE (6″)

Finmore Close L. i. 257
v. Finemere Wood *infra*.

SHAKESPEARE FARM

The name is not old having replaced the name of the earlier Ship Inn, but it records the tradition first mentioned by Aubrey in the 17th cent. that Shakespeare visited Grendon and that the humour of the constable in *Midsummer's Night's Dream* (sic) was drawn from the village constable.

Kingswood

KINGSWOOD 94 G 10

In the perambulation of Bernwood Forest, dated 1298, and printed in VCH ii. 132, there is mention of 'the lord King's wood.' It is traditionally associated with Fair Rosamund and on an old map printed by Lipscomb (i. 513) a lane between the woods appears as 'Rosiman's Waye.'

MERCER'S FARM (6″)

Owned for nearly two centuries before 1829 by the Mercers' Company (*VCH*).

Ludgershall

LUDGERSHALL 94 G 9 [lə'gəsəl]

(*æt*) *Lutegareshale* 1015 KCD 722, 1164, 1185 P, 1227, 1241, 1247 *Ass*, 1255 *For*, 1262 *Ass*, 1331 Cl
Lotegarser 1086 DB
Luttegersahala Hy ii (1285) Ch
Luttegareshall 1233 Ch
Ludegarshal 1241 *Ass*

Lottegarsale 1257 Ipm
Lotegershal(e) 1262 *Ass*, 1302 FA, 1315 Fine
Luttegareshale 1298 Ipm
Lutegarsale 1302 Fine, 1334 Cl
Ludegershale 1315 Fine
Lotegarssale 1346 Cl
Lutegarshale ib.
Ludgareshale 1347 Pat
Luteger(s)shale 1348 Ipm
Lutegarshalle 1381 IpmR
Lodegarshale 1382 Cl
Lurgessale 1509 LP
Lurdgarsall 1526 LP
Lurgosall 1536 LS
Lurgesall Eliz ChancP, 1627 Vern
Ludgarsell 1766 J

This is a puzzling name and its history cannot be separated from that of Ludgershall (W), Ludgarshall (Gl) and Lurgashall (Sx). All names end in healh and all three developed the same pronunciation, to judge from the latest spellings of them—*Lurgasill* for the Wilts one and *Largeshall* (sic) for the Gloucestershire one. The difficulty lies in the first element. There is very little variation in the early forms of it. In the Wilts name the forms follow those of the Bucks one closely, those with initial *Lud-* being definitely of late development. For the Gloucestershire name the forms are in order of appearance from 1220 to 1310, *Lutegares-*, *Letegares-* and *Lotegares-*. For the Sussex one we have *Letegares-* in 1136 and *Lodegars-* in 1428. The only other names that come in for consideration at the same time are an unidentified *Ludegarstun* in a late copy of a Worcestershire charter and *Lutgaresberi* the old name for Montacute (So), cf. IPN 115. If this is the gen. sg. of a pers. name as seems almost certain from the forms, the second element of that name is *-gar*, a very common name-element. The only OE name on record with initial *Lut-* is an 11th cent. *Lutsige* (KCD 1334) but that there was at least one other name with this prefix is clear from the place-names Lotherton (Y), *Luttringtun* in BCS 1352, Lutterington (Du), *Lutringtona* in Boldon

Book, and Lutterworth (Lei), *Lutresurde* in DB. Each of these seems to contain a personal name *Luthere* and the name *Lutting* found in LVD is probably a patronymic form from *Lutta*, a pet-form of this name, which is not found independently but is found in a strong form in *Luttes crundel* (BCS 327). A mutated diminutive **Lytel*, *Lytila*, is the origin of Lidlington (Beds) and (C), Littleton (Mx) and Littlecote below[1].

SHARP'S HILL

Probably derives its name from the family of John Sharpe, who paid tithes in 1659 (*VCH*).

TETCHWICK [tetʃik], [tʌtʃik]

Tochingewiche 1086 DB
Totingwich 1175 P, 1182 P
Totingewich 1176, 1180 P
Thochewik 1237–40 Fees 1448
Thochewic(h) c. 1240 *Mert* 2442 (p), 1255 *For*
Togwike 1242 Fees 874
Tochewic 1255 *For*
Tuchewyk 1258 Pat (p)
T(h)ochewyk 1262 *Ass*
Tothwych 1276 RH
Touchewyk 1302 FA
Tochewyk(e) 1316, 1346 FA, 1323 Pat
Tutchwike c. 1570 Map in L. i
Tochewicke Eliz ChancP
Titchwick field 1674 *Terr*
Tetchwich 1756 ib.

The OE form of this name was probably *Totingawīc*, and in that case we must take the DB form as corrupt, owing to the scribe's anticipation of the *ch* which comes later in the name. The full meaning of the name is therefore 'wic of Tota's people.' *Totingewik* > *Totigewik* > *Totgewik* > *Totchewik* with

[1] The persistent *e* may be explained as a svarabhaktic vowel already developed between *t* and *g* in OE, cf. Baldwin Brown, *Arts in Early England* (v. 270), on the Bewcastle *Cyniburug* and other names, and *v. Dudeman, Dudemær, Dudewine* in Searle, *Onomasticon*.

devocalising of *ge* after *t*. For the whole phonetic development we may compare the history of Atcham (Sa), DB *Atingeham*. One would have expected [tɔtʃik] or [tætʃik] rather than either of the pronunciations now found locally. Cf. Tathall End *supra*.

North Marston[1]

North Marston 94 E 13

Merstone 1086 DB
Normerstone 1233 WellsR
Nordhmerston 1237–40 Fees 1448

'Marsh-farm' *v.* mersc, tun. *North* in relation to Fleet Marston.

Oving

Oving 94 F 13 [u·viŋ]

Olvonge 1086 DB
Huuinga Mainfelini 1167 P
Vuinges R i *P*, 1237–40 Fees 1448, 1320 Ch
Uving(k)e 1222 WellsR
Ovinge 1240 Gross, 1242 Fees 884, 13th AD vi
Ouinges 1241, 1262 *Ass*
Vuinge 1247 *Ass*
Ovinghes 1255 *For*
Ouvinge 1273 Ipm
Owyngge 1276 RH
Evinge 1284 FA, *Evynge* 1316 FA
Howyng 1307 *Mert* 385
Ovyng 1321 BM, 1358 AD iii, 1488 Ipm
Ovynk 1323 Cl
Ouvyng 1353 Cl
Ovyngge 1380 Pat
Uuing 1675 Ogilby

OE *Ufingas*, 'Ufa's people,' *v.* EPN 41 (last paragraph). Oving (Sx) is identical in origin as well as in modern form.

[1] In FA this parish is placed now in Ashendon, now in Waddesdon Hundred. Perhaps it was divided between the two. It is here reckoned as part of Ashendon Hundred.

Quainton

QUAINTON 94 F 12 [kweintən]

Chentone 1086 DB

Quenton 1175 P, 1220 Fees 314, 1224 WellsR, 1241 *Ass* (p), 1247, 1262 *Ass*, c. 1290 *Mert* 862, 1300 Ipm, 1316 FA, 1329 Cl, 1370 Pat, 1371 Cl

Quentune c. 1190 *Bodl Berks* 9, 10

Queinton 1235 Fees 461, 1247 *Ass*, 1252 BM, 1262 *Ass*, 1329 Cl

Queynton 1247 *Ass*, 1275 Ipm, 1284 FA, c. 1290 *Mert* 861, 1331 Cl, 1356 Ipm, 1392, 1397 Pat, 1485 Ipm, 1524 AD vi

Quenthon 1255 *For*

Quintone 1290 Misc, *Quynton* 1375 Cl, 1396 Pat

Quaynton 1569 AD v

The clue to this somewhat difficult name is probably to be found in the history of Quinton (Gl). This is *Quenintone* in DB, *Quentone* in BCS 453 (14th cent. transcript), *Queinton* and *Quenton* in 13th cent. forms given by Baddeley (PNGl). If there has been similar loss of a medial *n* between two vowels in the Buckinghamshire p.n. we have a ready explanation of the early and persistent *ei* forms which must result from the crasis of the two vowels after the *n* is lost[1] (cf. the forms of Wing and Wingrave *supra* after similar loss of a medial consonant). We must then take the original form of this name to be *Cwēningtun*, an ingtun formation from a pers. name *Cwēna*, used as a pet-form for one of the OE feminine names in *Cwēn-*. This stem remained in use long after the Conquest, and *Quenild* (OE **Cwēnhild*) was one of the commonest feminine names in the 12th century Danelaw. Quainton and Quinton are interesting as additions to the brief list of place-names in which a feminine personal name was originally followed by the element *ing*.

BINWELL LANE FARM

Binnol Lane c. 1570 Map in L. i

Benwells 1826 B

Benwell, *Binwell* or *Binnol Lane* L. i. 418

[1] Professor Ekwall suggests that alternatively the development may have been *Cwenington* > *Quengton* > *Qweinton*, with the same development of a diphthong as in ME *mengde* > *meinde*, *drencte* > *dreinte*.

OE *Bynnan-wielle*, 'Bynna's spring' or possibly OE *binnan wiellum* = between the springs. *v.* **wiell**.

LOWER BLACKGROVE (Fm) (6")

Blagrove field 1706 *Terr*

Self-explanatory.

DENHAM

Dunindun c. 1220 *Marst* 55
Dunindon 1237–40 Fees 1448
Dundon 1242 Fees 874, 1569 AD v
Donydon 1247 *Ass*
Duningdon 1247 *Ass*
Dunigdon, *Dunydun* 1256, 1258 *FF*
Dundham 1766 J
Denham Hill c. 1825 O

OE *Dun(n)ingdun*, 'Dunn's hill,' the *ing* in *-ingdun* having the same sense as that recorded for it in **-ingtun**. The change of vowel in the modern forms is curious. *un* must have become *in*, at least in pron. as in Dinton *infra*, and the form *Dinham* seems then to have been assimilated to that of the more common name *Denham*. The loss of the second *d* must be due to assimilation, *nd* becoming *nn*.

DODDERSHALL

Dodereshell' Roberti 1167 P
Doderesberge[1] 1204 FineR
Dodereshille 1207 Fines
Doderhull 1227 *FF*
Dodereshull 1235 Fees 461, 1241, 1247 *Ass*, 1255 *For*, 1284, 1316 FA, 1343 Misc
Dodhereshull 1255 *For*
Dodreshulle 1316 FA
Dodershull 1342 Cl, Misc
Doreshull 1374 Pat
Dedersell 1392 Pat

[1] In this entry Robert de Baskerville is fining for a writ touching 'Sorteleg' and D. The chirograph was made in 1207, and the place there appears as *Dodereshill* (u.s.).

Daddersill 1539 LP
Dadersyl Laund c. 1570 Map in L. i

'hill' *v.* **beorg, hyll**. It may be suggested that Doddershall contains a personal name consisting of the well-recorded OE name-element *Dod*, extended by an *r* suffix. Such formations do not seem to be recorded independently in OE, but their existence is virtually proved by place-name evidence. Hothersall (La) and Huddersfield (Y) present problems which are best solved by assuming that a bare *Hūd*, occurring in the recorded name *Hūda* (cf. Hudnall *supra*), was extended in this way to form a new personal name, cf. Ekwall PNLa. It is probable that other examples will appear when place-name material has been more minutely analysed. *Ivershagh* from Oxton Grange (Nt), e.g., is much more likely to contain such an extension of the bare *If(a)* contained in Ivinghoe, above, than a hypothetical compound *Ifhere*.

FINEMERE WOOD [fainmu·ə]

Fiuemere (sic) 1179 BM
Fynemere 1325 Cl
Fynemer 1535 VE
Fine Moor Hill c. 1825 O

Finemere Wood and Hill lie on the parish boundary so that the second element may be **gemære** but the first is difficult of explanation. The spelling *Finmore* given by Lipscomb for Finemerehill *supra* suggests that the vowel ought to be short and that the modern pronunciation is purely a spelling one. There are OE words *fīn*, 'heap or pile,' *fīna*, 'woodpecker,' which might be the source of the first element but the sense of the compound is not clear.

SHIPTON LEE

(*a*) *Sibdone* 1086 DB
Scipdon 1207 Fines
Sypdon 1247 *Ass*
Sybdon 1247 *Ass* (p)
Schibdon 1291 Tax, 1302, 1346 FA
Shipton by Lutegarsale 1312 Pat
Shipdon 1365 Ch, 1392 Pat, c. 1718 Map in L. i

Shepton 1391 Pat
Shibdon 1391 IpmR

(*b*) *Lye* 1237–40 Fees 1448
la Lee 1255 *For*
Shipden lye 1517 Encl

v. sceap, dun, leah. As Lipscomb says (L. i. 413), 'Is it fanciful to suppose that the sheep pastured here, supplied its name?' The names of two distinct manors have here been run together into one.

SORTELE (lost)

Sortelai 1086 DB, 1163 P
Sorteleg 1204 FineR
Scottele (sic) 1207 Fines

'Short clearing' from OE *scort*, short and leah. *Sortelai* is mentioned next to Shipton in DB (274 *b*, 275 *a*), both manors being held TRW by one *Alsi*. It is quite possible therefore that we should identify *Sortelai* with the manor of Lee in Shipton Lee. In the last two passages mentioned above it is associated with Doddershall which is in the immediate neighbourhood of Shipton Lee. If it is not to be identified with Lee and taken as a shortened form of it, it is clear that 'short lea' was so called in contrast to Lee.

WOAD HILL

Wodhull 1321 BM

v. wad, hyll.

Winchendon

WINCHENDON (Upper and Lower) 94 H 12 and J 11 [witʃən-dən]

yincandum (sic) 1004 (E iii) St Frides 6
wincandon Ethelred (E ii) ib.
Witchende 1086 DB
Wichendone 1086 DB, 1182 P, 1227 WellsR
Wikendon(a) 1155 NLC, 1199 Cur (p)
Wichindone 1160–5 NLC
Winchenton 1175, 1176 P
Winchendon 1176 P, 1204 Fines, c. 1218 WellsL, 1221 Bract

Wichinton 1178 P
Whychindone c. 1220 WellsR, *Whychinton* 1241 *Ass* (*parva*)
Wichedona 1221 Bract
Wynchendone c. 1232 WellsR
Winchedone 1232 WellsR, 1242 Fees 881 (*Inferior*), 1255 *For* (p)
Whichedon 1242 Fees 1404
Wynchindon 1255 *For* (p)
Wynchedon 1262 *Ass* (*Nether*), 1285 QW, 1316 FA, 1349 Pat
Wychendon 1262 *Ass* (*Superior*), 1335 Pat
Wynchyndone 1302 FA, 1375 Pat (*Over*), 1435 AD vi
Wechendon 1447 Pat (*Nether*)
Wynchingdon 1535 VE. *Over Winchingdon* 1575 AD vi
Nether Witchingdon 1627 Vern

Possibly OE *Winecan-dūn*, 'Wineca's hill.' This pers. name, originally a diminutive of one of the numerous compound names in *Wine-*, is found in *Winecanfeld* (BCS 778) for Winkfield (Berks). The form *Winch-*, rather than *Wink-*, offers difficulty but may possibly be due to the influence of the related form *Winec(e)* found in *Winecesburug* BCS 1099 and *Wincesburch* (ib. 1164) for Winsbury (So). The early and persistent loss of *n* before [ʧ] in the local pronunciation is noteworthy. Upper and Lower are respectively Great and Little Winchendon. Winkburn (Nt) probably contains the same personal name *Win(e)ca*.

THE LINCES (6″)

Lynch c. 1825 O

v. hlinc. *Lince* is a French spelling of this word (cf. Linslade *supra*) but it is inpossible to say whether it or *Lynch* is the genuine form here. *lince* is a common local term applied to old terraces of cultivation, cf. 'The Linces' on Westend Hill near Cheddington.

MAINSHILL

The farm was known as *Mainsground* in the 17th cent. and takes its name from the *Mayne* family of Dinton (*VCH*).

PIGGOTTS (6″)

Pickets 1826 B

This farm-name is manorial in origin and probably takes its name from the family of that Robert Pycot who was a juror in Ixhill Hundred, just across the parish-border, in 1302 (FA).

Wotton Underwood

WOTTON UNDERWOOD 94 H 10

wudotun 848 BCS 452
Oltone (sic) 1086 DB
Wutton' 1167 PR
Wotton Marescalli 1237–40 Fees 1448
Wotton juxta Brehulle 1288 Orig
Wotton-under-Bernewode 1415 AD iii

v. wudu, tun. In the 9th cent. Wotton must have been within the forest which appears as Bernwood in the 10th cent. The name is still appropriate. *Marescalli* because it was a manor of the Earl Marshal.

GRENVILLE'S WOOD (6″)

Wotton was a Grenville manor (Fees 881) and in the perambulation of Bernwood Forest in 1298 (VCH ii. 132) the wood is referred to as 'the wood of Richard Grenvoile (sic) of Wotton.'

LAWN FARM (6″)

Takes its name from *Wotton Lawnd*, a common mentioned in 1580 (*VCH*).

NEW WOOD (6″)

Newewod 1255 *For*
Self-explanatory.

TITTERSHALL WOOD

Todleshall (sic) 1298 VCH ii. 132
Tudreshull 1372 Ipm (*VCH*)
Tydershall Wood L. i. 601

The forms are too scanty and doubtful to admit of any certainty. Professor Zachrisson suggests that the first element may be a dimin. *Tyddel*, with mutation of the stem vowel, corresponding to the unmutated *Tuddul* which is found in Old English. Hence 'Tyddel's hill.' The *r* would then be due to

the common AN confusion of *l* and *r* (IPN 106). In this case the ME *o* and *u* represent the *u*-development of OE *y* while the modern form show St English *i*. *v*. Introd. xxiii.

YEAT (Fm)

This may possibly take its name from the old name of the R. Ray. In the Wotton charter (BCS 848) we have the phrase *ut bi geht*, 'out along Geht,' which certainly refers to this stream and gives us the old name of the river on which Islip (O) stands, explaining the early forms for that name.

XI. IXHILL HUNDRED

Tichessele, *Ticheshele* 1086 DB
Yxhelle 1175 P
Hikeshelle 1189 P, *Hikeshulle* 1265 Misc
Ixhulle R i *P*, 1227 *Ass*, 1238 Fees 1373, 1241 *Ass*, 1346 FA
Ickeshulle 1232 Fees 1358, 1255 *For*
Ixhill 1242 Fees 1404, 1247 *Ass*
Ikeshulle 1241, 1262 *Ass*, 1316 FA
Yckeshulle 1263 Misc

The Hundred meeting-place was at Ixhill in Oakley, on comparatively low-lying ground, the parishes of Boarstall, Brill, Chilton and Long Crendon forming a well-marked half-circle of hills round it. For the etymology *v*. Ixhill *infra*. The DB form is corrupt, perhaps through prefixing of the final *t* of the preposition *æt* to it. *v*. æt.

Aston Sandford

ASTON SANDFORD 105 A 12

Estone 1086 DB, 1199 Fines
Aston' Sanford' 1242 Fees 883
Eston Sandford 1291 Tax
Aston Saunford 1302 FA, 1350 Ipm, 1396 IpmR
Aston Saundford 1350 Cl
Aston Sam(p)ford 1404, 1417 IpmR
Cold Aston 1418 IpmR

'East farm' and distinguished by the name of the feudal holder. Joh. de *Sanford* is party to a Fine in Aston in 1199. Lipscomb (i. 41) suggests that it is 'east' in distinction from *West* End on the opposite side of Haddenham. Haddenham and Aston had the same lord in DB (TRE).

Boarstall

BOARSTALL 94 H 8

Burchestala 1158, 1159 P
Burcstala 1159, 1160 P
Borchestal 1169 (14th) *Miss* f. 131
Borestall 1175 P
Borkestall 1185 Rot Dom, 1200 Cur
Burkestall' 1199 Cur
Borgstalle 1200 FineR
Burstalle 1214 FineR, 1210–2 RBE
Borestal 1232 Fees 1358
Borstalle 1237–40 Fees 1447

Forms with *Bor(e)s-* and *Burs-* alternate down to 1400, then we have

Borestall 1450 Godr
Bostoll 1538 LP
Bostall 1545 LP
Boorstall in Books 1703 *Terr*

v. **burhsteall**. Lipscomb quotes (i. 55) from Hearne's Preface to Robert of Gloucester his statement that 'The people of Borstall are mightily pleased when any one tells them that B. is the same with the Saxon word which signifies "a seat on the side of a hill," which exactly answers to this place.' For this confusion of **beorg** and **burh**, *v.* EPN 11.

ARNGROVE (Fm)

Armegrove 1348, 1355 Cl
Arrengrove 1766 J

The evidence is too slender and late to admit of any certainty of interpretation. No OE pers. names in *Earm-* are known, though there is a rare OHG name *Armo* (*v.* Förstemann PN

146). More probably we ought to take *Arme-* as from an earlier *Erme-*, with the common development of *er* to *ar*. This would bring the first element into comparison with that in Armley (Y), DB *Ermelai*, and Armston (Nth), DB *Mermeston*, Nth Surv. *Armeston*, FA *Ermeston*. These all point to the existence of an OE pers. name *Eorma* used as a short form for the names in *Eormen-*. Such a pet-form is found in OHG in *Ermo* and the patronymic *Erming* (Förstemann ib. 470–1). The modern form may have been influenced by that of Arncot (O), little more than two miles away. Professor Ekwall suggests however that the true OE form may be *earna-graf*, 'eagles' grove,' and that the change from *n* to *m* in the ME forms is due to distant assimilation of *n* to *f*.

DANES BROOK

Denebrok(e) c. 1294 St Frides, 1300 *For*

'Valley brook' *v.* **denu, broc.** The modern form is corrupt. For a possible second name for this stream *v. infra*.

DEERHIDE (lost)

Derhyde 1260 Pat, 1285 QW, 1289 Ipm
la Derhide 1276 RH

v. **deor, hid.** This 'hide' was supposed to have been granted to Nigel, lord of Boarstall, by Edward Confessor together with the hereditary custody of Bernwood Forest, in reward for his slaying of a formidable boar. Whatever the truth of this story of the hide it is clear that it can gain no support from the name of Boarstall itself for the first element in that name clearly has nothing originally to do with *boar* (OE *bār*).

HONEYBURGE

Honybrugge 1298 VCH ii. 132
Honey Bridge 1826 B

This bridge spans Danes Brook but there is mention in OE charters of more than one stream called *hunig-burna*, *hunigbroc* (*v.* PNWo 86) and this stream was doubtless alternatively a 'honey-brook' and the bridge 'Honey-brook-bridge.' For the loss of the middle term cf. Saunderton Lee *infra*. For *-burge*, *v.* Introd. xxiv.

MARLAKE HOUSE (6″)

Merlakebrugge 1298 VCH ii. 132
Merlake 1316 FA
Merlake, *Marlake* 1540 LP

Marlake House is a public house actually in Oxfordshire, in Murcot parish, but it preserves the name of a lost Buckinghamshire manor, associated with Nashway Farm (*infra*) in Feudal Aids. *Merelake* is also mentioned in a perambulation (temp. Edward I) quoted by Lipscomb (i. 52). It is clearly the boundary-stream (*v*. **mære, lacu**) which divides the two counties here, running parallel to Boarstall Lane. Cf. VCH *u.s.* 'to *Merlakebrugge* and so always by the bounds of the counties of Bucks and Oxon.'

ORIEL WOOD (6″)

Representing 8 acres of 'woode' ground owned by Oriel College in 1586 (*VCH*).

PANSHILL (Fm) [pænsəl], [pænsɔ·l]

Pansehale 1230 Cl
Pauncehale 1231 Cl
Pauncehaye 1233 Cl
Paunsehale 1241 *Ass*
Pancehale 1255 *For*
Paunshale 1315 Fine
Paunsale 1347 Misc
Pawnsell 1533 LP
Pawncells 1540 LP
Pauncill Walk 1611 D
Pansole 1766 J, 1826 B

v. **healh**. Professor Ekwall has probably provided the solution of this name in the following note:—There is a well-evidenced forest-name *Penchet* of Celtic origin. We have it in *Penceat*, the source of Penge (Sr). Further in Pancett or Pauncett Wood, formerly the name of Clarendon Forest, Wilts. This is *Penchet* (1279 *For. Proc. Chanc. Misc. Bundle* 12, 4), *Pancet* (Hy iii *For. Proc. MS Stowe* 798 f. 9), *Pansett* in a perambulation in Registrum S. Nicholai, Sarum (Salisbury 1912) in Wilts. Arch. Soc. The original *Penchet* became *Pancet*, *Pauncet* through Norman

influence. The change of *a* to *e* we have in Pamber (Ha), *c* for *ch* is well-known. This forest-name is probably the first element in Panshill. For the loss of *t* cf. Penge *supra* and Trunch (Nf), DB *Trunchet*. It may be added that Panshill is in an ancient forest and hunting district.

TOUCHBRIDGE (Fm)

Touchburge Fm c. 1825 O

For the suffix *v.* Introd. xxiv. It is difficult to deal with the first element on the basis of the present form alone but it may possibly be the same as that found in Tetchwick (*v. supra*) a few miles to the north-east.

Brill

BRILL 94 H 9

Burhella 1072 (1225) Abingd
Bruhella 1072 (1200) Abingd, 1109–11 AC, 1184, 1189 P, 1202 PR, 1227 *Ass*
Brunhelle 1086 DB
Bruelle c. 1150 WM
Brehill(a) Hy ii *Bodl O* 6 *b*, 1217 Pat, 1230 Ch, 1232 Cl, 1449 Pat, 1489 Ipm
Bruhill 1176 P
Brohill 1176 P, 1247 *Ass*
Bruhull R i P, 1202 PR, 1204 RC, 1227 *Ass*, 1232 Cl, 1232 Fees 135, 1241, 1247 *Ass*
Brohulle 1200 FineR, 1255 *For*
Brehulle 1204 Cur, 1213 FineR, 1217, 1226 Pat, 1232 Cl, 1237–40 Fees 1447, 1241, 1247 *Ass*, 1255 *For*, 1262 *Ass*, 1315 Fine, 1339 Cl, 1344 Ipm, 1417 Pat
Briwhille 1227 *Ass*
Broehull 1232 Cl
Breohull 1262 *Ass*
Bryhylle 1476 Pat
Bryll super montem 1535 VE

A compound of the same type as that found in Bredon and Breedon (IPN 25), the first element being a Celtic word for a hill and the second the OE **hyll**.

CLEARFIELDS (Fm)

Les Cleres de Ludgershell 1305 St Frides
Les Clers 1305 Pat
Cleresplace 1361 Ipm, 1362 Cl
Claresplace 1366 Pat, Cl

OFr *clere*, 'glade' (*v.* Godefroy, *Dict. de l'anc. langue française*). 'The glades' would be an apt name for a farm in this forest-district.

MALECUMB (lost)

Malecumbe 1237 Cl, 1255 *For*

This was near Boarstall and Brill. The second element is clearly *cumb*. The first is uncertain. An OE name *Mala* is very doubtful. Possibly the first element is OE **mæl**, and the reference may be to some cross in the valley.

MUSWELL HILL

Mussewell 1255 *For*
Mosewell 1305 Pat, 1362 Cl
Musewell 1346 Cl, 1356 Ipm
Mesewell 1362 Cl

'Moss-spring' *v.* **meos**, **wielle** and cf. Muzwell *supra*[1]. The spring is also called *Warborughwell* (1228 VCH ii. 132), *Seyntburwell* (1273 Fine (p)) and this second name is due to association with St Werburgh, who actually lived at one time at Weedon (Nth). Cf. L. i. 106 and Pat (1251), which speaks of the 'hermitorium' of St Werburg in Brill.

NASHWAY (Fm)

Lesa 1086 DB
Esses 1227 *Ass*, 1241 *Ass* (p), 1242 Fees 874, 1255 RH
Esse 1237–40 Fees 1447, 1255 RH, 1316 FA
Aysshegh 1298 VCH ii. 132

This Domesday manor has hitherto not been identified. Round (VCH i. 268) showed that it was identical with the *Esses* of the *Book of Fees*, that it was probably on the Oxfordshire border, and that it was the *Esses* and *Esshe* of FA. It is clear

[1] The *ss* in the earliest form would point rather to a p.n. **Mussa* found in Robert fil. *Musse* but that would leave the 1362 form unexplained.

also that it is the *Esses* in Ixhill Hundred of the Assize Rolls and the *Hasse* in the same Hundred and the *Esses* in the manor of Brill in RH. In the *Book of Fees* it is mentioned between Boarstall and Addingrove and also between Winchendon and Worminghall. In FA it is associated with a lost *Merlake* (117). In a perambulation of the forest of Bernwood printed in VCH (ii. 132) we have, in a list of boundary-marks, Tittershall Wood, Grenville's Wood, *Phippenhoo* (*v.* Chilton Park *infra*), Brill Forks, Moorley's Farm which we can identify, and then we have *Aysshegh*, followed by a messuage of Walter de *Byllyndon*, which must be the *Byllyngdons* in Oakley and Addingrove of 1489 (Ipm). Later on we come to Field Fm, Honeyburge and *Merlake*. Nashway Farm lies right in the line of this boundary and it is clear that here we have the last relic of the lost manor. *Nahsway* should really be *Nashhay* (*v.* hæg) and that must take its name from the lost manor of *Ash*, with prefixed *n* as in Nash in Whaddon and so many other *Nashes*, *v.* æsc. The *l* of the DB form is probably the French definite article.

POLETREES (Fm)

Poole Trees 1574 *VCH*
Poultrees 1766 J

'Pool-trees,' i.e. trees by the pool. There is a stream by the farm.

Chilton

CHILTON 94 J 10

Ciltone 1086 DB
Chilton' 1152–8 NLC *et passim*
Chilton Marescalli 1237–40 Fees 1448

Probably OE *cilda-tūn*, *v.* cild. A manor of the Earl Marshal's.

CANONCOURT (Fm)

Cannon Farm al. *Courte* 1542 LP

'Acquired its name from the Canons of Notley who, in the reign of King John, received a grant of half a hide of land here' (L. i. 134).

CHILTON GROVE

Le Grove 1316 Ipm (*VCH*)

Self-explanatory.

CHILTONPARK FARM

Fippenho 1255 *For*
Phippenhoohurne 1298 VCH ii. 132

About 1544 140 acres of waste were enclosed at *Fyppenhoe* and known henceforward as Chilton Park (*VCH*). This seems to contain some lost pers. name, cf. John *Phippe* in Beds (Ipm 1310).

EASINGTON

Hesintone 1086 DB, 1152–8 NLC
Esitona 1155 NLC
Esinton 1185 RotDom, 1186 NLC, 1237–40 Fees 1448 (*Marescalli*), 1302 FA
Esington 1241 *Ass* (p), 1242 Fees 880, 1301 Orig (*juxta Brehull*)
Essintone 1284 FA
Esynton 1305 Fine
Essyngton 1325 Cl, 1526 LP
Esyngdon 1337 Cl, 1484 Pat, 1535 VE, 1542 LP
Essington 1348 Ipm, 1373 IpmR
Esyngton 1366 Pat
Esigdon 1366 Pat
Esindon 1420 IpmR
Eastoundon 1627 Vern

OE *Ēsingtun*, 'farm of *Esa* or *Ese*.' For *Ēsa* and *Ēse*, *v.* Redin 75. *v.* **ingtun**. At one stage there seems to have been a tendency to shorten the *e* in the trisyllable but this did not maintain itself. The position of Easington led to frequent alteration of its suffix to *don*, as if from **dun**. Easington (O, Y) is an identical name.

HORNAGE (Fm)

Harnage 1541 L. i. 135, 1607 *VCH*, 1739 L. i. 135

There are not many forms to go upon and those are late but as the farm lies on the bounds of Chilton parish, with the ground falling away to the valley below it may be suggested that it is from OE *hāran ecge* (dat.), 'boundary edge.' *v.* **har**.

Long Crendon

LONG CRENDON

Credendona 1086 DB
Crehendon(a) c. 1145 (c. 1300) *Miss* 95 *b*, 1186 P
Crandon Hy ii (1313) Ch, 1366 Pat
Crendona 1155 NLC, 1176 P, 1195 Cur(P), 1200 Cur, 1227 *Ass*, 1237–40 Fees 1448 (*Marescalli*), 1247 *Ass*, 1301 Ipm, 1302 FA, 1346 Pat, FA, 1357 Ipm, 1485 *Bodl Berks* 149
Craendoñ 1163 P
Creendon 1175 P, 1177 R i P, 1195 Cur(P), 1200 BM, RC, 1202 PR, 1230 Cl
Croinden 1182 P, c. 1230 AD i
Crandun, *Crendun* 1218 Pat
Creindon c. 1218 WellsL
Crenden 1231, 1328 Ch
Croendene 13th AD i
Crundon 1247, 1262 *Ass*, 1276 RH, 1294, 1296 Pat, 1301 Ipm, 1347 Pat, 1388 IpmR
Grendon 1278 Ipm (*by Tame*), 1342 Pat, 1362 Fine
Grandone 1284 FA
Crondon 1316 Pat, 1322 Misc, 1335 Orig, 1356 Cl, 1357 Ipm, 1358 Pat
Croyndon 1362 Fine
Cryndon 1373 Cl
Cranden by Tame 1376 Cl
Crayndon 1524 LP
Long Crindon 1626 Vern

OE *Creodan-dun*, 'Creoda's hill,' *v.* dun. Intervocalic *d* was early lost, as in Tingewick *supra*, the intervocalic *h* which appears in some forms is the result of an attempt to get over the resultant vowel-hiatus, and the other forms result from the difficulties arising from the crasis of the two vowels. *Long* aptly describes the village and the epithet is supposed to have arisen from the need for distinguishing it from the not very distant Grendon Underwood. The forms of Crendon show that at one stage in its history confusion was quite likely.

The name *Creoda* is ancient. It was borne by a son of Cerdic the first king of the West Saxons, who is ignored by the annals

which form the basis of the OE *Chronicle*, but appears in the most trustworthy texts of the West Saxon royal genealogy as the father of King Cynric, and thus the ancestor of the later West Saxon kings. An almost contemporary *Creoda* (*Crioda*) occurs in the Mercian royal genealogy as father of Pybba, the father of the famous King Penda of that race. Other examples of the name occur in local nomenclature, as, for example, in Credenhill (He).

NOTLEY

Nutele 1204 Fines, John BM, 1228, 1233 Cl
Noteley(*e*) c. 1218 WellsL, 1232 WellsR
Nuteley(*a*) c. 1218 WellsL, 1220 Fees 295
Nutelegh(*a*) 1221 Bract
Nuttele 1228 Cl, 1242 Fees 881, 1251 Gross, 1284 *Winton*, 1291 Pat, 1305, 1318 Cl, 1325, 1399 Pat
Nutle 1232 Cl
Notele 1242 Fees 865
Nutlegh 1247 *Ass*
Nuttelegh 1262 *Ass*
Nottele 1304 Ipm, 1305 Cl, 1340 Pat, 1347 Cl, 1380 Pat
Nutteleye 1341, 1442 Pat
Notteleya 1348 *Wigorn*, 1445 BM, 1468 AD iii
Notlee 1411 Pat
Notley 1485 BM, 1493 AD ii

'Nut clearing' *v*. **hnutu, leah**. This is the history of Notley (Ess), 998 *Hnutlea* (Crawford 9).

Dorton

DORTON 94 H 10 [du·ətən]

Dortone 1086 DB, 1152–8 NLC, 1237–40 Fees 1447 (*Marescalli*), etc.
Dortun Hy ii (1313) Ch
Durton 1291 Tax, 1420 IpmR, 1535 VE, 1536 LS
Dourton 1325 Cl, 1362 IpmR, Fine, 1368 Cl, 1392 Pat, 1420 IpmR, 1626 Vern, 1806 Lysons
Dorton by Brehull 1343 Pat
Dorton under Bernewode 1371 Cl

v. dor, tun. The place was so called because it stands at the entrance to the narrow pass between Dorton and Brill hills, through which the railway now makes its way.

HOWE WOOD (6″)

Hough gate 1766 J
Hough Wood 1826 B

v. hoh. There is a clearly marked spur of land here.

Ickford

ICKFORD 105 A 9

Iforde 1086 DB
Ycford 1175 P (p), 1220 Fees 414
Ikeforde 1226 WellsR, 1235 Cl, 1235 Fees 555, 1246 Gross, 1247 *Ass* (*parva*), 1300 Ipm
Hick(e)ford(ia) 1231 Bract, 1361 Fine, 1588 BM
Hicford 1235 Fees 463, 1247 *Ass* (p)
Icford 1237 Cl, 1255 *For*, 1284, 1302 FA, 1489 Ipm
Ikesford 1241 *Ass* (p)
Ikford 1247 *Ass*, 1313 Fine
Hyk(e)ford 1289 Ipm, 1366, 1504 Pat
Ikkeford 1377, 1392 Pat
Hikforde 1526 LS

There is a well-established *Icel* used as a pers. name in OE. To this corresponds OHG *Ichilo*, which is a diminutive of a well-established *Icho*. This must be the cognate of OE *Ic(c)a* known only from p.n. *Icangeat* (BCS 240), *Iccannore* (ib. 64), Itchenor (Sx) and such names as Ickborough (Nf), DB *Icheburna*. There must have been two forms of the name *Icca*, one with and the other without palatalisation of the *cc*. Cf. similarly Eckington (Wo) and Etchingham (Sx) from OE *Ecca* or *Ecci*. Hence 'Icca's ford.'

The central part of the parish is known as Great or Church Ickford (cf. LP xv. 613, 21), Little Ickford lies to the south-east (*VCH*).

BRISSENDEN (Fm) (6″)

Brisendon 1826 B
Brisenden c. 1825 O

It is difficult to do anything with these late forms. There is an OHG name *Briso* which may have had an English cognate **Brisa*.

ICKFORD BRIDGE (6″)

Wodebrigge c. 1250 (1400) St Frides

Self-explanatory.

Ilmer

ILMER 105 B 12/13

Imere 1086 DB
Ilmere 1161–3 Reg Roff 391 (p), 1230 *FF*, 1229 Pat, 1232 Fees 1358, 1241, 1247 *Ass*, 1306 Ipm, 1338, 1339 Cl, 1346 FA
Ylmer 1208 Fees 20, 1260 Ipm
Illemere 1210–2 RBE, 1284, 1302 FA
Ilemere c. 1218 FellsL, 1222 WellsR
Ymmere 1244 Fees 1154
Ylemere 1250 Fees 1172, 1338 Cl
Illmer 1472 AD iii
Elmer 1485 Ipm, 1535 VE
Ilmere, *Elmere* Eliz ChancP

Possibly 'boundary or mere of *Ylla*.' *v*. mere, mære. There does not seem to be any actual mere though the parish lies so low that we might assume one. Alternatively, it is perhaps significant that the parish lies on the borders of Bucks and Oxon. If so, the form *Illemere* suggests that the first element here is a pers. name. In Searle's *Onomasticon* two names are entered, either of which might explain the present name: *Ylla*, from LVD, and *Illa*, implied in *Illan leah*, now Monks Eleigh (Sf) (BCS 1289), but *Illa* is probably only a 10th cent. form for *Ylla*, cf. *Giddingcforda* for a site near Gedding (Sf) (< OE *Gydda*). *Ylla* is the only recorded name which will explain Ilmer, Monks Eleigh (Sf) and Ellington (Nf). Taking mere as the second element Ekwall suggests with a good deal of likelihood that the first element is OE *igil*, *il*, 'hedgehog,' cf. *ilmere* (BCS 1037).

Oakley

OAKLEY 94 J 8

Achelei 1086 DB, R i *P*
Aquelie 1106–9 Fr
Akeley 1155 Fr, 1189 *P*
Acleya 1222 WellsR
Acle 1222 WellsR, 1227 *Ass*, 1234 WellsR, 1238 Fees 1373, 1247 *Ass*, 1255 *For*, 1284 FA, 1318 Pat, 1355 Cl
Akle, 1227 *Ass*, 1346 FA
Aklye 1237–40 Fees 1447
Acley 1241 *Ass*
Ocle 1242 Fees 883, 1316 FA, 1339 Cl (*in Bernewode*), 1366 Pat, 1485 Ipm
Ecle 1247 *Ass*
Akele 1262 *Ass*
Accle 1289 Ipm, 1322 Pat
Acle alias *Ocle* 1318 Abbr
Occle 1336 BM, 1358 Pat
Okele(y) 1341 Ch, 1348, 1357, 1375 Pat, 1408 AD vi, 1619 BM
Okle 1354 Cl
Ocley 1525 LP
Okeley al. *Whokeley* 1607 *VCH*[1]

v. ac, leah. 'Oak clearing.' This is probably the history of this name but the later forms have been influenced by the independent word *oak* and the normal development to *Ackley* or *Ockley* stopped.

ADDINGROVE (Fm) (6″) [ɑ·ngrouv]

Eddingrave 1086 DB
Edingraue 1142 (1400) St Frides, 1152–8 NLC, 1198 Fines
Edinggraue 1185 Rot Dom, 1276 RH
Adingraue 1198 Fines, 1237–40 Fees 1447, 1241 *Ass* (p), 1255 *For*, 1262 *Ass*, 1284, 1302 FA, 1322 Pat, 1489 Ipm
Adegrave 1235 Fees 462
Edyngrave 1318 Cl

[1] The series of entries for Oakley in the Lincoln Registers runs as follows: *Acle* (1290–1300), *Akele* (1300–20), *Acleia* (1320–42), *Ocley* (1347–62), *Accle*, *Ocle* (1363–98), *Ocle* (1405–20), *Okeley* (1420–31), *Okley* (c. 1450), *Acleia* (1472–80), *Akeley* (1480–96), *Ocley* (1496–1514), *Ackeley* (ib.), *Okeley*, *Ockley* (1522–47), *Okeley* (c. 1550).

Addyng(g)rave 1325 Cl
Adyngrave 1361 Fine, 1428 Pat
Adyngrove 1408 AD vi
Addingrove c. 1825 O

OE *Ædding-grāf(a)*, 'Æddi's grove,' *v.* **graf(a)**, with the same use of *-ing-* as in **-ingtun**. In modern times [ɑ·d(ə)ngrouv] has become [ɑ·ngrouv] by assimilation of *dn* to *n* (Introd. xxiii). *v.* Adstock and Addington *supra*.

CATSBRAIN (Fm)

Cattesbreyne 1348 Cl

'Catsbrain' is very common as a field-name in Bucks and is also found in Oxon and Berks[1]. It is clearly the term *cat-brain* used dialectally to describe a soil consisting of rough clay mixed with stones.

FENEMORE'S (Fm)

Fennymere 1250 Fees 1212 (p)

'Fenny-mere.' It lies on a stream. The pseudo-genitival *s* is probably wrong.

IXHILL

Hixulle 1255 RH
Hixhull 1311 Cl
Hikkeshull 1337 Pat
Ixhull 1347 Pat
Hikeshille 1397 Pat
Ixsill 1533 LP
Ickshill 1826 B

(For further forms *v.* Hundred-name.)

This name points to an OE pers. name *Hicc*. This name is later found as *Hick*, cf. the interlude of *Hicke Scorner*. Hence 'Hicc's hill.' *v.* **hyll**.

[1] Professor Ekwall has furnished an interesting parallel in the form *Catesbragen* in the Cartulary of St Nicholas Hospital, Salisbury (Wilts Rec. Soc.) 204 f. the name of a place in Broad Chalke (W). This form and the *braȝen* in Layamon B suggest to him an alternative OE *bragen* from a stem **bragun-*, in contrast to the usual *brægen* from **bragin* and this may ultimately in its turn have a bearing on the mysterious *Bragen* in Brayfield *supra*.

MOORLEY'S (Fm) (6")

Morlesmede 1298 VCH ii. 132

This identification is pretty certain and if it is right the name in the medieval form is probably to be explained as 'Moorley's meadow,' i.e. the meadow land belonging to Moorley (*v.* **mor**, **leah**). The ground is well watered.

Shabbington

SHABBINGTON 105 A 9

Sobintone 1086 DB, 1208 PR, c. 1218 WellsL, 1220 Fees 314, 1237 Gross
Sopinton 1163 P
Soppinton' Jordanis 1167 P
Shobinton 1227 *Ass* (p), 1231 Cl, 1247 *Ass*, 1255 *For*
Shobenton 1237 Ch
S(c)hobington 1241 *Ass*, 1278 Ipm, Eliz ChancP
Schobbington 1241 *Ass* (p)
Shopindon 1247 *Ass*
Sobiton, *Shobiton* 1262 *Ass*
Sc(h)obintone 1284, 1302 FA
S(h)obynton 1299, 1330 Ch, 1346 FA, 1359 IpmR
Sobintun 13th AD i
Shobyndon 1320 *Bodl Berks* 60, 1324, 1346 Pat, 1375 Cl, 1376 IpmR, 1379 Cl, 1420 IpmR, 1523 AD i, 1542 BM
Shobyngdon 1456 IpmR, 1485 *Bodl Berks* 149, 1490 Ipm, 1535 VE
S(c)hobingdon 1526 LS, 1542 BM
Shabbington or *Shobbington* 1806 Lysons

'Sc(e)obba's farm' *v.* **ingtun**. The name *Sc(e)obba* may be safely inferred from *Scobbanora* (BCS 932), *scheobanwerzthe* (ib. 438) and *scobban byrigels* (KCD 673). The modern form shows unrounding of the vowel. *v.* Introd. xxxiii.

Towersey

TOWERSEY 105 B 11/12

Eie 1086 DB, 1227 *Ass* (*Parva*)
Eye 1235 Fees 469
Turrisey 1237–40 Fees 1448

Turesye 1241 *Ass*
Thureseya 1241 *Ass* (p), 1262 *Ass*
Turseya 1241 *Ass* (p), 13th AD vi
Turresheye 1255 RH
Tureseya 1262 *Ass*
Thoreseye 1284 FA
Turesheye 13th AD ii
Tour(e)sey(e) 1302 FA, 1326, 1337 Cl, Pat, 1346 FA, 1360 Pat, 1392 IpmR, 1434, 1445 Pat, 1485 Ipm
Touresheye 1351 Pat
Towresey 1422 AD ii, 1427 AD vi

v. eg. The village is surrounded on three sides by water. The first part of the name is derived from the *Tours* family who held land here in the 13th cent. Hence, 'Tours'-island' to distinguish it from the neighbouring *Kingsey* or 'King's island.'

PENN FARM

Pennys 1471 AD i

This is pretty certainly a manorial name derived from some unknown settler from Penn in the south of the county.

Worminghall

WORMINGHALL 105 A 8/9 [wə·nəl]

Wermelle 1086 DB
Wurmehal' 1163 P
Wurmehala Willelmi 1167 P
Wurmaala 1167 Chancellor's Roll
Wurmehale c. 1210 *Bodl O* 85
Wirmenhale c. 1218 WellsL
Wrmenhale c. 1220 WellsR
Wirmehale 1229 WellsR
Wrmehale 1237–40 Fees 1447, 1241 *Ass*, 1302 FA
Wurmehale 1241 *Ass*
Wurmenhale 1246 *Ass* (p)
Wormehale 1247 Fees 874, 1284 FA, 1296 Ipm
Wyrmehale 1247 Gross
Wyrmenhale 1247 *Ass* (p), 1291 Tax

Wirmehalle 1255 *For*
Wermehale 1255 *For*, 1292 *Bodl O* 110
Wormenhale 1280 Ipm, 1316 FA, 1333, 1341 Cl, 1346 FA, 1375 Pat, 1376 Ipm, 1382 Cl
Worminghall c. 1450 *Linc*, c. 1550 ib.
Wormynale 1503 Pat
Wornall 1525 LP
Wurnall 1535 VE
Wormenhall(e) 1535 VE, 1806 Lysons

There must have been OE names *Wurma*, and, with mutation of the stem-vowel, *Wyrma*, though the only OE name on record with a *Wurm-* element is *Wurmhere*. We certainly have a patronymic form from *Wyrma* in Wormegay (Nf) for which Ekwall (PN *-ing* 172) quotes *Wirmyngeye* BM 1383 and in Warmington (Nth), *Wyrmingtun* BCS 1130. Hence 'Wyrma's **healh**.' In the modern form *mn* has been assimilated to *n*.

FIELD FARM

Wormenhael field (sic) 1298 VCH ii. 132

Self-explanatory.

REDDING WICK and REDDING'S FARM (6″)

La Ruding Hy iii BM
Reddings 1826 B

v. **hryding**. The genitival *s* is misleading.

RIGNALL

Ricknall 1612 L. ii. 376
Rignald 1766 J

OE *Rīcan-heale* (dat.), 'Rica's nook.' *v.* **healh**.

SANDWICH WOOD (6″) [sændridʒ]

Sandridge Wood 1826 B

The second element should clearly be *ridge* from **hrycg**. No sand is known here (Harman).

SPURLANDS END [spɑ·liŋgz]

Sparlynges 1574 L. ii. 395
Spurling End 1826 B

This must take its name from the family to which Wm Sperling, mentioned in NI (1340), belonged. *er* regularly becomes *ar*. The final *d* is a vulgarism for which Wyld u.s. gives parallels. The modern form is either corrupt or due to a spelling pronunciation of *Sperling*. Cf. the vulgar *Durby* for *Derby*.

XII. WADDESDON HUNDRED

Votesdone, *Votesdune* 1086 DB
Wottesdone 1175 P, 1195 Cur(P), 1227, 1241, 1247, 1262 *Ass*
Wat(te)den 1179 P
Wattisdun 1195 Cur(P)
Wotesdone 1227 *Ass*

The exact site of the Hundred meeting-place is unknown. It may well have been on the prominent hill to the south-east of the village. For the etymology *v.* Waddesdon *infra*.

East and Botolph Claydon

EAST CLAYDON and BOTOLPH CLAYDON 94 E 11 [bɔtl]

Claindone 1086 DB
Claidone 1086 DB
Cleindona c. 1200 Eyns
Cleydon 1220 Fees 313

Forms with inflexional *n* remain in fairly common use until about 1320, after which the sole forms are *Claydon* and *Cleydon*. The application of 'East' has first been noted in *Est Cleydon* (1247 *Ass*). For *Botolph* we have

Botle 1224 *Bodl Berks* 13, 1255 *For*, Hy iii Ipm
Bote 1227 *Ass*, 1235 Fees 466, 1320 *Bodl Berks* 60
Botte 1235 Fees 461, 1299 Ipm, 1302 FA, 1321 *Bodl Berks* 67
Bottel(e) 1241, 1247 *Ass*, 1345 Pat, E iii Orig
Botil 1330 Ch
Botul 1355 Cl, 1356 Ipm
Bot 1362 Cl, 1366 Pat
Botel 1420 IpmR
Bottle 1576 BM

Claydon St Botolph c. 1825 O
Bothel or *Bottle* 1826 B

but the most important reference is that to *la Botle* in 1255 (*For*) which proves that the first element in that name is **botl** and that the association with (St) *Botolph* is purely fictitious. Botolph Claydon is a name compounded of **botl** and *Claydon*, this particular Claydon having presumably been distinguished by some prominent 'building.' Whether the *Botyl Well* (6") is named from the **botl** or does really take its name from St Botolph and was sacred to his name, it is impossible to say.

BERNWOOD (Fm) [bə·nud][1]

Byrnewudu c. 950 (921 A) ASC
Bernewude R i *P*
Bernewode 1255 *For*

This is henceforward the normal form except for

Brenewode 1366 Cl, Pat
Barnewode 1489 Ipm
Berwood 1529 LP
Barnwood 1610 D

This farm-name is the last relic of the name of the great forest of Bernwood. It is difficult to dissociate the name of that ancient forest from that of Bicester (O), DB *Bernecestre*, 1274 QW *Burcestre* (*v.* PN O). Each seems to contain an OE *Byrne-* as its first element. If this association is correct, it is impossible to derive either name from a personal name *Byrna* (*v.* Burnham *infra*) for the ASC form of Bernwood is long previous to any possible reduction of *Byrnan-* to *Byrne-*. Bicester lay outside the bounds of the medieval forest of Bernwood, but was only 2½ miles west of them (*v.* Nashway Fm *supra* for the bounds at this point), but the original Bernwood may have extended far to the west of these limits and even have linked up with the wooded country round Shotover and Woodstock. Such an extension would accord with the statement in the Chronicle (*loc. cit.*) that the Danes harried the land between Bernwood and Aylesbury, a phrase more appropriate to a forest centring on Bicester than

[1] No trace can now be found of the pron. [bɑ·nwud] which must at one time have prevailed.

to the forest of the 13th cent. perambulation, whose boundary was the Thame, only 1¼ miles from Aylesbury[1].

The etymology of the name cannot be fixed with absolute certainty but it may be noted that to the south of Bicester there is a conspicuous hill, now called Gravenhill, and Professor Ekwall suggests that the *Byrne-* of Bicester and Bernwood may be the British word corresponding to Welsh *bryn*, 'hill,' with the same metathesis which we find in Malvern (Wo), containing *fryn*, a mutated form of *bryn*. *v.* IPN 25. It may be suggested that this British word was contained in the unknown Romano-Celtic name of the settlement at Alchester near Bicester, and passed from that into the ME forms of Bicester quoted above. It would be more satisfactory for our purpose to assume a settlement at Bicester itself but no remains have hitherto been found which would justify this assumption.

COPPICE LOWHILL (Fm)

Coppesley-hills 1517 L. i. 169
Copsley Hill 1766 J, 1826 B

Probably 'Copp's clearing' *v.* **leah**. There is an OE name *Coppa*, of which *Copp* would be the strong form. The modern form is curiously corrupt.

MONKOMB (Fm)

Muncomb (House) 1826 B

Middle Claydon

MIDDLE CLAYDON 94 D 11

Claindone 1086 DB
Middelcleydon 1242 Fees 874

The *n*-forms persist to the middle of the 14th cent.

Cleydon Cantelou 1320 Pat

So called from its position between East, Bottle and Steeple Claydon. It was a manor of the Cantilupe family.

KNOWL HILL

(Wm de) *la Cnolle* 1241 *Ass*

v. **cnoll**. Self-explanatory.

[1] Similarly the name *Sciryuda* which must be connected with Sherwood (Nt) appears in the 10th cent. in the boundaries of Sutton near Retford, many miles to the north (*v.* Stevenson's note in *Yorkshire Charters*, i. 11–12).

Grandborough

GRANDBOROUGH 94 E 12

Grenebeorge c. 1060 (1250) KCD 962
Grenesberga 1086 DB
Grenebur' 1242 Fees 875
Greneburne 1284 FA
Greneberne 1285 QW
Grenebury Hy ii (1301) Ch
Greneborewe 1302 FA
Grenebourwe 1316 FA
Greneburgh 1330 Pat
Grenbourn 1348 Pat
Grenesbor(o)w c. 1400 St Alb
Grenborough 1535 VE
Granborowe Eliz ChancP
Granborowe 1614 *Grandborough*
Grandborow 1653 ib.
Gainborough 1675 Ogilby
Granborough 1766 J

v. **grene**, **beorg**. 'Green hill.' Cf. L. i. 247, 'Probably from a swelling hill or rising ground on which the village is built.' Cf. *OE Gnomic Verses* 34, 'beorh sceal on eorþan grene standan.' There has been much uncertainty as to the suffix from the earliest times and we hear in the 14th cent. (*Hist. St Albans*, Rolls Ser. ii. 253) that the Sheriff of Bucks was required to hold an enquiry as to the identity of *Grenesbury* and *Grenesborow*. The jurors declared on oath that the two were one and the same and not different vills. For the form cf. Grandborough (Wa).

BIGGIN (lost)[1]

le Byggyghe 1280 Ipm
Biggeng 1302 FA
la Bygginge 1316 FA
Biggynge 1330 Pat

[1] An enclosure in Biggin Field is said to mark the site of the former farm or manor-house of Biggin (HMN 120).

Byggyng 1540 LP
Biggin 1766 J
'Building' *v.* bigging.

Hogshaw

HOGSHAW 94 E 12

Hocsaga 1086 DB
Hogsaue 1199 Cur
Hoggeshag 1199 Cur
Hogseage 1201 Fines
Hoggeshage 1209 Abbr
Hogeshag c. 1218 WellsL
Hoggesaghe Hospitalariorum 1237–40 Fees 1448
Hogeshawe c. 1240 Misc
Hoggesschawe 1255 *For*
Hogsher 1614 Edgcott

OE *hogg-sceaga*, 'hog-wood,' and cf. Evershaw *supra*, or perhaps, as it is so near Hoggeston (*v. supra*), 'Hogg's wood.' *v.* sceaga. The Knights Hospitallers had view of frankpledge in Hogshaw (RH i. 24).

FULBROOK (Fm)

Folebroc 1197 Fine, 1242 Fees 894, 1302 FA
Fulebroc 1199 Cur, c. 1200 Eyns, 1227 *Ass*, 1255 *For*, 13th AD iv
Folebrook 1241 *Ass*
Fullebroc 1242 Fees 874
Fulebrok 1255 *For*
Fulbroc 1284 Ipm
Folbrok 1302, 1346 FA
Folbroc 1305 Ipm
Folebrok(e) 1316 FA, 1363 Cl
Fulbrok(e) 1332 Ch, 1347 Ipm

'Dirty brook' *v.* ful, broc. 'The waters of the moat and pond which feed the brook are still of a dirty, yellow colour, caused by clay soil' (Harman).

Fleet Marston

FLEET MARSTON 94 G/H 13 [flit mɑ·sən]

Merstone 1086 DB
Fletemerstone 1223 WellsR, 1245 Gross, 1300 Ipm, 1302 FA
Flettemerstone 1284 FA
Fletemershtone 1300 Ipm, 1316 FA, 1375 AD vi
Fletmerston 1336 Pat, 1346 Misc, 1349 Pat
Fletemarston 1509 LP
Flittmarston 1526 LS
ffet marson 1670 *Terr*
Fleet Masson 1690 *Terr*

'Marsh farm' *v.* **mersc**, **tun**. The distinctive epithet is from **fleot** which survives in the 'fleet' of brackish water still existing and running by the side of the high road (Harman).

Pitchcott

PITCHCOTT 94 F 13

Pichecot(e) 1176 P, 1199 Fines (p), 1220 Fees 313, 1237 Gross, 1241 *Ass*, 1284 FA, 1292 Pat, 1300 Ipm, 1302 FA, 1328 Ch
Picchecota 1177 P, 1380 Pat
Pichekote 1179 P, Hy iii Ipm
Pichescote 1227 *Ass* (p)
Puchecote 1241 *Ass*, 1300 Ipm
Pychecote 1255 *For*, 1262 *Ass*, 1300 Abbr, 1316 Cl, 1346 Pat
Pichecote juxta Cuvyng (sic) 1348 Pat
Pechecote 1376, 1377 Pat
Pychcote 1400 AD ii
Pycchecote 1422 Pat
Pyttescott 1536 LP
Petchecott 1584 *Archd*

'Cottage(s) of *Picca*.' *Pīc* is on record in OE (Redin 22) and *Picca* may be inferred from *Pican stapele* (BCS 299) and *Piccingawurþ* (KCD 812). The related diminutive **Picel* occurs in Pitstone eleven miles S.E. from Pitchcott. For *Puche-* cf. Chicheley *supra*.

Quarrendon

QUARRENDON (6"), cf. 94 H 13 St Peter's

Querendone 1086 DB, c. 1140 (c. 1225) *D and C Linc. Reg. Antiquiss.* f. 36, 1176 P, 1218 Bract, 1227 *Ass*, 1232 Cl, 1247 *Ass*, 1250 Fees 1172, 1275 Ipm, 1279 AD i, 13th AD iv, 1315, 1344 Pat, 1374 Cl, 1488 AD v
Cuerendon 1189 P, 1232 Pat
Querrendon 1232 Cl
Querndon 1255 *For*, 1284 FA, 1299 Fine, 1330 Ipm, 1332 Cl, 1342 Ipm, Pat, 1397 Pat
Querdon al. *Querndon* 1297 Ipm
Querindon 1297 Cl
Querdone 1316 FA
Quernedon 1370 Cl
Kerungdon 1398 Pat
Querundon 1399 Pat
Querenden 1491 Ipm
Quarendon 1499 Pat, 1510 LP
Quarryngdon 1509 LP
Quarnedon 1512 LP
Quarington 1592 D, 1766 J
Quarrington 1826 B

OE *cweorn-dūn*, 'mill-hill,' *v.* cweorn. The reference here must be to a mill rather than a mill-stone for such could never have been quarried here (Harman).

Waddesdon

WADDESDON 94 G 12 [wɔdzdən]

Votesdone 1086 DB
Wettesdon' 1167 P
Watisdun 1195 Cur(P)
Votesdune c. 1200 BM
Wottesdon 1211–2 RBE, 1220 Fees 317, 1220–34 WellsR, 1220 Bract, 1247 *Ass*, 1255 *For*, 1292 Ipm, Pat, 1302 FA, 1305 Cl, 1327 Pat
Wotthesdune 1212 Fees 117
Wettesdena 1222 Bract, *Wettesdon* 1227 *Ass*, 1337 Pat

Wottesdun 1224 Pat, 1225 Abingd
Wotesdon 1227 *Ass*, 1232 WellsR, 1240 Gross, 1241, 1247 *Ass*, 1315 Pat
Wotteston 1240 Gross, 1265 Misc
Whotesdon 1241 *Ass*
Wocdesdone 1284 FA
Wodesdon 1327, 1346 Pat, 1423 IpmR
Wotysdon 1356 AD iii
Woddeston 1365 Pat
Woddesden 1377 Cl
Woddesdon 1474 Pat, 1477 AD iii
Wodeston 1509 LP
Wottesdon al. *Odesdon* 1512 LP
Wotesdon or *Waddesdon* 1755 BW

Cf. *Wottesbroc* in the bounds of Winchendon (St Frides 8).

'Wott's hill' *v.* dun. *Wott* gave his name not only to the hill but to the brook which runs south-west from it and his name may be preserved in Watbridge *supra*. This name is otherwise unknown[1]. *Wota* in Searle, inferred from *wotan hlinc* (BCS 1216) probably has no justification as it is almost certain that *þæne wotan hlinc* should read *wohan*, 'crooked.' *v.* woh.

BEACHENDON (Fm)

Bichedone 1086 DB
Bicchendon 1175 P (p)
Bichendone 1198 Fines, 1235 Fees 461
Bichindone 1198 Fines, 1262 *Ass*
Bychendone 1241 *Ass*, 1316 FA
Bychindone 1284 FA, 1300 Ipm, 1326, 1332, 1335 Cl
Bechyndon 1384 Pat
Bichyndon 1367 Cl
Bechenden 1500 Ipm, Eliz ChancP
Bechington 1535 VE
Beachington 1766 J, c. 1825 O, 1826 B

Cf. *bican broc* in boundaries of Winchendon (St Frides 8). The personal name *Bica* appears again in Bicknor (Gl), Bickenhill (War).

[1] We may note however a Ricardus *Wot* in Tillingham (Ess) in the Domesday of St Paul's (60) and a *Wotgar* in Heybridge in 1222 (ib. 56).

Just as *Wott* gave his name to a hill and a stream so did *Bic(c)a*, the stream in the second case being that to the west of Beachendon. The name should have become *Bitchingdon*, or possibly, with lowering of *i* to *e*, *Betchingdon*, but as in Beechburn (Du), earlier *Bitchburn*, unpleasant associations have probably been avoided by lengthening of the vowel, or association with the common noun *beech* has affected the pronunciation. A similar change has taken place in Beachampstead (Hu), 1248 FF *Bichehamstede*, which seems to contain the same personal name.

BLACKGROVE

Blagraue 1227 *Ass*, Hy iii BM
Blakegrave Hy iii Ipm
Blagegrave 1300 Ipm
Hamme Blakegrave 1302 FA
Blacgrove 1545 LP

Self-explanatory. For *Hamme*, *v.* Woodham *infra*.

CRANWELL

Cremedewelle 1165 P, 1185 Rot Dom
Crendewelle 1227, 1247 *Ass*, 1302 FA, 1360 Ipm
Crundewell 1227 *Ass*, 1242 Fees 883, 1325 Fine
Crandewelle 1316 FA
Grundewell 1325 Fine, 1326 Orig
Cryndewelle 1379 Cl
Crendwell 1459 IpmR, 1514 AD vi
Cranewyll 1501 Ipm
Cranwell 1517 Encl

The first element in this name must be from *crymbed* the past part. of the OE vb. *cryman*, to bend, and the whole name meant 'bent, crooked, or winding spring.' For this sense development cf. Cromwell (Nt) from the adj. *crumb*. For the *e* and *u* forms *v.* Introd. xxiv. The *a*-forms are perhaps due to association with the common **cran** (cf. Cranwell, Lincs). They are also found in the not very distant Crendon, *v. supra*. *mbd*>*md* (with loss of *b* from cons. group)>*nd* by assimilation.

EYTHROPE (Pk) [iˑθrəp]

Edropa Ricardi 1167 P

Eddropa 1167 Chancellor's Roll
Etrop(e) 1220 Fees 313, 1247 *Ass*
Herope 1235 Fees 461
Ethrop 1242 Fees 883, 1379 Cl
Ettrope 1247 *Ass*
Ethorp 1255 *For*, 1284 FA, 1459 IpmR, 1806 Lysons
Eydrop 1262 *Ass*
Edrop(e) 1262 *Ass*, 1316 FA, 1325 Fine, 1326 Orig
Estrop al. *Ethorp* 1300 Ipm
Etheroppe 1501 Ipm
Ethrop 1528 LP
Heythrope 1535 VE

'Island-farm' *v.* eg, þorp, or perhaps better *ēa-þorp*, 'river-farm,' for Eythrope lies close by the Thame. There are hardly enough streams to justify the former sense.

LITTLETON MANOR (Fm)

Liteletona 1231 Bract (p)

Self-explanatory.

SHEEPCOTHILL WOOD

Shipcot 1766 J
Shipcot Hill c. 1825 O

Self-explanatory, *v.* Introd. xxvi.

WORMSTONE [wɔ·mstən]

Weremodestun c. 1200 (14th) *Miss* 132 *b*
Warmodeston 1220 Fees 313, 1247 *Ass* (p), 1262 ib., 1284 FA, 13th AD vi
Warmoteston 1241 *Ass* (p)
Waremodeston 1241 *Ass* (p), 1292 Ipm (p)
Warmundeston c. 1250 *Mert* 413
Wermundestone c. 1290 *Mert* 412
Wermedeston, *Wormodeston*, *Waremeston* 1255 *For*
Wermeston 1262 *Ass* (p), 1360 Pat (p), 1442 IpmR
Warmestone 1334, 1367 Cl (p), 1423, 1469 IpmR, 1540 LP
Wermodeston 1346 Pat (p)

'Farm of *Wǣrmōd* or, possibly, of *Wǣrmund*.' The former name is not on independent record but may be inferred from

p.n. evidence (*v.* Searle and cf. Warmscombe (O)). If that is the name the *n* in some of the ME forms must be explained as due to the common introduction of inorganic *n* in the unstressed element in polysyllabic words (cf. PN NbDu 265 for further examples). It certainly occurred in Aymestrey (Heref) which appears as *Æþelmodes treow* in BCS 1006, *Aylmondestre* in FA.

Westcott

WESTCOTT 94 G 11

Westcote c. 1200 BM

v. **west, cot.** 'Westcote is the most considerable hamlet attached to Waddesdon, from which it is nearly two miles distant westward' (L. i. 490).

Woodham[1]

WOODHAM (6")

Wodehamme 1370 BM
Woods Ham 1766 J

'A district called Ham extended into the parishes of Waddesdon and Wotton Underwood. The part in Waddesdon was situated in Eythrope and called the manor of Ham or Woodham, and that in Wotton was called Ham, Fieldham or Ham cum Wotton' (*VCH*). *v.* **hamm.**

COLLETT (Fm)

Colewyck 1276 RH
Colewyk(e) 1315 Ch, 1316 FA, 1337 Pat, 1535 VE
Colwyk 1346 FA
Col(y)wykes 1539 LP
Colik c. 1530 Map in L. i
Collick 1766 J, c. 1825 O
Colwick, *Collet* or *Collick* 1806 Lysons

The first element is the OE pers. name *Cola*. Cf. Colwick and Collingham (Nt) which are certainly from a pers. name, but perhaps from the Scand. cognate.

[1] Woodham is partly in Waddesdon and partly in Ashendon Hundreds in FA. Here it is included in the former.

HAM (Fm)

Hamme 1255 *For*, 1274 Fine, 1379 Cl, 1488 Pat
Feldhamme 1255 *For*, 1299 Ipm, 1302 FA
Feldham 1316 FA
Feltham 1370 BM
Ham 1509 LP

v. hamm. This *hamm* was distinguished from Woodham *supra* by the epithet feld, the contrast being between the woodland and the open country. *v.* feld and cf. Field and Wood Plumpton (La).

The name is carried back to the 12th cent. by the form *Hama Willelmi* 1167 P, but it is uncertain whether this form relates to Woodham or to Ham Green.

MERCER'S WOOD (6″)

Cf. L. i. 603, 'The Warden and Community of the Mystery of Mercers were seized of the Manors of Wotton and Ham.'

OVINGHILL (Fm)

Woving Hill c. 1718 L. i. Map, 1766 J, c. 1825 O

The forms are too late to do much with. Oving is not far away and it may be that *Ovinghill* has something to do with it. In that case the *w* is a dial. development. Cf. Oakley and Hawridge *supra* for a similar spelling. Such a pronunciation is common in Bucks (EDG 207–8).

XIII. AYLESBURY HUNDRED

Elesberie 1086 DB
Eillesbir' 1195 Cur(P)

For the etymology *v.* Aylesbury *infra*.

Aston Clinton

ASTON CLINTON 95 J 2 [a·stən klintən]

Estone 1086 DB, R i *P* and *passim* to 1414
Aston Clinton 1237–40 Fees 1448
Eston et Clynton 1244 Fees 1154
Aston 1247 *Ass passim*

Astonclyngton 1342 Ipm
* *Asen* 1675 Ogilby
Arston Clinton 1702 *Buckland Terr*

'East farm,' the distinctive second name being derived from the Clinton family, of whom Willelmus de Clinton held *Eston* in 1208 (Fees 20). This seems the correct explanation though the entry *Eston et Clynton* given above is difficult to account for and that in *Ass* (1262) 'venit apud Weston et Clynton' and 'i virg. tre. in Weston et Clinton,' which look as if there was a hamlet of Clinton as well as Aston. The *Weston* is Weston Turville and Weston and Aston must be so called in contrast to one another.

The connexion of the family of Clinton with this place is carried back to the 12th cent. by an entry in the Pipe Roll of 1196 touching 'Eston Willelmi de Clinton' (Fowler, *Calendar of Pipe Rolls*, Beds. Hist. Rec. Soc. vii. 119).

BITTAM'S WOOD (6″)

'Hill called *Byttons next Bradneg*' 1543 LP

BRADNIDGE WOOD (6″)

Bradneg 1543 LP
Bradnedge 1639 *Terr*
Broadnedge 1703 *Terr*

OE *bradan ecge* (dat.), 'broad edge,' *v.* brad, ecg.

* OLD BRUN'S (Fm)

Brunes 1544 L. ii. 474

CHIVERY

Cheurehaye 1262 *Ass*
Chiveray 1341 Fine, 1346 FA
Chevereye 1382 IpmR
Aston Chewery 1532 LP
Aston Cheverey 1543 LP
Aston Chevery 1579 BM
Cheverye 1631 *Foster*

OE *cefer-(ge)hæg*, '(cock)-chafer enclosure,' so called because infested by this creature. Cf. *ceafor-leah* BCS 622. *cefer*

and *ceafor* are related forms of the same word, *v.* NED s.v. *chafer*. *v.* (ge)hæg. The modern form shows the common dialectal raising of *e* to *i* before *v* as in *ivver* for *ever*.

* DUNDRIDGE (Fm) [dʌnridʒ]

Dunrege 1202 Fines
Dunrugge 1227 *Ass*, 1285 Ipm, 1320 Cl
Dunregge 1241 *Ass* (p), 1250 Fees 1213
Dunrich 1247 *Ass*
Dunrugh, *Dunrigh* 1250 Fees 1171, 1211
Dunruge 1262 *Ass* (p), 1276 RH (p)
Dounregg 1298 Pat
Donrigg 1302 Ch
Donrygge 1399 Pat
Dounrigg 1400 Pat
Dunriche 1544 L. ii. 96
Dunrigge 1544 L. ii. 474

v. dun, hrycg. The *dun* here probably describes open hill country, so that the whole name would mean 'bare ridge.'

HARELANE BRIDGE (6")

Hareway 1639 *Terr*

This is on the parish boundary and the name should perhaps really be *Harway* (*v.* har), the modern form having been influenced by the animal name.

MARL COPSE (6")

Marrwell 1639 *Terr*

'Boundary-spring' *v.* mære, wielle. Marl Copse is on the parish boundary.

MERRYMEAD (Cottage) (6")

Merrimeade 1639 *Terr*

'Pleasant mead' *v.* myrig, mæd.

* ST LEONARD'S

(capella) *Sancti Leonardi de Blakemere* 1250 Fees 1171, 1212

'Black mere.' There is no mere there now but there is a probability that there used to be one near the church (Harman).

VATCHE'S FARM [vetʃiz], [viˑtʃiz], [fiˑtʃiz]

Manor of Aston Clynton al. *Vache* 1513 LP
land de la Vach North 1639 *Terr*
Vetches Farm 1826 B

The farm takes its name from the family of *La Vache* (*v.* The Vache *infra*) who already held land in the manor of Aston Clinton in 1271 (*FF*).

Aylesbury

AYLESBURY 95 H 1

Aegelesburh c. 900 (871), ASC(A)
Aegelesbyrig (dat.) c. 970 (12th) BCS 1174
Eilesberia 1086 DB, 1195 FF(P)
Ailesberia 1176, 1189 P
Aeilisberi 1178 P
Aillesbiri R i *P*
Aylesberia 1199 (1320) Ch
Alesbiry 1257 Pat

Later forms are not of any interest except to note that down to c. 1320 the suffix is generally *-biry*, *-byry* but after that forms in *-bury*, which hitherto had been comparatively rare, are almost universal.

'Aegel's *burh*' *v.* burh. *Ægel* is not on independent record in OE but is contained in Aylesworth (Nth), *Ægeleswyrð* BCS 1131, Aylesford (K), *Æglesford* (Thorpe 202), Aylesbeare (D) and Aylestone (Lei).

DUNSHAM (Fm) [dʌnsəm]

Dunesham 1276 RH
Dunsome 1826 B

'Dun(n)'s hamm.' This particular *hamm* lies near a stream but on the outside of a bend and not within it. The name *Dun(n)* occurs also in Dunston (St, Nf) and in Dunchurch and Dunsmore (Wa).

WALTON
Walton 1237–40 Fees 1448
Walton near Ayllesbury 1339 Cl
v. weala and Introd. xix.

Bierton with Broughton

BIERTON 95 H 1 [biːətən]
Bortone 1086 DB
Burton 1227 *FF*, 1237–40 Fees 1448, 1241 *Ass* (p), 1259 Abbr, 1297 Cl, 1298 Ipm, 1308 *Burton near Aylesbiry* Pat, 1315 Pat, 1334 Ipm
Byrton 1362 Inq aqd, 1382 IpmR, 1616 HMN
Byerton 1363 Cl
Beyreton 1370 Cl
Bierton 1382 Pat, 1461 IpmR, 1536 LS
Berton al. *Bureton by Ailesbury* 1404 Pat
Beerton 1415 AD vi, 1432 AD i, 1474 Pat, 1483 IpmR, 1546 LP, 1627 BM
Bereton 1462 Pat, 1465 IpmR, 1497 BM
Berton 1467 Pat, 1538 LP
Beyrton 1488 Pat
Berton al. *Byerton* 1540 LP
Bearton 1766 J[1]

The forms of this name down to 1334 point clearly to an example of the common burh-tun, here descriptive of a farm by Aylesbury *burh* or simply of some fortified farm and this etymology is perhaps strengthened by the neighbouring Burcott (*v. infra*) which may also contain the element burh.

If that is the etymology however the forms from the middle of the 14th cent. must be due to some definite intention to alter the name. Possibly there was danger of confusion with Bourton by Buckingham even though that is fairly distant. That such confusion was thought possible is shown by the frequency of the addition of the phrase 'by Aylesbury,' which has been noted in four cases beside those given above.

[1] We may note in addition the forms in the Lincoln Registers: *Burton* (1290–1342), *Byrton* (1347–62), *Birton*, *Bureton*, *Beerton*, *Burton* (1303–98), *Beerton*, *Bereton*, *Byrton* (1408–20), *Bereton* (1452–72), *Bireton*, *Bereton* (1480–96), *Berton*, *Byreton* (1496–1514), *Bireton* (1522–47).

Professor Ekwall would prefer to explain this difficult name by starting from an OE compound *byrh-tun*, containing the gen. sg. of *burh*. For such a compound he adduces the parallel of *Byrhfunt̃* (BCS 1161). The DB form he would explain as due to the more common compound *burh-tun* and those in *Bur-* as representing, in a good many cases at least, ME *u* from OE *y*.

He identifies *Byrhfunt* with a good deal of probability with Boarhunt (Ha). This can readily be done if we assume that the *f* in the OE form is a mistake for *h*, due to unconscious anticipation of the next name, viz. *Hafunt*, that the scribe places on record. Admitting that, the OE form can then be brought into relation with the later forms for Boarhunt, viz. DB *Borehunte*, 13th cent. *Bur(g)hunte*, 14th cent. *Bourehunte* and these forms may in their turn throw light on the development of Bierton.

* BROUGHTON 95 H 1

Brotone 1086 DB
Broctona c. 1155 (14th) *Miss* 125 *b*
Parva Brouton c. 1220 (14th) ib.
Magna Broughton 1273 Abbr
Little Broghton by Aylesbury 1350 Ipm
Broughton Lovell juxta Aylesbury 1456 IpmR
Abbotts Broughton Eliz ChancP

'Brook farm' *v.* **broc, tun**. There were two manors, 'Great' or 'Abbot's,' in the possession of Missenden Abbey, and 'Little,' which belonged to the Lovells in the 14th cent.

BURCOTT

Burcote 1183 P (p), 1465 IpmR
Borecote 1241 *Ass* (p)
Purkett 1627 BM

v. **burh, cot** and Burcott and Bierton *supra*. See Addenda.

CALDECOTE (lost)

Caldecote c. 1230 (14th) *Miss* 119 *b*
Caldecote by Aylesbury 1355 Ipm

v. **cald, cot**. The exact site is unknown, but in the Missenden Chartulary the place is associated with Broughton and is near *pratum de Wendover*.

Buckland

* BUCKLAND 95 J 3
Bocheland 1086 DB
Bochland 1157 P

Except for

Bucland 1265 Pat

forms with *o* prevail till 1378, after which we have

Buklond 1378 Cl, 1476 AD v
Boklond 1382 Pat
Bokland 1383 Cl
Bokelond 1400 Pat, 1424 ib. (*by Aillesbury*)
Bukland 1449 Pat, 1488 AD v, 1504 Pat

v. **bocland**. In 1066 the manor was held by Godric brother of Wulfwig bishop of Dorchester. As Godric was his brother's tenant, and could not alienate the land without his licence, it is probable that Buckland was an ancient possession of the see of Dorchester. If so, the place may well owe its name to the fact that it had been granted to some early bishop by *boc*, or royal charter.

LAYLAND'S FARM
(Joh. ate) *Leye* 1340 NI
Lealands c. 1825 O

'Land by the clearing' *v.* **leah**. The pseudo-genitival *s* is misleading. Cf. Leyland (La).

NORTH HILL WOOD (6″)

This wood is probably referred to in the *Norringer Way* of a 1702 Terrier. *Norringer* is clearly *North-hanger*. *v.* **hangra**.

SPENCERSGREEN

The name is due to the fact that this was a Despenser manor (FA i. 123).

Ellesborough

* ELLESBOROUGH 106 A 1
Esenberge 1086 DB, *Esenbergh* 1241 *Ass*
Esberga 1182 P

Eselbergh 1195 Cur(P), 1196 FF(P), R i Cur, 1227, 1241, 1247 *Ass*, 1251 AD i, 1275 Ipm, 1315 Pat, 1382 Cl
Hisilberga 1195 Cur(P)
Heselberge 1199 Cur, 1227 *FF*, 1371 Cl
Iselberg 1199 Cur
Hesseberge 1200 Cur
Yselberwe 1227 *FF*
Eseburg' 1227 *Ass*
Heselburuwe 1235 Fees 461
Eselburgh 1237–40 Fees 1448, 1241 *Ass*, 1351, 1373 Cl, 1470 IpmR
Heselburg 1247 *Ass*
Esselburg 1251 AD i
Eselburwe 1274 Ipm, 1308 Cl, 13th AD i
Eselborne 1283 Misc
Eseleberewe 1323 Cl
Esulb(o)urgh 1350 Ipm
Eselberugh 1430 AD i
Elisborough 1491 AD iii
Ellysburgh, *Ellesburgh* 1509 LP
Ellesborowghe 1580 AD iii

OE *esol-beorg*, 'ass-hill,' i.e. where it grazes. *v.* **beorg**. The present form seems to have arisen from late-metathesis, strengthened probably by the natural tendency to make the first half of the name genitival in form. For *n*, *v.* IPN 106.

* APSLEY

Aspeleia c. 1210 (14th) *Miss* 125
Appesley 1247 *Ass*, 1316 FF (*VCH*)
Aspley 1486 Ipm
'Aspen-clearing' *v.* **æspe**, **leah**.

* BUCKMOOR-END

Bockmer-end 1847 L. ii. 180

The forms are too late to do anything with. It is not evident that there was ever a *mere* here and as the place is not on the parish-boundary it is not clearly a case of **mære**. Perhaps the suffix is **mor** after all.

CHALKSHIRE

No early form has been found, but cf. VCH i. 15 'It (i.e. the Middle Chalk) is from eight to ten feet thick and has been observed at Chalkshire.'

CHEQUERS COURT

Chekeres 1401 FF (*VCH*)

The manor takes its name from the family to which Henry de Scaccario i.e. of the (Ex)chequer belonged, who held a quarter-fee in Ellesborough in 1242 (Fees 883).

COOMBE

Cumbingacre 1195 (14th) *Miss* 123 *b*
Cumbacres 1202 Fines

v. cumb and æcer. The *-ing-* of the first form is curious. Have we here a trace of an earlier form *Cumbing* or *Cumbingas*? *v.* EPN 41 and, more fully, Ekwall, PN in *-ing*.

NASH LEE, NORTH LEE

Lalega 1199 Fines
Nashleyfield 1706 *Terr*

v. leah. This 'clearing' seems to have been divided into two parts, the first of which was distinguished by some prominent ash-tree or trees.

TERRICK

Tirrock 1533 LP
Terwick 1766 J, 1826 B
Turwick c. 1825 O

This is clearly a wic but beyond that we can hardly go.

WHORLEY WOOD (6″)

Wardeleie 1195 (14th) *Miss* 123 *b*
boscus de Wardle 1199 Fines

'Watch-clearing' *v.* weard. That this site might well have been used for such is suggested by the name *Beacon* Hill just to the north.

WIDNELL WOOD (6″)

Vidhale 1196 FF
Wydehale 1235 *FF*

OE *wīdan heale* (dat.), 'wide nook,' *v.* **wid, healh.**

Great and Little Hampden

* HAMPDEN (Great and Little) 106 C 1 [hæmdən]

Hamdenam 1086 DB
Hamedene c. 1250 Rec. xi. 344 (p)
Hampdene c. 1200 (14th) *Miss* 111 (p)
Hamdene 1227 *Ass* (p), 1247 *Ass* (*Parva*), 1284 FA (*Magna*)

Forms with intrusive *p* are rare before 1400 and it is not heard in the local pronunciation of the name to this day.

This may be *hām-denu*, 'homestead-valley,' so called because marked by such, but compounds with initial **ham** are doubtful in English though Förstemann ON (s.n.) gives several such for OHG *heim*.

ALDRIDGE GROVE (6″)

Eldrigge 1227 *Ass* (p)

There is hardly enough to go upon. Possibly the first element is OE **alor** or **elle(r)n**, hence 'alder' or 'elder-ridge,' or the pers. n. *Ealda* is conceivable.

* HONOR END (Fm)

Hanora Hy ii (14th) *Miss* 50
Honore 1291 Tax, 1302 Ch

The second element in this name is **ora**. The first is OE *hān*, 'rock, *hone*.' There is a stone quarry here from which a very fine textured sandstone is obtained, which can be used as a whetstone (Harman).

Hulcott

HULCOTT 95 G 1 [hʌkət]

Hoccote 1200 Fines
Huccote 1227 *Ass* (p), 1237–40 Fees 1448, 1238 Gross, 1241 *Ass*, 1284, 1316 FA, 1291 Tax, 13th AD vi, 1304 Ipm, 1309 Pat, 1330 Cl, 1331 Ipm, 1346 Fine, Pat, 1372 Cl

Hulecote 1228 Pat (p)
Holekote 1242 Fees 885
Hucote 1262 *Ass*
Huckote 1262 *Ass* (p), 1331, 1340 Ipm, 1390 ImpR (*juxta Aylesbury*)
Hockote 1291 Tax
Hukkote 1371 Cl
Hukcott 1405 Pat
Hocote 1453 IpmR, 1497 BM
Hulcote 1535 VE
Huckott 1539 LP
Hulcott 1546 LP
Huckett 1626 Vern

The first element is either OE *hulu*, 'hull, husk,' used in ME of a 'hovel,' or the derivative OE *hulc*, with the same sense. The compound *hulu-cot(u)* or *hulc-cotu* was presumably used to describe some hovel-like cottages. The *l* was early lost from the cons. group *lcc*. When it reappears in the 16th cent. the *l* is probably due to association with such names as Holcote al. Hulcote (Beds) in which the first element is *holh*, 'hollow.'

ASCOTE (lost)

In the Missenden Chartulary (111 *b*) we have a grant in *Escote* which includes land neighbouring on the land of *Huccote* and the meadow of *Blakehegge*. We seem to have here a lost *Ascott*.

Lee

* LEE 106 B 3

Lega 1181 P
La Legh 1241 *Ass*
La Leye 1284 FA
Lye 1537 LP
v. leah.

Great and Little Missenden[1]

* MISSENDEN (Great and Little) 106 C 3

Missedene 1086 DB
Mesendena 1154 AC

[1] In Stone Hundred in DB, later in Aylesbury Hundred.

Mussend' Hy ii *AOMB* 33/170
Messemd' 1182 *AddCh* 10593
Missend' c. 1182 *AddCh* 10595
Messenden 1181 P, 1195 Cur(P), 1200 Fines, 1232 Fees 1358 (*Parva*), 1237–40 ib. 1448 (*Magna*)
Messedena 1185 Rot Dom
Mussend' c. 1200 *AddCh* 10597

In the 13th cent. 24 *e*-forms have been noted, 2 *u*-forms and 1 *i*-form. In the 14th, 8 *e*-forms, 4 *i*-forms, and 24 *u*-forms; in the 15th, 3 *i*- or *y*-forms, 1 *u*-form and 3 *e*-forms. No *u*-form is found in the 16th, and no *e*-form after 1535. Other forms that may be noted are

Massendone 1227 *Ass*
Massendena 1231 Bract
Messingdon 1247 *Ass*
Massyngdene 1374 Cl
Mussingden 1387 IpmR
Missyngdon 1399 Pat
Messenden Sancti Petri, *Messenden Attewhytechirch* 1262 *Ass*

This difficult name may best be explained by reference to the history of Mursley *supra*. It has been there suggested that this contains a pers. name *Myrsa*. The early forms of Missenden point clearly to a pers. name *Myssa*, a perfectly regular formation from *Myrsa* (cf. IPN 173), with assimilation of *rs* to *ss*. As each name is a *hapax legomenon* and the places themselves are only 16 miles apart it is difficult to think that they are entirely unconnected[1]. The settlers from whom they took their names may well have been of the same family, and the name which shows the assimilation be later in date than the other, a definite piece of evidence that the Chiltern slopes above the Vale of Aylesbury were settled from the north and not from the south. If this is the history of Missenden, the Misbourne river (*v. supra*) must contain the same pers. name. Cf. Waddesdon, Pitstone, Beachendon *supra*. For the variant vowel, *v.* Introd. xxiv. The

[1] A similar pair of pers. names found in close local contiguity occurs in Derbyshire, where the village now called Markeaton, clearly contains OE *Mearca* (cf. forms in PN Db), and adjoins a village called Mackworth, containing OE *Mæcca* (12th cent. *Mache*), these two pers. names showing the same type of assimilation that we have in the two names under discussion.

church of Great Missenden is dedicated to St Peter. Little Missenden Church is a 12th cent. building and must have been known as the 'white church.'

AFFRICK'S FARM

Anfric (sic) c. 1250 (15th) Godst, 1450 Godr
Auffrikke 1553 L. ii. 395
Aufricks 1670 L. ii. 395
Afflecks 1806 Lysons

BALLINGER [bælindʒə]

Baldinghore 1195 Cur(P)
Beldyngore 1297 Ipm
Baldynghore 1374 Cl
Belynger 1504 Pat
Bal(l)inger 1535 L. ii. 370, 1550 ib. 372

OE *Bealding-ōra*, 'Beald's bank,' *v.* ora. *-ing* is here used as in the ingtun- names. *B(e)ald* is found as a pers. name in OE (*v.* Cockayne, *Leechdoms*, ii. 298) and is a normal shortened form of such names as *Bealdhūn*, *Bealdrēd*. For the [indʒ] pronunciation cf. Fingest *supra*.

BEAMOND END

Beamonde juxta Myssenden 1535 VE
Beamonde 1538 LP
Beaman-end 1639 *Terr*
Beaumont 1670 L. ii. 395
Beman End c. 1825 O
Beaumont 1826 B

The regular development of AN *beumont*, 'beautiful hill.' Modern forms in *Beau-*, pronounced with initial [bou] are entirely artificial. For loss of *d*, *v.* Introd. xxvi.

BREACHES WOOD (6″)

great Brach 1639 *Terr*

v. Bourton Brake *supra*

GRANGE FARM

Grangia 1250 Fees 1172

Self-explanatory.

HALEACRE WOOD [haˑləkə]

Halligar Wood 1826 B

The modern form is probably artificial, at least in the pronunciation it suggests. As the wood is on the side of a steep hill the second element may be **hangra** and we may, for the phonetic development, compare Binegar (So). Equally possible, as Ekwall suggests, is OE *healf-æcer*, 'half-acre.' *v.* **æcer**.

HOLMER GREEN [houmə]

Holemer Hy ii *AOMB* 33/170
Homer Green 1766 J
Homers c. 1825 O

'Hollow **mere** or pool.' There is still a pool in a hollow. *v.* **holh**, **mere**. For the pronunciation cf. Homer (Sa) which has the same history.

HYDE (Fm) (6″)

Hide 1535 VE
Missenden Hyde 1550 L. ii. 372

v. **hid**.

MANTLE'S FARM

Mauntells Court al. *Fee* 1424 IpmR
Maundell al. *Mauncell Manor* 1500 Pat
Mantils farm 1703 *Terr*

The name of this farm is a survival from the manor of half a hide which Turstin Mantel held TRE in DB (267 *a*).

MARTIN'S END (6″)

Martynesende 1486 Rec. xi. 68

v. **ende**. The first element is the ordinary Christian name.

NINNEYWOOD (Fm)

Nynning (wood) 1540 L. ii. 372
Ninningwood 1714 Rec. xi. 178

One may suspect that this is corrupt and that the true form is *Nyming* and that it is the word *niming* used of 'taking in' some piece of wood, noted by Ekwall, PN *-ing* 25.

* PETERLEY

Piterleia c. 1150 (14th) *Miss* 45, *Piterleya* c. 1161 (14th) ib.
Puterle 1291 Tax
Peterleye 1302 Ch, 1426 Pat
Peterley 1542 L. ii. 370
Petterlow 1550 L. ii. 372
Petterley 1559 L. ii. 373
Peterly Eliz ChancP

Cf. also via de *Piterleistan* (c. 1180 (14th) *Miss*).

The first element may be an OE pers. name *Peohthere* which is not found but is a very likely compound, or *Peohtrǣd* which is on record, though in either case we should have expected a genitival *s*. The forms make the ordinary *Peter*, found in Petersfield (Ha), unlikely. *v.* leah.

* POTTER ROW

Le Pottererewe 1311 BM
Pottersrowe 1509 LP

Self-explanatory.

* PRESTWOOD

Prestwude c. 1180 (14th) *Miss* 45
Prestwood 1535 VE

Self-explanatory. It belonged to Missenden Abbey.

Stoke Mandeville

* STOKE MANDEVILLE 95 J 1

Stoches 1086 DB
Stokes 1200 Cur (p), 1237–40 Fees 1448, 1247 *Ass*
Stoke Mandeville 1284 FA
Stok by Aylesbury 1302 Fine
Middelstoke 1378 *Bodl Berks* 120
Stoke Mandil 1676 Rec. viii. 147

v. stoc. It was held by the Mandeville family in the 13th cent. (RH i. 20).

HALLING (lost)

Hallinges c. 1200 (14th) *Miss* 125

Halling(e) 1241 *Ass* (p), 1247 ib. (p), 1287 Pat (P), 1316 FA, 1382 IpmR
Stokehallinge 1295 Ch
Stok Halling 1304 Ipm
Stokhallinge 1305 Abbr

There was certainly a manor of *Hallinges* in Stoke Mandeville, but it is by no means certain that its site was Hall End as has been suggested. However that may be, Halling is from OE *Heallingas*, 'Heall's people.' *v.* Ekwall PN *-ing* 37, 180.

Wendover

WENDOVER 106 A 2

Wændofran (dat.) c. 970 (12th) BCS 1174
Wendoure 1086 DB, 1155 P, 1183 BM, 1199 FineR, R i *P*
Wenduura 1167 P
Wandoura R i *P*
Wendore 1220 Bract
Wendovere 1231 Bract

v. IPN 25. Probably an old stream-name.

* BACOMBE

Backham 1826 B

The forms are insufficient for an explanation to be offered.

DUTCHLANDS (Fm)

'Land called *Dutchland*' 1541 L. ii. 474

* THE HALE

La Hale 1223 *FF*
Wendover le Hale 1442 Ipm (*VCH*)

v. **healh**. The topography is indicated by Lipscomb, who says (ii. 481) that it stands at the foot of an eminence.

* WENDOVER DEAN

The second element in this name is not, as one might expect, the word *dean*, 'valley,' but is a feudal addition of which the explanation is found in Bracton's *Note-Book* (ii. 440) where we read that Robert Decanus (i.e. dean) of Wendover had a lay fee in Wendover.

XIV. STONE HUNDRED

Stanes 1086 DB, 1161 Reg Roff 391, 1182 P, 1195 Cur(P), 1232 Fees 1358, 1247, 1262 *Ass*, 1284 FA
Stone 1302 FA

The exact site of the Hundred meeting-place in Stone is unknown. *v. infra.*

Cuddington

CUDDINGTON 94 J 11/12

Cudintuna 1115–25 Reg Roff 383, 1176 BM
Cudinton 1186 P, c. 1218 WellsL, 1247 *Ass*, 1297 Pat
Cudington c. 1218 WellsL
Codington 1231 Reg Roff 387, 1536 LS
Cudyngton 1295 Ch
Codintone 1302 FA
Codyngton 1339, 1377 Pat, 1396, 1398 IpmR, 1485 Ipm, 1535 VE, 1539 LP

'Cuda's farm' *v.* ingtun.

It is hardly possible to recover the original form of the pers. name present here. According to the medieval spellings it may have been any of the pers. names *Cudda*, *Cuddi*, or *Cuda* (the last marked long by Sweet).

DADBROOK (House)

Dodbrook Hill c. 1825 O

Possibly 'Dod(d)a's brook.' For *a* from *o*, *v.* Introd. xxiii.

SPURT ST (*v.* HMS 113)

La Sperte 1320 Ch

This may be an early example, much earlier than any recorded in the NED of *spirt*, 'jet of liquid.' Cf. *Spertemede* in Denham (*HarlCh* 85 C 56). In Holly Tree Lane, the direct continuation of the present very short Spurt St, there are several springs (Harman).

Dinton

DINTON 94 J 12

Danitone 1086 DB
Dunitun c. 1205 *Bodl O* 51
Duninton 1208 Fees 19, c. 1210 *D and C Linc* D ii 69/2, 42, 1227 *Ass*, 1237–40 Fees 1448, 1247 *Ass*, 1316 FA
Duniton 1220 Bract, 1302 FA
Dunington c. 1218 WellsL, 1241 *Ass*
Donington c. 1218 WellsL, 1245 Gross, 1526 LS
Deniton 1227 *Ass*
Doninton 1247 *Ass*
Dunigton 1253 Ch
Donigton 1262 *Ass*
Donyton 1325 Fine
Donynton 1342 Pat, 1346 FA, 1374 Cl
Donyngton 1384 Cl, Pat
Dinton c. 1450 *Linc*
Dunton 1480–96 *Linc*
Donyngton al. *Donton* 1500 Pat
Donyngton, *Dunton* 1509 LP
Denton 1514–21 *Linc*, 1586 AD vi
Dynton 1526 LS
Dynton al. *Dennington* Eliz ChancP

'Dunna's farm' *v.* ingtun. Cf. Dinnington (Nb) and Dinton (W) which have the same history.

ASTON MULLINS

Eston 1232 Fees 1358, 1242 ib. 874 (*Hilmere cum*)
Aston 1247 Fees 1404
Ilmeresaston 1273 Cl
Estonebernard 1284 FA
Astone cum Illemere 1302 FA
Aston Barnard al. *Aston Molins* 1426 IpmR
Aston Mulling 1766 J

'East farm.' Known as *Ilmer's* Aston from its close association with Ilmer, Aston *Bernard* from Thomas son of Bernard who held the manor in the 12th cent. and *Mullins* from the Moleyns family who held it in the 14th cent. (FA 1346). Cf. Round, *King's Serjeants* 303–310.

FORD

Forda c. 1200 (14th) *Miss* 111 *b*
Donyngtonsford 1262 *Ass*

Self-explanatory. *v.* Dinton *supra*

MORETON (Fm)

Mortun c. 1218 WellsL
Morton 1227 *Ass*

v. mor, tun. It lies in low well-watered ground.

UPTON

Upetone 1086 DB
Opetone 1086 DB
Uppetone 1197 Fines
Upton 1204 Cur
Uptone Superior 1316 FA
Uptone cum Stone 1346 FA
Upton by Donynton 1358 Ipm

Self-explanatory. It lies a little higher than Dinton itself.

WALDRIDGE

wealdan hrigc 903 BCS 603
Wadruge 1086 DB
Waldruge 1086 DB
Walderug' 1195 Cur(P)
Walderugge 1227 *Ass*, 1262 ib. (p), 1284 FA, 1298 Abbr, 13th AD vi
Waldrugge 1237–40 Fees 1447, 1247 *Ass*
Waldrigg 1267 Ch, 1278 Abbr
Waldrych 1384 Pat
Waldriche 1384 Cl

'Wealda's ridge' *v.* **hrycg**. Cf. Waldingfield (Sf), Woldingham (Sr).

WESTLINGTON

Westinton 1384 Cl
West Dinton c. 1825 O

The modern form is corrupt. *Westinton* is probably from earlier *Westdinton*.

Haddenham

HADDENHAM 105 A 12 [hædnəm]

Nedreham 1086 DB
Hedreham Wm ii Reg Roff 383
Heddraam c. 1125 WMP
Hedenham 1142–8 Reg Roff 385, 1161–3 ib. 391, 1176 BM, c. 1195 Reg Roff 395, c. 1218 WellsL, 1235 Fees 462, 1247 *Ass*
Hadenham 1196 FF(P), Cur, 1227 *Ass*, 1242 Fees 875, Gross, 1255 *For*, RH, 1295 Ch, 1302 FA, 1333 Misc, Cl, Pat, 1343 Pat, 1346 Cl, 1373 Pat
Hadnam 1471 AD i

OE *Hǣdan-hām*, 'Hæda's homestead.' Cf. Haddenham (C), *Hædanham* (BCS 1268), *Hadreham* DB. The name *Hæda* is not actually on record but *Hædda* is (Redin 66). A similar variation between forms with and without gemination is found in *Had(d)a* (ib.). The *r* for *n* of some of the early forms is a common AN error. *v.* IPN 106–7.

BIGSTRUP (Fm) (6″)

Bichestrope 1161–3 Reg Roff 391 (p)
Bikelestorp 1179 P
Bikestrop c. 1195 (14th) *Miss* 124 *b*, 1204 Cur (p), 1234 Bract (p)
Bistrop 1200 Cur (p)
Bygestrope 1235 Fees 462
Bigestrop 13th AD i
Biggestrope 1302 FA
Byggesthrope 1346 FA
Bigstropp 1703 *Terr*

There is an OE name *Bic(c)a*. The diminutive *Bic(c)el* is not on record in OE but is found in Biggleswade (Beds), while its OHG cognate *Bichilo* is well-established. Hence 'Biccel's farm.' *v.* þorp. It is worthy of note that the name *Bic(c)a* is found in Beachendon (*v. supra*), only four miles away and we may note the similar pair—Kiddington and Kidlington (O), though these are rather farther apart.

Halton[1]

HALTON 95 J 2
Healtun c. 1033 (13th) KCD 1321
Haltone 1086 DB, 1195 Cur(P)
Halkhton 1237–40 Fees 1448
Haulton 1766 J

v. healh, tun. The sense of healh here is aptly fixed by Lipscomb (ii. 319) who says that Halton is situated in a sandy track on the side of the Chiltern Hills.

BODDINGTON HILL

Lipscomb says (ii. 481) that this hill is vulgarly called Bottendown Hill. If so it may really be OE *Bōtandūn*, 'Bota's hill.'

BYE GREEN

(Joh. atte) *Grene* 1340 NI

The first element in this name is probably due to the fact that the place lies in the extreme west corner of the parish and it is an example of those compounds in *by-*, of which several are given in the NED, in which *by-* denotes 'out-of-the-way.'

Hartwell

HARTWELL 94 J 13
Herdewelle 1086 DB
Hertwell 1205 FineR, c. 1210 (14th) *Miss* 112 *b*, 1220 Fees 313, 1269 Ch, 1270 AD iii, 1302 FA, 1325 Fine, 1325 Ch, 1341 Pat, 1502 Pat
Hurtwella c. 1210 (14th) *Miss* 112 *b* (p), 1284 FA
Ortwell 1235 Fees 1557
Hertwell Rode 1303 Cl
Hartwell 1509 LP

'Hart-spring,' i.e. where the stag waters. For *hurt* *v.* IPN 136.

CULLEY (Fm) (6″)
Couselowe 1320 Ch
Cally Farm 1826 B

[1] Is in Stone Hundred in DB and in Aylesbury in FA.

Perhaps for OE *Cūsan-hlāw*, 'Cusa's hill,' *v.* hlaw. *Cūsa* is a well-established OE name. *sl* > *ll* by assimilation, just as *sr* becomes *rr* in Courage (Berks), earlier *Cusanhricg* (BCS 900).

SEDRUP

Surop' 1236 *FF*
Suthrop 1241 *Ass* (p)
Southorpe 1507 L. ii. 458
Southrop 1706 *Terr*, 1766 J, 1826 O
Southwarpe c. 1825 O

'South thorpe' *v.* suð, þorp. The weakening of the vowel in the first syllable is noteworthy. Cf. Southcott in Linslade and Southcote *infra*. 'South' in relation to Hartwell.

Great and Little Kimble

KIMBLE (Great and Little) 106 A and B 1

Cynebellinga gemære 903 BCS 603
Chenebelle, *Chenebelle Parva* 1086 DB
Kynebelle c. 1180, *Oseney* 153 (p)
Kinebelle 1196 FF(P)
Kenebelle 1197 Fines, 1204 Cur
Magna Kynebell c. 1218 WellsL

In the 13th cent. 18 *e*-forms, 8 *i*- and *y*-forms and 6 *u*-forms have been noted; in the 14th, the figures are 2 *e*-, 7 *i*- and *y*- and no *u*-forms. The first assimilation of *nb* to *mb* is in

Kymbell 1369 Cl

Later forms are

Kymble 1408 Pat
Kembel(l) 1441, 1451 Pat
Kumbell 1446 AD i
Kymbell 1485 Ipm, 1509 LP
Kymball al. *Kembyll* 1510 LP

This is a name with regard to which no certainty can be attained. Professor Ekwall suggests that the second element may be an OE *bell(e)*, meaning 'hill,' a word the existence of which we have good reasons for assuming. It is found as *bell* in modern dialects (cf. Yeavering Bell in Nb) and the cognate

bjalli is common as a hill-name in Norway and Iceland. The first element he would take to be OE *cyne*, 'royal.' There is a very conspicuous hill at Kimble which must undoubtedly have impressed itself on the minds of the first settlers in the neighbourhood and they might well have distinguished it from its neighbours as the 'royal' hill, or it may be that early in the history of the settlement it came, by reason of some royal burial or other event, to earn the epithet 'royal' in more direct fashion. For a compound of this type we may compare Kingston-on-Soar (Nt), DB *Chinestan*, which must be from OE *cyne-stān*. For the variant vowel, *v.* Introd. xxiv.

GRANGE (Fm)

'A *grange* house at Great Kymble' 1580 AD iii.

MARSH

la Mersa c. 1195 (14th) *Miss* 123 *b*
Mersch 1277 AD iv
Estmersh, *Westmersh* 1373 Cl
Self-explanatory.

PULPIT WOOD (6″)

Bulpittwood 1639 *Terr*

The modern form is clearly due to folk-etymology. The 'bull-pit' is an ancient hill top camp. Cf. VCH ii. 15.

SOLINGER (Fm) [sɔ·liŋgə], [sæliŋgə], [sæligə]

Salangre c. 1210 (14th) *Miss* 124

'Willow-wood' *v.* sealh, hangra and cf. *seal hangra* (BCS 890), *seal hyrst* (BCS 758). The goat-willow (sallow) is common in the hedges near by (Harman).

KIMBLE WICK

Wyk(a) Hy ii (1313) Ch, 1227 *Ass*
'Kimble dairy-farm' *v.* wic.

Stone

STONE 94 J 13

Stanes 1086 DB, c. 1218 WellsL, 1219 Bract, c. 1220 WellsR, 1235 Fees 462, Hy iii BM, 1284 FA, 1320 Ch, 1346 Pat

Staines Hy iii AD i
Stanes juxta Ayllesbur' 1286 Orig
Stone E ii AD iv, 1324 Cl, 1344 Ipm
Stane 1320 Ch

OE *stānas*, 'stones,' the reference being to some boundary or other stones, possibly those that marked the Hundred meeting-place.

* BISHOPSTONE

Bissopeston 1227 *FF*

'Bishop's farm,' probably so called because it was that part of the manor of Stone, which was held by Odo, Bishop of Bayeux, TRW. If so, it is a remarkable example of a place-name created by a very brief tenure of an estate.

BURN HILL

Burnhull 1276 RH
Bourn Hill 1722 Rec. ix. 264 n.

There is no stream here so that association with the OE burna is ruled out. The hill is however marked by an ancient barrow which has been examined and found to contain skeletons of the Early Iron age or of the Anglo-Saxon period (*v.* Rec. ix. 263 f.). It is therefore clear that the first element is OE *byrgen*, 'burial-place,' an element which Bradley and Ekwall independently showed to be present in the second part of Hebburn (Du). Hence 'hill marked by a burial place.' Cf. Burn in Brayton (Y), c. 1030 *Burne* Yorkshire Charters, *Birne*, *Burne* Feudal Aids.

CHILBOROHILL (Fm)

Chillsbury Fm 1826 B

Possibly OE *Cēoles*-burh or -beorg, *Ceol* being a well-established OE pers. name. It might also contain the name *Cild*.

SOUTHCOTE (lost)

Sudcote 1086 DB
Suthcote c. 1200 (14th) *Miss* 112 *b*
Sircotes or *Sithcotes lands* 1511 LP

Self-explanatory but the 16th cent. forms are worthy of note. Cf. those for Southcott and Sedrup *supra*.

STANDAL'S FARM [stændəlz]

Standhills c. 1825 O

Standhill (O) goes back to OE *stangedelf*, 'stony trench or quarry' (*v.* (ge)delf), and that is what we may have here, perhaps in the plural. There is a stone quarry a mile to the north.

WHADDON HILL [wɔdən]

Whetduna c. 1210 (14th) *Miss* 112 *b*
Watton Hill c. 1825 O
Wotton Hill 1826 B

OE *hwǣte-dūn*, 'wheat-hill.' Cf. Whaddon *supra*. The assimilation in this case was in the original instance *td* > *tt* rather than *td* > *dd*.

Weston Turville[1]

* WESTON TURVILLE

Weston 1086 DB
Westone Parva 1284 FA
Weston by Aylesbury 1297 Ipm
Westone Turvile 1302 FA
Weston Turfild 1417 Encl

'West' farm in relation to *Aston* Clinton. The Turville family held land here already in the reign of Stephen. A motte and bailey representing their castle still stands.

BEDGROVE (Fm)

Begrave 1086 DB
Be(l)begraue c. 1220 (14th) *Miss* 117
Babbegraue 1227, 1262 *Ass*
Bebbegraue 1247 *Ass* (p), 1262 *Ass*, 1297 Ipm
Pebbegrave 1276 Pat
Belegrave 1284 FA, 1339 Pat
Bedgrave 1461 Pat
Bedgrave al. *Bedgrove* 1541 LP
Belgrove 1627 BM

[1] In Stone Hundred in DB but afterwards it is always in Aylesbury Hundred. Possibly Weston Turville and Halton once formed a detached part of Stone Hundred.

The *d* in the modern forms of this name is clearly not original and it is hard to say whether it is due to some form of dissimilation, *Beb-* becoming *Bed-*, or whether it is a sheer corruption. Apart from that the forms are not easy. OE names *Bebba* (f) and *Babba* are on record and a form *Bæbba* may also have existed, which would explain the first, third, fourth and fifth forms given above, but they leave untouched the *l* which appears sporadically. No OE name *Bælba* or *Belba* is known though it is just conceivable that such may have existed as a pet-form for such a name as *Bealdbeorht*, which itself is not actually found in OE but is a quite likely name. The question therefore of the name of the owner of this 'grove' must be left open.

HYDE (lost)

Hyda 1302 FA

v. **hid**. The name of this manor is now lost from the map but it corresponds to Manor Farm (*v.* VCH ii. 369–70).

XV. RISBOROUGH HUNDRED

Ris(e)berg 1086 DB, 1155 P, 1247 *Ass*
Risemberge 1130 PR
Rysebergh, *Rysenberg* 1262 *Ass*

The site of the Hundred meeting-place is unknown. For the etymology of the name *v. infra.*

Bledlow

BLEDLOW 105 C 13

Bleddanhlæw 1012 (12th) Thorpe 553
Bleddehlæwe 1023 (13th) Thorpe 331
Bledelai 1086 DB
Bledeslewes Hy ii AD vi
Bledelaw(e) 1175 P, R i *P*, 1227, 1241 *Ass*, Hy iii BM, 1228 Bract, 1235 Fees 462, 1247, 1262 *Ass*, 1284 FA, 1292 Pat, 1294 AD i, 1295 Ipm, 1302 FA, 1353 Pat, 1361 AD vi
Bleddeleaus R i (1332) Ch
Bledeslawe 1247 *Ass*

Bladelawe 1262 *Ass*
Bledelowe 1315, 1352 Cl, 1353 Pat
Bledelewe 1336 Cl
Bledlow 1485 Ipm

The first element is an OE pers. name *Bledda*, not actually found but a regular pet-form for an OE name in *Blǣd-*, '*Bledda's* hill or barrow' *v.* **hlaw**. The settlement must have taken its name from the hill above it, or possibly from the tumulus by Bledlow Cross (Harman).

BLEDLOW CROSS

atte Crouche of Bledelowe 1350 Pat

OFr. *crouche*, 'cross,' as in Crouch End (Mx).

BLEDLOW RIDGE

Bledelowerigge 1247 *Ass*
Bledelawerugg 1262 *Ass*, 1325 Cl
Bledlowerugge Hy iii BM

Self-explanatory.

DREWELLS (lost)

Mesle 1302 FA
Mesele al. *Druels* 1474 Pat
Drewells c. 1825 O

Simon *de Rual* (al. *Simon Druel*) held land in Bledlow in the 13th cent. (Fees i. 462, ii. 875) and this is the origin of the manorial name. The other name is from OE **meos** and **leah**, hence 'mossy clearing.'

* THE FORD

Forda 1302 FA (p), 13th AD vi

Self-explanatory.

* THE LYDE (6")

la Lithe c. 1250 Rec. xi. 344 (p), *atte Lithe* 1287 Misc (p)
la Lithe 1290 AD iii (p)
ate Lythe 1346 FA (p)

The Lyde is the name of a steep wooded combe with which is associated the rhyme

> They that live and do abide
> Shall see the church fall in the Lyde.

This is clearly OE **hliþ**, 'slope.' The word long survived in the form *lithe* and NED quotes from White's *Selborne* the use of *lithe* to denote 'steep pastures.' The vowel has been lengthened in the open syllable of the oblique case form *hliþe*.

SHIMMELL'S FARM (6″)
Shinnalls c. 1825 O
Shingles Fm 1826 B

Horsenden

HORSENDEN 105 C 13
Horsedene, *Horsedune* 1086 DB
Horsendon 1175 P, 1200 Cur

The suffix varies between *-don* and *-den* from the earliest times onwards. From the 14th cent. *-don* forms prevail and the *-den* form now in use is quite modern. We may note also

Horsindone 1221 WellsR, 1262 *Ass*, 1333 Ch, 1337 Cl
Horsingdone 1221 WellsR, 1262 *Ass*, 1766 J, 1797 Desb
Horsyngton 1359 IpmR
Horsyngdon 1360 Ipm, 1474 Pat, 1477 IpmR
Horsington 1512 LP, 1526 LS
Horssingdon 1535 VE

OE *Horsan-dun* or *-denu*, 'Horsa's hill or valley,' with later corruption of *en* (from *an*) to *ing*.

In actual situation *-den* best suits the village as it lies on the flat in the centre of the Risborough Gap (Harman).

This name is exceptionally interesting, for it helps to prove the existence of an OE pers. name *Horsa*, borne according to tradition by the brother of Hengest the leader of the mercenaries invited by Vortigern. The fact that this name is not otherwise found in OE has been sometimes taken to throw doubt on the authenticity of the tradition. The argument falls to the ground in face of the present name and Horsington (L), an equally certain compound of an OE *Horsa*.

Monks and Princes Risborough

RISBOROUGH (MONKS and PRINCES) 105 B 14

þæm easteran Hrisanbyrge (dat.) 903 (11th) BCS 603
Risenbeorgas c. 1000 (12th) KCD 714
Hrisebyrgan be Cilternes efese 1006 ( ) KCD 715
Risebergh 1086 DB, 1175, 1180 P, 1199 Cur, R i *P*, 1243 Ch, 1262 *Ass*, 1336 Pat, 1337 Pat (*Earl's*), 1341 Cl, 1349 Pat
Risesbirie c. 1155 *Bodl O* 49
Risemberga 1173–4 Fr, Hy ii (1313) Ch, *Rysemberg* 1300 AD i, Ipm, 1315 BM
Risenberg 1175 P, 1195 Cur(P), R i *P*, 1200 RC, 1227 *Ass*, 1241 ib. (*Simylly*), 1262 *Ass*
Riseuilla 1226 Bract
Risingbergham 1226 Bract, 1244 Pat
Magna Riselburwe 1235 Fees 468, *Riselbergh* 1241 *Ass*
Riseburg' 1237 Ch
Parva Risenburgh 1237–40 Fees 1449
Riseburne 1241 *Ass*
Rysenberg' 1244 Ipm, 1262 *Ass*
Ryseberg 1247 Fees 1405, 1247 *Ass*, 1290 AD iii (*Monks*), 1318 Fine
Rissenberg 1247 *Ass*
Rissebergh 1262 *Ass*
Rysburgh 1290 Ipm (*King's*), 1399 Pat, 1359 IpmR (*Principis*)
Ryseborowe 1302 FA
Risborough 1308 AD i
Risburgh 1318, 1343 Pat, 1374 Cl
Riseburgh 1341 Cl
Ryseburghe 1344 Ipm, 1346 FA
Monekenrisbourgh 1346 Pat, *Munken Rysebergh* 1392 Pat
Risburgh Moyne 1347 Pat
Pryns Risburgh 1433 Pat
Monkyng Rysburgh 1509 LP
Pryncyn Ryseborough 1509 LP

The forms of this name may be explained if, as suggested by Professor Ekwall, we take the first part of the name to be the OE adj. *hrīsen*, a regularly formed adj. from **hris**. The hills

above the two Risboroughs could not be better described than as grown over with *hris* or brushwood and their name must have been *þā hrīsenan beorgas*, 'the brushwood-covered hills.' The hill above Monks Risborough was called the 'eastern' Risborough, while in the third form quoted above we have the picturesque description of the two Risboroughs as 'by Chiltern eaves.' The medial *en* in *hrisenan* would early have been lost. The forms with *m* are due to assimilation of *nb* to *mb*, those with *l* are AN spellings (IPN 106).

Monks or Little Risborough was so called because it belonged to Christ Church, Canterbury, from pre-Conquest days.

Prince s or Great Risborough was so called from the Black Prince into whose custody the manor passed in 1343 (Cl). It was originally a royal manor and was often in royal hands, hence 'King's.' When it is called *Earl's* in 1337, it was in the possession of the Earl of Cornwall[1].

ASKETT

Astcote c. 1250 Rec. xi. 344
Ascote 1300 AD i
Ascot(t) 1541 LP, 1766 J, c. 1825 O

'East cottage(s)' in contrast to a lost *Westcote* mentioned in 1227 (*Ass*). *v.* east, cot.

GREEN HAILEY

hegleage 903 (late OE copy) BCS 603
Green Healy c. 1825 O

'Hay-clearing' *v.* heg, leah and cf. *higleage* (BCS 731).

[1] The *Hrisbyri* of BCS 552, identified by Birch with Princes Risborough cannot be reconciled with the other certain forms for Risborough and there are other grounds too on which the identification should probably be rejected. It is therefore left out of count here. The charter in which it occurs purports to have been made in a Mercian witenagemot at *Hrisbyri* in 884. The charter, which is only known from Smith's edition of Bede, is probably genuine, but it is very difficult to believe that in 884 central Buckinghamshire was sufficiently settled under English rule to permit the holding of a witenagemot at Princes Risborough. The charter itself relates to land at Himbleton (Wo).

MEADLE

Madhulle 1227 *Ass*
Medhulle 1227 *Ass*
Medell 1541 LP

OE *mǣd-hyll*, 'meadow-hill,' *v.* mæd, hyll.

* OWLSWICK [elsik]

Wulueswik c. 1200 (14th) *Miss* 111
Ulueswike c. 1200 (14th) *Miss* 111, 1237–40 Fees 1449, 1241 *Ass* (p)
Ulueswicke 1227 *Ass*
Wulueswyk 1242 Fees 875
Olueswik 1247 *Ass* (p), 1284 FA
Ulueswyk 1262 *Ass* (p), 1
Ulfysyke 1262 *Ass*
Ulveswyke 1541 LP
Owleswicke 1617 L. ii. 424

'Dairy-farm' (*v.* wic) of *Wulf* or *Úlfr*, the forms from early times showing hesitation between the English and Scandinavian forms of this name. *Wulf*, uncompounded, is rarely found as a personal name before the Conquest, and it is far from common afterwards. *Ulf*, from ON *Úlfr*, is one of the commonest pers. names in the 11th and 12th cents. It therefore seems probable that the present name is late and that it contains the Scandinavian *Ulf*, Anglicised for a time to *Wulf* by the surrounding English population. The name may be even later than the Conquest, by which time many men bearing Scandinavian names were holding estates in Buckinghamshire.

WHITELEAF

Whitt Light 1541 LP
Whitcliffe Cross 1766 J

The modern form is corrupt. The hill and cross must have been named from the white chalk hill in which the cross is cut. Cf. Whitcliff (Gl) which is *Whytleyff* in 1540 LP. No trace of the pronunciation with short vowel can now be found.

* ALSCOT

Elsicote 13th AD vi

OE *Ælfsiges-cot(u)*, 'Aelfsige's cottage(s).' *v.* cot.

The name *Elsi*, still surviving in the 13th cent., might also represent OE *Æthelsige*.

COOMBE

This is almost certainly the home of the William atte *Coumbe* who in 1354 left a bequest of 'one sheep' to the church at Bradenham (Hist. MSS. Com. Rep. v, App. i, 562), for Coombe is close to Bradenham Parish. *v.* cumb.

CULVERTON

Culu'don 1199 Cur, 1200 Fines, 1241 *Ass* (p)
Culverdon 1247 *Ass*, 1434 Pat
Coluerdon 1262 *Ass* (p), 13th AD i, 1325 Cl
Colveredon 1290 Ipm

'Wood-pigeon hill' *v.* culfre, dun. The same place seems to be referred to as *Culuerhamhull* (*v.* ham, hyll) in *FF* 1271.

DARRILLSHILL

Darvell Hill 1766 J
Darvars Hill 1826 B

The first element is almost certainly OE *dēor-fald*, 'animal- or cattle-fold,' which lies behind Darvell (Sx). The *s* of the most recent forms is misleading.

LACEY GREEN [li·əsi]

Leasey Green 1766 J

Leasey is probably a weakened form of *leasowe*, 'pasture,' the regular descendant of OE læs.

LONGWICK

Long Wyke 1320 Cl
Longewyke 1485 Ipm

v. wic. The hamlet, of which the dairy farm must have formed the nucleus, is long and straggling.

LOOSLEY ROW

Losle 1241 *Ass* (p)
Lesley Row Eliz ChancP

OE *hlōse-lēah*, 'pigstye-clearing,' i.e. one marked by the presence of such. *v.* hlose. Cf. Loseley (Sr).

STOCKEN (Farm) (6")

Stockyng 1301 Ipm

v. stocking.

WARDROBES

Juliana atte Wardrobe in 1338 (AD vi) demised land at King's Risborough. She was probably of the same family as Joscelin de la Wardrobe who held land in Aylesbury (1229 Bract).

* *CHILTERN HUNDREDS*

*Ciltern*es *efese* 1006 ( ) KCD 715
Ciltern 12th (1009 E) ASC, 11th BCS 297
Ciltre 1241 *Ass*, 1305 Pat, 1335 Ipm
Ciltrie 1309 Cl

A name certainly of pre-English origin.

XVI. DESBOROUGH HUNDRED

Dustenberg 1086 DB
Dusteberg 1175 P, R i *P*, 1227, 1241, 1247 *Ass*
Dustleberg R i *P*, 1316 FA
Dustelberg 1195 Cur(P), 1241 *Ass*
Dustebrug' 1195 Cur(P)
Duslebergh 1241 *Ass*
Dosteberge 1255 RH
Dustleberewe 1262 *Ass*
Dusteburgh 1265 Misc
Desburue 1284 FA
Dusteborwe 1302 FA
Dosteborowe 1346 FA
Dysborowe 1526 LP

The site of the Hundred meeting-place must have been at Desborough Castle, an ancient earthwork which lies on the top of a hill. *v.* Desborough *infra*.

Bradenham

BRADENHAM 106 D 1 [brædnəm]

Bradeham 1086 DB, 1195 Cur(P), 1234 Bract, 1237–40 Fees 1450, 1253 Pat
Bradenham 1227 *Ass*, 1235 Gross, 1242 Fees 879, 1316 FA
Bradingham 1255 *For* (p)
Bradenhamme 1535 VE

Probably 'Brada's homestead' rather than OE *brādan ham* (dat.) 'broad homestead.' For *Brada v.* Redin 73. The VE form suggests the possibility that the suffix may be **hamm** rather than **ham** but is unconfirmed by definite early evidence and if it is a *hamm* it is not one on a river.

Fawley

FAWLEY 105 H 12

Falelie 1086 DB
Falle 1199 Fines
Faulega 1219 Bract
Fauley c. 1225 *Mert* 2444 (p)
Falele 1234 Cl

After this the forms have uniformly *Fall-* until

ffawley 1639 *Terr*

'Fallow clearing' or 'fallow-coloured clearing' *v.* **fealh**, **fealo**, **leah**. Similarly Fawley in Ha and He. Fawsley (Nth) and possibly Fawley in Berks come from a pers. n. **Fealu*.

BOSMORE

Bossemere c. 1240 *Mert* 2451, 2 (p), c. 1250 ib. 785 (p), 2438, 9 (p)
Bosmere 1479 AD vi

'Bossa's boundary' *v.* **mære**. The name *Bosa* is well established (*v.* Redin 86) and survived into the 12th cent. It gave rise to several place-names of which Market Bosworth (Lei) and Bosham (Sx) are famous, and Bozeat (Nth) refers to a site close to Buckinghamshire. There can however be little doubt that Bosmore comes from a geminated form **Bossa*. This form can hardly be connected with Bosa, of which the ultimate origin is

uncertain. It may well be a short form of a compound pers. name beginning with *Bōt-*. If so, an original **Bōtsige* may be suggested. **mære** seems more likely than **mere** here for the farm lies near the bounds of the parish and county and there is certainly no 'mere' here now.

OXEY GROVE (6″)

Oxefrid 1241 *Ass* (p)

The identification seems probable, as in the enquiry with reference to the killing of Juliana daughter of Richard of *Oxefrid*, the vills of Hughenden, Saunderton, West Wycomb, Radnage, all neighbouring parishes found the accused party guilty by inquest. If so the old name is 'ox wood.' *v.* **fyrhþ**. For the reduction of the final element cf. Hoastley Park (Ess), earlier *Horsfreth park* (Cl).

Fingest

FINGEST 105 F 13 [findʒəst], [vindʒəst]

Tingeherst Hy ii (1329) Ch, 1233 WellsR, 1246 Gross
Tingehurst 1163 D and C *Linc* D ii 88/1/57
Tinghurste 1209–19 WellsR, 1227 *Ass*, 1284 FA, 1291 Ipm
Tynghurst(e) 1209–19 WellsR, 1237–40 Fees 1450, 13th AD vi, 1302 FA, 1342 Inq aqd
Tinghirst 1227, 1247 *Ass*
Tingherst 1233 WellsR, 1262 *Ass*
Thinghurst c. 1240 *Mert* 2453, 1535 VE
Tyngehyrst 1247 *Ass*
Tingehirst 1247 *Ass*, 1526 LS
Tingehurst 1265 Misc
Tynggehurst 1270 *Mert* 2426 (p)
Tyngehurst 1316 FA, 1329 Ch, 1335 Pat
Tynghirst 1324 Cl
Thynchehurst 1402 Pat
Fingest 1660 *Foster*

'Assembly-hill' *v.* **þing, hyrst**. For the full significance of this name *v.* Introd. The change from initial *th* to *f* is not uncommon in dialect and place-names generally and exactly the same change has taken place in Finedon (Nth). For *v* from *f*, *v.* Introd. xxv. The pronunciation of *ng* as [ndʒ] is noteworthy.

CADMORE END

Cademere 1236 *FF*

'Cada's boundary.' The name *Cada* may be inferred from *Cadanhangra* (KCD 780) and numerous other place-names. *v.* Förster in *Liebermann Festschrift* 180. **mære** rather than **mere** seems certain as the place is right on the county border.

MUZWELL (Fm) [mɔzəl]

Mosewell 1340 NI (p)
Mozzels c. 1825 O

'Mossy spring' *v.* **meos, wielle** and cf. Muswell Hill (Mx).

Hambleden

HAMBLEDEN 105 H 13 [hæməldən]

hamelan dene (dat.) 1015 KCD 722
Hanbledene 1086 DB
Hameleden 1182 P, R i *P*, 1227 *FF*, 1237–40 Fees 1450
Hamele 1208 Fees 19
Hameldene 1227, 1241 *Ass*
Hamoledene 1227 *Ass*

Further forms are unnecessary. There are a good many cases of forms with *-don* for *-den*, no *b* has been noted before the 19th cent. and it is not pronounced locally now.

It is probable that we have the adj. **hamel** here. It may describe the valley here for it winds a good deal and its sides are much indented with combes, but in our ignorance of the precise significance of *hamel* it is difficult to say more. A personal name, ***Hamela*, is also conceivable.

BACRES

Baker's Fm 1714 *VCH*
Beakers 1766 J

The farm takes its name from the family-name *Baker* (VCH).

BURROW (Fm)

le Berewe al. *la Burgh* 1290 IPM
Burrough Craft 1680 *Terr*

It is difficult to say whether this is from **beorg** or **burh**.

CHISBRIDGE (Fm) [ʧizbidʒ]

Chissebech 1175 P (p), 1241 *Ass* (p), 1246 *Ass* (p), 1307 *Cocks* (p)
Chessebech 1228 Bract
Chisbeach 1766 J, 1826 B
Chisbidge c. 1825 O

OE *Cissan-bæc*, 'Cissa's hill,' *v.* **bæc**. There is no stream here for us to suspect the other **bæc**. If it were not for the persistent double *s* in the early forms one might suspect OE **cis**, for Chisbridge stands on a ridge of gravel (Harman). The OS form is corrupt and is not accepted locally.

The name *Cissa* is rare and early. It was borne by a son of Ælle, king of the South Saxons, and it is probable that the name Chichester (OE *Cissan ceaster*) takes its origin from him.

COLSTROPE

Collmanstrop 1634 (Hambleden Churchwardens' Account Book)[1]
Coltthorp 1797 Desb
Coltstrope c. 1825 O
Coldthorpe 1826 B

'Colman's village or hamlet' *v.* **þorp**. There is no native pers. name *Colman*. Whatever the origin of Colman, the 7th cent. bishop of Lindisfarne, he came from 'Scotia,' and was indeed the spokesman of the Celtic party at the Synod of Streoneshalch. After him, the name is not found in English sources till DB. There are no English names compounded with *Col-* and there can be little doubt that Björkman was right in deriving the medieval English name *Coleman* from a Continental Germanic source.

* FRIETH

ffrith c. 1307 *Cocks* (p)
Freeth 1766 J, 1826 B

v. **fyrhþ**. Until quite recently it was called locally 'the Frieth.' Cf. Oxey *supra*.

[1] This reference is due to Mr A. H. Cocks' *Church Bells of Bucks*, 398.

GREENLANDS

Greneland 1546 LP

Self-explanatory.

HOLYWICK [hɔliwik], [hæliwik]

Halwic Joh Abbr (p)
Haliwyk 1291 Tax
Hallywicks 1537 LP
Hollowicks Wood c. 1825 O

Clearly 'holy wic,' presumably so called because the farm belonged to Medmenham Abbey (1291 Tax) though it should be noted that the Abbey itself was only founded in 1204. *v*. halig.

HOWE

atte *Hoo* 1391 Pat (p)
Howgrounde 1545 LP

v. hoh. It lies on a definite spur of ground.

HUTTON'S FARM

Hottens 1826 B

In 1227 Thos. de *Hotton* was a party to a fine in Hambleden and his family doubtless gave their name to this farm.

LUXTERS (Fm)

The name of this farm must be associated with an entry in a Fingest Terrier (1674) which speaks of '5 lucksters which is about ten acres.' No further light can be thrown on this 'double' acre.

PARMOOR

Pyremere 1290 Ipm
Permere 1509 LP
Parmoor 1766 J

OE *pirige-mere*, 'peartree-mere.' There is a small pool here. *v*. pirige.

POYNATTS (Fm) [painəts]

Pinets 1766 J, 1796 Desb
Pinots 1826 B

This manor takes its name from the Poynaunt family who in 1284 (FA) held the sixteenth part of a knight's fee in Hambleden.

ROCKWELL END [rɔkəl]

(de la) *Rocolte* c. 1307 *Cocks* (p)
(ate) *Rokholte* 1340 NI
Rockall End c. 1825 O

'Rook wood' *v.* **hroc, holt.** The vowel has been shortened in the first part of the compound. For loss of final *t v.* Introd. xxvi. The name *Rockoll* is frequent in the Great Marlow Registers.

SKIRMETT

la Skiremote c. 1307 *Cocks*
Skirmot 1347 FF (*VCH*)
Skyrmote 1412 Pat (p)
Skyremot al. Skymot 1417 IpmR
Scermit 1797 Desb
Skirmitt c. 1825 O
Scirmet 1826 B

There is no doubt that the second element in this name is OE (*ge*)*mōt*, 'meeting,' and that the first element is a Scandinavianised form of OE *scīr*, 'shire.' In the passage in 1417 (IpmR) there is mention of the *viam vocat' Skyremot quae ducit versus Henley*. For the full significance of this name *v.* Introd. xvii.

WOOLLEYS

Wolveleg' 1227 *FF*
Wuluelegh 1241 *Ass* (p)

OE *wulfa-lēah*, 'wolves' clearing.' *v.* **leah.** The modern *s* is a corrupt form. Woolley in Chaddleworth and Woolley Green (Berks) have the same origin.

YEWDEN MANOR

Yueden 1255 RH
Iweden 1265 Misc
Yveden 1338 Ipm, 1346 FA
Iueden 1357 Cl, 1478 AD ii
Ewden 1546 LP

'Yew-valley' *v.* **iw, denu.** There is still an ancient avenue of yews here.

*

Hedsor

HEDSOR 106 H 3

Heddesore R i *P*, 1195 Cur(P), 1220 Fees 314, 1241 *Ass*
Hedleshore 1195 Cur(P) (checked against MS)
Hadessore 1203 Fines
Heddesour 1208 Fees 21
Hedesores 1212 Fines
Hedeshore 1212 Fees 119
Hadeshowere c. 1218 WellsL
Heddenesora 1223 Bract
Eddeshowre 1227 WellsR
Hedesore 1235 Fees 461, 1241, 1262 *Ass*
Edesovere 1235 Fees (p) 555
Heddesovere 1235 Fees 555
Heddeshore 1284 FA
Hedsore 1316 FA, 1489 Ipm
Haddesovere 1316 AD i
Hadsore 1539 LP
Heddesworth 1561 BM
Headsworth 1643 Desb 13

Were it not for the forms *Hedleshore* and *Heddenesora* one would suggest that the first element in this name was the gen. sg. of the pers. name *Hædde*, but they suggest a pers. name **Hæddel* a dimin. of this name with *n* for *l* in the second form under AN influence. The second is ofer. Hedsor stands on a cliff well above the river.

LUDPITS WOOD[1]

Ludeput c. 1210 (14th) *Miss* 93
Ludpytts 1540 LP

OE *Ludan-pytt*, 'Luda's pit.'

WOOLMAN'S WOOD

Wulneneham (sic) *Miss* 93 (*VCH*)
Wolmans 1509 LP

Probably OE *wylfena-hamm*, 'she-wolves' enclosure.' The *s* is a modern corruption.

[1] This is not on the O.S. maps but is mentioned as existing in Rec. viii 490 n.

Hughenden

HUGHENDEN 106 E 2 [u·əndən]

Huchedene 1086 DB
Hichedena c. 1125 (c. 1230) *Kenil* 75 *b*
Hichenden(a) c. 1145 (c. 1230) ib. 21, 1241 *Ass*
Hugendene Hy ii *Bodl O* (p), 1195 Abbr, R i *P*, 1204 Fines
Huggenden 1189 P, R i *P*, 1236 Pat, 1241 *Ass*
Hugeden R i *P*
Huggedene 1198 Fines, 1227 *Ass*
Huchenden 1199 Cur, c. 1210 (14th) *Miss* 146 *b*, 1228 Bract
Hichendon 1237 Gross
Hucchenden 1241 *Ass*

After this the prevailing forms are *Huc(c)h-* and *Hug(g)-* till the end of the 14th cent., only one other *Hich-* form has been noted before 1400 and two in *Hech-*. In the 15th cent. we have one each in *Hich-* and *Hech-* and two in *Huch-*. After that we have

Hichenden 1535 VE, Eliz ChancP
Huchinden 1526 LS
Hychenden 1537 LP
Huchenden 1539 LP
Hutchenden Eliz ChancP, 1607 *Terr*, 1633 *Archd*
Hugendon 1633 *Archd*, 1643 Desb 14
Hitchenden 1703 *Terr*, 1806 Lysons
Hitchingdon 1766 J
Hitchendon c. 1825 O[1]

OE *Hycga* is not on record as a pers. name but would be a pet-name of regular formation from an OE compound name in *Hyge-* (cf. IPN 174) such as OE *Hygered*, and it is probable that the OE name of this place was *Hycgan-denu*, 'Hycga's valley,' though the early *ch-* forms offer difficulties. This name would explain the variant vowel of the ME and EModE forms (*v.* Introd. xxiv). In Modern English we should have expected both *Hutchenden* and *Hitchenden* but no trace of these pronunciations can now be found and in their stead we have a

[1] The forms of this name in the Lincoln Registers show *Huch-* from the earliest times to 1547.

pronunciation based upon an entirely artificial 19th cent. spelling with *Hugh-*. Cf. Hitcham and Hedgerley *infra*.

BOSSLANE (Fm)

Cf. *Bossemede* quoted from the 15th cent. in VCH. It is clear that both take their name from the same person and that he bore the name found in Bosmore *supra*.

BRAND'S HOUSE

The *Brand* who has left his name here was father of Robert son of Brand, who in 1196 was party to a final concord concerning land in Kingshill. (Hunter, *Fines* 156.) Brand's name was afterwards used as a surname by the family descended from him. From a plea of 1227 (*Ass*) it appears that Brand, who belongs to the time of Henry II, was the son of a woman named Sayve (OE *Sǣgifu*) and a man named Turkill (ON *Þorkell*), and that Sayve had two brothers named respectively Sarich (OE *Sǣrīc*) and Svertrich (a hybrid compound of ON *Svartr* and OE *rīc*). These people are interesting as a family, obviously of pre-Conquest descent, maintaining a good position until the 13th cent. The names Brand, Turkill, and Svertrich are evidence of a Scandinavian element among the 12th cent. landholders of this district, which bears upon the problems presented by the local names Fingest and Skirmett.

BRYANT'S BOTTOM

From mention of *Brians house* in a perambulation of 1714 (Rec. xi. 177) we may assume that the first element is the common Christian name.

COLLINGS HANGER (Fm)

Collins Hanger 1766 J

From this form and from *Callins's Closes* (Rec. xi. 176) it is clear that the first element in this name is really *Collins*.

COOMBE'S FARM

ate Coumbe 1340 NI (p)
atte Coumbe 1346 FF (p)

v. cumb. As there is a 'valley' here it is probable that the proper name of this farm should be simply *Coombe* Farm and that the *s* is only another example of pseudo-genitival *s*.

COURNS WOOD

(boscus qui vocatur) *Chornore* 1248 *FF*

There can be little doubt of the identity of these two places, whatever the exact relationship of the two names. Courns Wood lies on ground sloping steeply down to the valley called North Dean, and **ora** as the source of the ME suffix would suit well. The first element would seem to be **corn** but in what sense is quite uncertain.

NORTH DEAN

(atte) *Northdene* 1325 Cl (p)

Self-explanatory. 'North,' because it lies in the northern part of the valley from which Hughenden itself takes its name.

DENNER HILL

Denore 1241 *Ass* (p)

OE *denu-ora*, 'valley-bank,' *v.* **denu**, **ora**. This aptly describes the position of the farm on the slopes of the valley which gives its name to Hampden lower down.

GREAT KINGSHILL

✱ *Kingeshulle* 1196 Fines
Kingsell 1675 Ogilby

Self-explanatory. The manor of Kingshill was held of the Crown after it was forfeited by Odo of Bayeux (*VCH*).

MOSELEY (Fms) (6″)

Musleghe 1237–40 Fees 1440
Mosleye 1284 FA
Mesleye 1302 FA
Moos(e)ley 1714 Rec. xi. 175
Mouseley c. 1825 O

'Moss clearing' *v.* **meos**, **leah.**

NAPHILL [næpəl]

Knaphill 1599 *Foster*
Naple 1766 J
Napple c. 1825 O

v. **cnæpp.** The Common is situated on the broad rounded top of one of the main ridges of the Chilterns (Harman).

THEED'S WOOD (6″)

This is named from the family of *Theed*, a fairly common surname in South Bucks. John Theed was churchwarden of Hughenden in 1714 (Rec. xi. 179).

Ibstone

IBSTONE 105 F 12 [ipstən]

Hibestanes 1086 DB
Ebestan 1086 DB
Ibbastana c. 1150 *Mert* 2437
Ibbestane 1184 *Mert* 2548

The later forms show an occasional initial *h* but it is clearly inorganic. The first *-ston* form is in 1262 (*Ass*). The first form to show unvoicing of *b* to *p*, as in the modern pronunciation, is

Ipston 1417 IpmR

'Ibba's **stan**,' but what the **stan** was one cannot say with certainty. As the county-boundary originally passed through the parlour of the manor-house (Langley, *Hund. of Desborough* 309) it may refer to a boundary stone on the old border of the two counties, before the adjustment took place in 1895.

In Ipstones (St) which superficially resembles this name, the first element is OE *yppe*, 'upper,' but the persistent *b* shows that this word cannot be present here. A duplicate of the present name occurs in the OE boundaries of Chieveley (Berks) in the phrase *to Ibban stane* (CS 892), and the pers. name *Ibba*, borne by a moneyer of Offa, king of the Mercians, forms the first element of Ibstock (Lei).

COPSON HILL (lost)

Coppesdon c. 1240 *Mert* 2441 (p)
Coppedon c. 1240 ib.
Copson Hyll 1550 *Mert* 1528, 1604 ib. 1539

This is the hill now known as Turville Hill. 'Copp's hill,' cf. *Coppa*, Redin 75.

MARLOW (Great and Little) 106 G and H 2

Merelafan (dat.) 1015 KCD 722
Merlaue 1086 DB, c. 1110 (1225) Abingd, 1182 P, 1196 FF(P), Steph (1275) Ch, 1237–40 Fees 1448 (*Magna*)
Merlaw(*a*) 1189 P, 1195 Cur(P), 1204 Fines
Merlauia 1208 Fees 313, 1209–19 WellsR (*Parva*)

After this the forms are not of much interest. *Mar-* first appears in 1447 (IpmR), *-low* in 1328 (Pat). Great Marlow is called Chipping Marlow first in 1304 (Cl *Chepyng*) from the market there, *v.* **cieping**. Little Marlow is also called *Minchin* Marlow from the nunnery there (cf. OE *myncen*, 'nun').

The second element in this difficult name must originally have been OE *lāf*, 'remainder,' used specially of what is left or bequeathed but also of what remains behind after some action, e.g. *hamera lāf*, 'hammers-leaving,' is used poetically of a sword, while *ȳðlāf*, i.e. 'wave-leaving,' is used in poetry of the shore. The *an* is Late OE for *um*, the dat. pl. suffix. The plural may simply record the fact that already in the 11th cent. there were two distinct settlements at Great and Little Marlow or it may be that OE *laf* when used in p.n. was used in the plural, like its OHG cognate *laiba*, which has given rise to many German p.n. in *leben*, originally a dat. pl. In the case of these names and in that of the cognate Dan. names in *lev* the first element is apparently always a pers. name but such seems impossible here. Rather, we must take the first element as OE *mere*, 'mere,' the reference being to the 'lakes,' as they are still called, which lie to the S.W. of the town of Great Marlow, near the Hare and Hounds PH. Mr A. H. Cocks of Poynatts says that doubtless the 'lakes' were larger before any drainage was done, and he had always taken Marlow to be 'hill by the mere.' Instead of taking the suffix to be **hlaw**, we must take it to be *laf*, and interpret the whole name as descriptive of the settlement which grew up on the northern shore (cf. *ȳðlāf supra*) of the *mere*, which doubtless shrank as it was drained. In other words, Marlow was built on what was left by the mere as it retreated. That this would suit the medieval topography of Marlow is curiously confirmed by a passage in William of Malmesbury's life of St Wulfstan (*Anglia Sacra*,

i. 260). He tells how the bishop was on his way to court and stopping at Marlow (*Merlave*) when, in accordance with his usual practice, he determined to go to church. It was a good way off and the road was muddy enough to deter anyone from going even by day. He got into difficulties even though he had a local guide, for in a fit of ill-humour his guide took him where the marsh was excessively watery and the road very steep. The result was that the bishop got up to his knees in mud and lost one of his shoes, ultimately returning to his inn with completely frozen limbs.

It is clear that the suffix was modified in later days under the influence of the similar sounding and more common *lawe*, *lowe*[1].

* ACKHAMPSTEAD (lost)

Hachamsted' 1199 Cur, c. 1225 Abingd
Achamsted 1199 Cur
Akhampstede 1429 Pat
Ackhumstead c. 1825 O

OE *āchāmstede*, 'oak-homestead,' *v.* ac, hamstede. For a similar compound in which reference is made to the trees, cf. Berkhampstead (Herts) from *beorc*. This is a lost parish. The site of the church is marked by ruins still to be found at Moor Farm (HMS 168).

BARMOOR (Fm)

Bomere 1295 Winton
Bormerefeld 13th c. *VCH*
Bermers 1766 J
Bormers 1797 Desb
Balmers 1826 B

The forms are not sufficiently consistent with one another to admit of any suggestion beyond the likelihood that the second element is mere.

BOVINGDON GREEN

Buuendon, *Bouendon* 1262 *Ass*

[1] Professor Ekwall calls attention to the phrases in a late copy of an OE charter (BCS 1187), *andlang lauen*, *fram þe lauen*, also dealing with a marshy district, which may possibly have to be brought into relation with this name.

Bovyndone 1332 Cl (p)
Bubington 1766 J

OE *bufan-dūne*, 'above hill,' *v.* **bufan**. The green stands on the top of a hill with the land falling away on either side of it.

FINNAMORE (Fm)

Fennym'e 1241 *Ass* (p)
Fenny More 1766 J
Finny Moor c. 1825 O

'Fenny **mor**.'

HARD-TO-FIND (Fm)

Harty Foine 1797 Desb

It is difficult to say which is original and which is corrupt of these two forms. The farm itself is remote and inaccessible.

HARLEYFORD (Manor)

Herleford 1269 *FF* (p), 1464 Pat
Harleford 1479 IpmR

The first element is probably the ancient pers. name *Heorla*, occurring in Harling (Nf, Sf), Harlton (C) and Harlington (Beds). The very unusual development of *an*, through *e* to '*ey*,' is probably due to the fact that Hurley (OE *hyrn leah*) Berks stands over against Harleyford on the south of the Thames. The influence of this name probably kept *Herle* trisyllabic.

MAREFIELD (6″)

M'ifeld 1227 *Ass* (p)
Mirifeld 1227 ib.
Mairesfeld 1227 ib.[1]

The etymology seems obvious but the ME forms do not support it and no suggestion can be made, especially as the ME forms are inconsistent with one another.

MONKTON

This was in possession of the Abbey of Medmenham in 1535 and doubtless takes its name from the monks.

[1] The identification of these forms is not absolutely certain but is highly probable.

MORTONS (lost)

Mortone 1284 FA
Mortons c. 1825 O

v. mor, tun. This is a lost manor of the Bishop of Winchester's in West Wycombe. To judge by the position of the name in the O.S. map as noted above it must have been ¼ mile east of Wood Barn in Little Marlow parish, and if so some adjustment of boundaries must have taken place.

RASSLER WOOD

Radeslo 1223 WellsR (p)
Radeslowe wood 1350 Ipm

In BCS 455 we have *in readan sloe* and in ib. 1176 *of þære readan slo*. These refer to some reddish-coloured 'slough' and that is doubtless what is referred to here also. For *Rad-* cf. Radclive *supra* and *v.* read.

SHEEPRIDGE [ʃipridʒ]

Sheperugge 1323 Pat (p)
Shoprichewood 1537 LP
Shipridge 1826 B

Self-explanatory. *v.* Introd. xxvi. The name occurs again in Berks but has then become Sheepbridge.

SPINFIELD (6″)

This is really a manorial name and should rather be *Spinfield's*, for Nicholas de *Espineville*, who held land in Great Marlow in 1230 (*FF*), must have given his name to it. *v.* Introd. xxv.

WESTHORPE

Westthrop 1766 J

'West farm' *v.* þorp. 'West' in relation to Little Marlow parish in which it lies.

WIDMERE

Withemere 1223 WellsR
Wythemere 1238 Gross, 1339 Cl
Wydemere 1333 Cl, 1349 Pat

Wydemore 1336 Pat
Wydmer 1535 VE

'Withy-mere' *v.* **wiðig, mere.**

Medmenham

MEDMENHAM 105 H 14 [mednəm]

Medmeham 1086 DB, 1198 Cur, c. 1218 WellsL, 1223 WellsL, 1237–40 Fees 1449
Medindeha, Meddemeha 1195 Cur(P) (p)
Medemeha 1195 Cur(P) (p)
Medemeham 1200 Fines
Mendham 1201 *Cart Ant* I 28

Late forms are usually *Medmeham* but we have

Medmenham 1284 FA, AD i, 1287 Ipm, 1358 AD iii
Medmyngham 1344 Cl (p)
Mednam 1643 Desb 14
Medmenham vulgo *Mednam* 1797 ib. 339

The first element in this name is the adj. *medeme* 'moderate-sized,' 'small,' the second element is probably **ham**, the full form of the name being *medemanhāme* (dat.). That the element *medeme* could form part of a word of topographical significance is shown by the use of the term *medemung* in BCS 788. The exact meaning of this term is unknown but it would seem to be one of the p.n. in *-ing* or *-ung* (sg.) discussed by Ekwall, PN *-ing* 1–26. We have the same adj. in *Medemenige* (BCS 64), Medmeney near Selsey (Sx) now misprinted in the 1-in. Pop. ed. of the O.S. map as *Medmerry*.

BOCKMER

Bockemere 1228 Bract (p)
Bokmerfeld 1537 LP
Bokmer, Bukmar 1538 LP
Bockmore c. 1825 O
Buckmoor 1826 B

Probably OE *Buccan-mǣre*, 'Bucca's boundary.' The farm lies on the parish boundary. *v.* **(ge)mære.**

BOLEBEC CASTLE (site of)

Bulbek 1485 Ipm, 1539 LP
Bulbank 1612 *VCH*

The site of the castle of the *Bolebec* family, who took their name from Bolbec near the mouth of the Seine.

BROOKS'S COPSE (6″)

It is just possible that this is the last trace of the Domesday manor of *Broch* (264 *b*). If we may trust the rubrication in DB that manor was in Desborough Hundred. This is the only name in that Hundred which in any way resembles it and it is to be noted that Lysons (605) speaks of a manor of *Brock* in Medmenham.

MARLINS GROVE (6″)

Merlyngesgrove 1461 IpmR

That there was an OE place-name element *Merling* is shown by Marlingford (Nf), DB *Merlingeford*. It is not on independent record as a p.n. in OE but would be a regular formation from a diminutive *Mǣrel* of a pers. name *Mǣra* from one of the OE names in *Mǣr-*. Such a diminutive and its derivative are on record in Gothic and OHG, *v. Merila* in Förstemann (PN 1102), and *Marlingon*, *Merlunghaim*, ib. ON 215. The first record of the name is however too late to allow of certainty in its interpretation.

Radnage

RADNAGE 105 D 13

Radenhech 1162 P, 1237–40 Fees 1450
Radenach(*e*) 1175 P, R i *P*, 1197 Fines, 1200 BM, 1202 PR, 1227 Ch, *Ass*, 1228 Cl
Radenech(*e*) 1176 P, R i *P*
Radenhirst R i *P*
Radenesche 1201 BM
Radeneghe 1241, 1262 *Ass*
Redenech 1276 RH

After this we have *Radenache* until

Radenage 1440 Pat

Radnesshe 1519 AD ii
Radnash 1535 VE
Radnidge 1643 Desb 14

OE *rēadan ǣc* (dat.), 'red oak,' the dat. form *æc* showing palatalisation of the final consonant. For the application of the term 'red' to an oak cf. *on hreadleafan æc* = to the red-leaved oak (BCS 625). For the voicing of final [tʃ] to [dʒ] cf. Chisbridge *supra*. This interpretation is confirmed by the interesting alternative form *Radenhirst* found once, meaning 'red wood.' Stevenage (Herts) shows the same phonetic development. *v.* **read, ac, hyrst.**

ANDRIDGE COMMON

Andrigge 1227 *Ass* (p)
Handridge 1826 B

A difficult name. The second element is **hrycg**. Does the first derive from the *Andr'* who is described as *Andr' de Andrigge* in the reference given above? If so, it is 'Andrew's ridge,' but that is very doubtful. Alternatively it may, like Anderton (La), contain OE *Ēanrǣd*.

ASHRIDGE (Fm) (6″)

Asherugg 14th *VCH*

Self-explanatory.

POND (Fm)

la Ponde c. 1291 Rec. xi. 346 (p), (*atte*) *Ponde* 1340 NI (p)

Self-explanatory.

Saunderton

SAUNDERTON 105 C 13 [sɔ·ndətən], [sɑ·ndətən]

Santesdone, *Santesdune* 1086 DB
Santresdon R i *P*, 1195 Cur(P), 1200 Cur
Sauntredon 1196 FF(P)
Santredon 1196 FF(P)
Sandresdon 1200 Cur
Sandreston 1200 Cur
Sandredon 1202 FineR

Santresdun c. 1205 *Bodl O* 51
Santerdone 1220 Fees 313, 1220 Bract
Santersdon 1227 *Ass*
Saunt' don 1227 *Ass*

After this the *Sa(u)nd-* forms gradually oust those in *Saunt-*. The genitival *s* has last been noted in 1364 Pat.

Names in *Sand-* are not on record in OE but their existence is made probable by the name *Sanda* which may be inferred from *sandan dene* (BCS 1225). *Sand-* names are common on the Continent and include *Sandheri* (Förstemann PN 1297) and it may be that an OE *Sandhere* lies behind this name. If so the early *Sant-* forms would have to be explained as due to the common confusion of *t* and *d* in AN spellings. Cf. IPN 109. Hence, 'Sandhere's hill.' *v.* **dun**.

FROGMORE (Fm)

Froggemora 1241 *Ass*

Self-explanatory.

HEMLEY HILL

Hemmeberg 1227 *FF*
Hemleyhill 1639 *Terr*

OE *Hemman-beorg*, 'Hemma's hill,' *v.* **beorg**. The modern *Hemley* suggests that there was also a **leah** named after *Hemma*.

SAUNDERTON LEE

Sant'ley 1227 *Ass*
Saunterle 1365 Ch

The ME forms may be for *Santerdonle* with loss of the middle element in the triple compound (cf. Ritter 88 ff. and Honeyburge *supra*).

SLOUGH

(ate) *Slo* 1340 NI (p)
Slowe 1649 *Foster*

OE *slō(g)e* (dat.), 'slough, mire.'

* Stokenchurch

STOKENCHURCH 105 E 12

Stockenechurch c. 1200 *Bodl Berks* 22 (p)
Stokenechirch c. 1205 *Bodl Berks* 36
Stokenechurche c. 1210 (14th) *Miss* 1466
Stokkenechurch' 1224 *Ass*

Forms in *Stokk-* and *Stock-* are much more common than those in *Stok-* and the next development is

Stockynchirche 1350 Pat
Stokynchurche 1355 AD vi
Stokyngcherche 1399 AD ii
Stokkyngchyrche 1407 AD vi
Stokhamchyrche 1424 AD vi
Stokkyng Churche 1517 Encl
Stokyngchurch 1542 LP

v. stoccen. The right pronunciation of this name is doubtless that with a short vowel but this seems to have been entirely replaced by a spelling pronunciation with long vowel.

ABFIELD (lost)

Abbefeld 1196 FF(P), 1105 (1225) Abingd
Ebbefeld c. 1200 Abingd
Abefeldia 1239 Bract
Abbeweld c. 1240 *Mert* 2459

OE *Æbban-feld*, 'Æbba's open country,' *v.* feld.

CHEQUERS (Fm)

This farm like Chequers in Ellesborough takes its name from a family deriving its name from their employment in the Exchequer. In 1279 this holding is referred to when we find Laurence de Scaccario holding six virgates of land in Stokenchurch (RH ii. 786).

EAST WOOD

Estwode 1239 Bract

Self-explanatory. It is on the east side of the parish.

HARECRAMP (Fm)

Erreorompe (sic) c. 1240 *Mert* 2454

MALLARD'S COURT

This originates from the 1 virgate of land held in Stokenchurch in 1279 by Robert Malet (RH ii. 786). Later forms are

Mallett Court 1627 FF (*VCH*)
Mallard's Court 1811 ib.

POPHLEY'S FARM

Poghleia c. 1210 (14th) *Miss* (p)
Poghele 1302 Ipm (p), 1325 Cl (p)
Poughele 1302 Ipm (p)
Poghlee 1364 Cl (p)
Paufleys 1766 J

As all these forms are taken from pers. names we may suspect that this is a genuine manorial name and that the holder of the manor came from Poughley (Berks).

STUDDRIDGE

Stodruge c. 1279 *VCH* (p)

'Stud-ridge' *v.* **stod**, **hrycg**.

TRENDELL'S WOOD (6")

Trindele 1227 *Ass*

We may compare *trindlea* in BCS 595 and 689, which clearly denotes a circular clearing, *v.* **trynde**, **leah**. The modern form is corrupt.

WORMSLEY

Wdemundesleia 1225 Abingd
Wydemundeleie 1235 Fees 456 (p)
Wudemundele, *Wodemundele* 1235 Fees 446, 452
Wodemundesle c. 1240 *Mert* 2449 (p)

The form of the pers. name which forms the first element is uncertain. It may be either *Widmund*, not actually found in OE but present in *Widmundesfelt* (BCS 81) or *Wudemund* which is not on record. The second element is **leah**.

Turville

TURVILLE 105 F 12

Þyrefeld 796 (c. 1250) BCS 281
Tilleberie 1086 DB
Tirefeld 1175 P, c. 1220 WellsR, 1227 *Ass*, 1231 Cl, 1237–40 Fees 1450, 1284 FA, 1326 Fine, 1333 Cl
Tyrefeud c. 1218 WellsL, 1227, 1241, 1246 *Ass*
Tyrefeld 1227 *Ass*, 1230 Cl, c. 1240 *Mert* 2443, 1242 Gross, 1262 *Ass*, 1315 Ch, 1337 Pat, 1339 Ipm
Treffeld 1227 *Ass*
Triffeud 1227 *Ass*
Thyrefeld c. 1240 *Mert* 1441
Turifeld c. 1280 *Mert* 2433
Tyrifeld 1286 *Mert* 2434
Thurefeld 1329 Ipm
Tirfeld 1422 AD i
Turfeld 1445 *Mert* 1532, 1508 ib. 2750, 1526 LS, 1548 *Mert* 2023
Thyrrefeld 1545 LP
Turfield 1766 J
Turville or *Turfield* 1826 B

The *Therfield* identification in Birch is certainly wrong for *Þyrefeld* was a St Alban's manor and so was Turville, while Therfield (Herts) (*Þerefeld* in KCD 809) was a manor of Ramsey Abbey. The identification makes it clear that the first element is the ODan. *Þýri* (*v.* Björkman, *Nordische Personennamen* 164) but at the same time confirms the spuriousness of that charter for it is dated 796, long before we could get a Danish pers. name in an English place-name. *v.* Introd. xviii. The manor described as *Tilleberie* in DB is clearly Turville but the scribe must have got hold of the wrong name. One cannot but think that somehow or other he has got it confused with the not very distant *Tilbury* of *Tilbury Wood*, *v. infra*.

Wooburn

WOOBURN 106 G 3 [u·bən]

Waburna c. 1075 *Linc Cath Chart*
Waborne 1086 DB

Wauburn 1200 Cur
Woburne 1201 Cur, 1227 *FF*, 1242 Fees, 1262 *Ass*, 1282 Ch
Wouburn c. 1218 WellsL, 1229 WellsR, 1262 *Ass*, 1299 Ch, 1301 Ipm
Wburne 1227 *Ass*
Wuburn 1231 Bract, 1232 Cl, 1237–40 Fees, 1241 *Ass*, 1247 *Ass*
Woburne 13th AD vi
Wyburne 1284 FA
Woubourne 1316 FA, 1341 Misc, 1360 Cl, Ipm, 1370 Pat
Woburn in Chilterne 1331 Cl
Woghburne 1331 AD vi
Woweburn 1393 Pat
Bishops Woburne 1402 Pat
Woborn Deyncourt 1442 Pat
Owborne 1484 AD iii
Oborn 1487 BM, 1490 Ipm
Ouburne 1489 Ipm
Obornes 1675 Ogilby

This name offers serious difficulties. The two earliest forms with an *a*-vowel and the isolated form *Wauburn*, cannot be reconciled with the later forms which would point to a compound of **burna** and the OE **woh**, applied appropriately enough to the winding stream on which Wooburn stands. Such a stream-name has its parallel in Woburn (Beds), for which we have the OE form *Woburningagemære* (BCS 1229). It seems impossible to reject the earliest forms, consistent as they are with one another, on the score that they do not fit in with the later evidence and one must therefore suggest a definite discontinuity in the history of the name, due to the replacing of a name which conveyed no meaning by an intelligible name, a common process of folk-etymology. The forms of Weybourne (Nf) offer a curious parallel to the early forms of Wooburn. They are as follows: DB *Wabrunne*, 1177 P *Wabrun*, 1275 RH *Waborne*, *Wauburn*, 1281 FF *Waburne*, 1291 Tax *Waubrun*[1]. If the parallel is a genuine one, then, since the later history of Weybourne seems to point to an original short *a*, we must

[1] Forms due to the kindness of Mr O. Schram.

believe the vowel in *Waburne* similarly to have been short. Beyond that we cannot go. 'Bishop's' from the Bishop of Lincoln's manor.

BOURNE END

(atte) *Burnend'* 1236 *FF* (p)
Brone End 1766 J
Bone End 1826 B

Self-explanatory. It lies where the Wye or (?) Wooburn falls into the Thames.

BURGHERS HILL

Beggars Hill c. 1825 O

A piece of late snobbery or squeamishness.

DEYNCOURT (Fm) [di·nkɔ·t], [deinkɔ·t]

The last trace of the manor of Wooburn Deyncourt, *v. supra*, which goes back to the 13th cent. (Fees 874). Written *Deancourt* in 1596 (D) and still often so pronounced.

GLORYHILL (Fm)

(de la) *Gloria* 1255 FF (*VCH*)
(atte) *Glone* (sic) 1325 Cl
,, *Glorie* 1329, 1340 Pat, 1344, 1364 Cl
,, *Glove* (sic) 1335 Cl
(de la) *Glorie* 1342 Pat

all of the forms being derived from pers. names.

(manor of) *Glory* 1490 Ipm

Professor Weekley suggests that this is the simplex of the French diminutive *gloriette*, common in French dialect, including Normandy, in the sense of a summer-house, 'a little banqueting house in a garden' (Cotgrave), apparently so called from its ornamental character. The dimin. is used also in English of a decorated chamber in a castle. One must take *Glorie* then as some term of praise describing the appearance or situation of the manor-house. In the *Dictionnaire Topographique* we have *La Gloire* (Marne and L'Aube).

HOLTSPUR

Ollesper (boscus de) 1241 *Ass*
Holspere 1241 ib.
Olspere 1370 Pat
Holdspere 1493 Rec xi. 200
Hotspur 1797 Desb

It is clear that the two elements in this name are holt and ME *sperre*, '*spar* of timber,' used also of a bar of wood to fasten a gate. The exact sense cannot be determined as, in the nature of things, the 'spar' is not likely to have survived. This element is found also in Rusper (Sx), meaning 'rough spar.'

LILLYFEE (Fm) (6")

Lyndeleg' 1239 *FF* (p)
Linlegh Hy iii Ipm
Lynleye 1300 Ipm
Lillyfield c. 1825 O

'Limetree clearing' *v.* lind, leah. 'fee' denotes possession or manor.

LUDE (Fm)

Lede 1086 DB
la Lude 1227 *Ass*, 1234 Bract, 1242 Fees 879, 1262 *Ass*, c. 1251 AD i, 1330 Cl, 1337 ib., all (p) except the first
(ate) *Lude* 1340 NI
Luda 1374 AD ii
(atte) *Luyde* 1393 Pat
Lide al. *Lewd* 1680 FF (*VCH*)
Lyde al. *Lowd* 1694 FF (*VCH*)
Lyde or *Lewd* 1736 FF (*VCH*)
Lewd Fm c. 1825 O
Lue Fm 1826 B

There is an OE *hlȳde*, used frequently of a noisy stream (cf. *hlūd*, 'loud'), but there is no stream now nor any likelihood of one, though there is an ancient trackway by the side, of a deep sunken character (Harman). Derivation from this word does not therefore seem very probable. BT also gives an OE *hlēde*, *hlȳde*, denoting 'seat, bench.' This is just possible as a farm-name. Cf. the use of *setl* in Settle (Y) and further ex-

amples of the use of the term in the charters as given by Middendorff s.v., though it should be noted that the word may here denote 'place where one settles' rather than 'place where one sits.' It should be added however that we have no knowledge as to whether *e*, *y* in this word go back to OE *ȳ* or, alternatively, if *y* is for earlier *ē* or *ī*, in which case it could not be brought in evidence.

OVER'S FARM

Richard Over purchased some land called *Lynchwell* in Wooburn parish in the middle of the 16th cent. (*VCH*).

RIDING LANE (6″)

'Two crofts called *Rydynges*' AD iii

v. hryding.

Chipping, High, and West Wycombe

WYCOMBE (Chipping, High and West) 106 E and F, 1 and 2

(æt) Wicumun c. 970 (12th) BCS 1174
Wicumbe 1086 DB, 1176 P, 1207 Fines, 1212 Fees 116
Wicumbedena 1157, 1158 P
West Wicumbe 1195 Cur(P)
Wycumbe c. 1220 WellsR, 1235 Fees 461
Weycumbe 1227 Ch

After this the forms vary between *Wi-* and *Wy-*. Then we may note

Wycombe Marchaunt 1340 Cl
Chepingwycomb 1478 IpmR
Wecome 1500 Ipm
Estwicombe 1509 LP
Magna Wykeham 1545 LP
Cheaping Wycombe Eliz ChancP
West Wickham Eliz ChancP

There are two Wycombes, High, known also as East, Great and Chipping Wycombe and West Wycombe respectively and this probably accounts for the *-un* of the first form. It is a weakened form of the dat. pl. suffix in *-um* (cf. Marlow *supra*). The first element in this name is presumably that of the river

Wye in spite of the tradition recorded in *Records of Bucks* (x. 90) that the stream was so called in the first instance by cadets of the Royal Military College when map-making. In the 16th cent. *Wicombe* came often to be written *Wickham* and thence arose the tradition that the name of the river was *Wick*. The second element is **cumb**. The application of the name *Wicumbedena* to the whole of the King's manor of Wycombe in 1157–8 is worthy of notice.

Chipping Wycombe

ASHWELL'S FARM

This is a genuine manorial name. In 1235 Stephen de *Hassewell* held one-fifth of a fee in Wycombe (Fees 556).

BUNCE'S FARM

In the Borough of Wycombe records (564) there is mention in 1549 of William *Bunse* and it is presumably from his family that this farm takes its name.

CRESSEX (Fm)

le Creys 1366 AD ii
The Cressche 1368 Wyc 557
La Cresche 1378 Wyc 562
Craseis 1489 Pat
Cressicks 1766 J
Crissex 1826 B

This, at least in its earliest forms, may be ME *crecche*, *cracche* < OFr. *cresche*, 'manger, crib,' but used also of a small cot (NED s.v. *cratch*), though, unless the form is borrowed direct from France, one would have expected *Crecche* rather than *Cressche*. The source of the suffix in the later forms is not clear. The *Dictionnaire Topographique* gives names *La Crèche* (L'Aube, Pas de Calais) and *Les Cresches* (L'Eure).

DEANGARDEN WOOD

This 'dean' is probably that found in the pers. name *Wm atte Dene* in Wyc 561.

FENNELLS WOOD

Fenelgrove by Wycombe 1391 Pat

The origin of this name is from a conveyance of land in Wycombe in 1283 by Roger Taylor of Little Marlow to Robert *FitzNeel* (FF from *VCH*).

FLACKWELL HEATH [flækəl]

Flacwelle, *Flakewelle* 1227 *Ass* (p)
Flakwell 1537 LP

The etymology of this is uncertain. It may be from an OE pers. name **Flæcca* found also in Fleckney (Lei), Flecknoe (Wa).

GINIONS FIELD (Fm) (Not on O.S. map)

This is the last trace of the manor of *Gynaunts Fee* which takes its name from one *Gynan* whose widow married Thomas of Wycombe (P 1171). It included a mill known as *Gwynauntes mulne* (*Miss* 142) or *Gyuant* (sic) *mylle* (Godst 89). It now forms part of Wycombe Marsh.

GOMM'S FARM

Gum's Fm 1826 B

John *Gomme* was a bailiff of Wycombe in 1451 (Wyc 564) and his family probably gave their name to this farm.

HANDY CROSS

le Onhandedecruch 1287 Misc

'One handed (i.e. ? armed) cross' *v.* Bledlow Cross *supra*.

HAZELMERE

Heselmere 13th AD i

Self-explanatory, *v.* **hæsel**, **mere**.

HILL (Fm)

(de) *la Hul* 1301 Wyc 561 (p)

Self-explanatory.

KING'S MEAD (6")

Kingesmede 1255 *FF*

Self-explanatory but the exact royal owner is unknown.

LOUDWATER

la Ludwatere 1241 *Ass* (p)
Ludewatir 1310 (15th) Godst
Lowdewater 1485 Ipm

The traditional explanation of this name is that given by Lipscomb (iii. 652), 'Its name is probably derived from the noise incessantly made by the rapidity of the stream, which rushes with great impetuosity towards Wooburn and its junction with the Thames.'

OAKRIDGE (Fm)

Okregge, *Ocregge* 1251 AD i
Okrugge 1281 Ipm

Self-explanatory.

ST JOHN'S WOOD, TEMPLE FARM (6″)

Both these names are relics of the manor held from 1227 (Ch) in Wycombe by the Knights Templars, whose property on the suppression of the order was transferred to the Knights of St John.

TERRIERS

Tarryers 1714 Rec xi. 179

This probably takes its name from a pers. name *Tarrier*, originally a nickname for some dilatory person.

TOTTERIDGE

Tuterugge 1179 P (p)
Toterugge 1179 P (p), 1416 Wyc 562

'Tota's ridge' or 'look-out hill' *v.* **hrycg**, cf. *Toothill* and the like.

WINCHBOTTOM (Fm)[1]

(*de*) *la Wynche* 1248 *FF* (p)

OE *wincel*, 'nook, corner,' is well-established as a topographical term; *wince* is only used of the 'winch' but it is clear

[1] This place has been commonly identified with *Hanechedene* (DB 236 *b*). If this is correct the DB form, as may well be the case, is so corrupt that it is useless for etymological purposes.

that the words are allied and that as Skeat points out (*Etymological Dictionary* s.v. *winch*) the root idea is that of something bent. Winchbottom is at the head of a little valley just where it makes a right-angled turn.

WYCOMBE MARSH

Merhs 13th AD vi

Self-explanatory.

High Wycombe

BASSETTSBURY (Fm) (6″)

Bassettysbury 13th AD vi
Bassetisbury 1437 Pat

Gilbert Basset had a holding in Wycombe in 1235 (Fees 467) and this farm takes its name from him. It is clearly a case of the manorial use of *bury*. *v*. burh.

BOWDEN MILL (6″)

Bughendune c. 1215 (14th) *Miss* 131*b*

OE *Bugan-dun*, 'Buga's hill,' *v*. dun. Cf. Bowden (Nt, Lei).

CRENDON LANE (Not on O.S. map)

Croendena c. 1220 AD A 401 (p)
Croindene Hy iii Wyc 559 (p)
Croyndoneslane leading to Croyndene E iv Wyc 556
Crendone Lane 1449 Wyc 564

It is difficult to avoid association with Croydon (Sr), a name which also offers great problems. This is *Crogdene* in BCS 529, a 13th cent. copy of a 9th cent. charter and *Croindune* in a ME version (BCS 530). Similarly it is *Crogdæne* in BCS 1132 (a 12th cent. text) and *Croindene* in a later version of the same (BCS 1133). The late Dr Bradley[1] suggested that these inconsistent forms might be reconciled by the assumption of two name-forms, (1) from the OE *crog*, *croh*, 'saffron' (cf. Crafton *supra*) and (2) from the corresponding adj. **crogig*. The dat. sg. *crogigan dene* would account for the alternative forms.

[1] *ex inf*. Mr Arthur Bonner, F.S.A.

EASTON ST (6″)

Estyntone 1444 Wyc 563
Estyntone 1528 ib. 557

This in the records is not the name of the street but the name of a part of Wycombe to which presumably the street led. It may be from OE *ēastan tune*, 'east of the tun,' or *ēast in tūne*, 'east in the tun.'

HUCKENDEN (Fm) [hʌkiŋtən], [hʌkiŋdən]

Hokendon 1316 *FF* (VCH)
Huckington 1766 J
Oakington c. 1825 O
Uckington 1826 B

'Hucca's hill.' There is evidence in Hucclecote (Gl) and other names for an OE pers. name *Huccel*, a diminutive of such a name as *Hucc(a)*.

LOAKES HILL (6″)

Lokes maner' 1483 IpmR

NEWLAND

la Newlande 1227 Ch

Self-explanatory.

PANN MILL (6″)

la Pande 13th AD i
la Penmell 1344 Cl
Penn Mill or *Pand Mill* or *Pond Mill* 1606 Ipm (*VCH*)
Pann mill or *Pondemill* Ch i Ipm (*VCH*)

This is a difficult name. No early forms of *pond* are on record with an *a* vowel but the history of that word itself is obscure (NED s.v.). Professor Ekwall suggests that this may really contain the word 'pawn,' cf. the 12th cent. Lat. form *pandum* in NED s.v. and that the name may be descriptive of a place held in pledge or the like.

THE RYE (6″)

atte Reye 1372 Wyc 561 (p)
The Reye 1451 Wyc 564
Rye Marsh 1826 B

The Rye is low-lying land almost surrounded by water and it is clear that *atte Reye* must be from *at ther eye*, 'at the island.' *v.* eg, æt.

West Wycombe

AVERINGDOWN (Fm)

Haveringedune 1222 WellsR (p), 1291 Tax
Haveringedon 1237–40 Fees 1451
Haveringdon in West Wycomb 1241 *Ass*
Haveringdon al. *West Wycombe* 1391 Pat
Havern Down 1766 J
Abraham Down 1826 B

This is the name of a lost village on the spur of the Chilterns just to the north of West Wycombe. The latter name seems commonly to have been applied to the manor, the former to the church. It is clear that the first element in this name is *Hæfering(a)*, a formation in *ing* from the pers. name *Hæfer* dealt with under Haversham *supra*. Hence 'hill of Hæfer' or 'of Hæfer's people.' It may be suspected that *Averingdown* is a modern archaistic revival and that the genuine local survival is to be found in the *Hearnton* of Hearnton Wood just by.

BOOKER

'The tithing of *Bokar*...is mentioned in the early 13th cent.' (VCH). No suggestion can be offered as to the etymology of this name, unless it be from OE *bōc-ora*. *v.* boc, ora.

CHAWLEY (Fm) (6")

Chaluelegh 1227 *Ass* (p)

'Calves' clearing' *v.* cealf, leah.

CHORLEY (Fm)

Chordele 1227 *Ass* (p)
Chardele 1251 *FF* (p)
Charley c. 1825 O

The forms of this name are not sufficiently consistent with one another to allow of any certainty as to its etymology. If *Chor-* is the correct form no suggestion can be offered. If the *Char* -form is the correct one then the name may be from OE *Cærdan-lēah*, 'Cærda's clearing,' with the same pers. name as

in Charndon and Chartridge *supra*. The modern Chorley may be due to the necessity of keeping the name distinct from the neighbouring *Chawley*.

DESBOROUGH CASTLE

Dusteburg 1227 *Ass* (p)
Dusteberg 1237 Ch (p)
Disborowe 1626 Vern
Disborough 1797 Desb

Taking the forms of this and the identical Hundred name (*v. supra*) the only etymology which can be suggested is that while the second element is **beorg** the first is the second element in the OE plant-name *dweorge-dwostle*, *dweorge-d(w)osle*, *dwyrge-dwysle*, 'penny-royal.' This might possibly appear as ME *dustel*. One does not know just what plant the uncompounded form may have been used for in England, for it is not found in the OE vocabularies. Ekwall suggests alternatively that we may have an English cognate of OHG *Dusilo*, such as may lie behind Desning (Sf). If that is the case the OE name **Dysel(a)* must early have developed *t* between *s* and *l*. In any case one must explain the variation between *l* and *n* as due to Anglo-French influence (IPN 106).

FASTENDICH (lost)

Fastindige 1197 Fines
Fastendich 1269 Ch
Fastyngdiches 1477 IpmR

This is probably a compound of **fæsten** and **dic**, hence 'stronghold-ditch.' The exact site is unknown but it was probably in this parish and may have been near Widdenton. It is probably the source of the Bucks family name *Fastnidge* noted in *Records of Bucks*, xi. 174–86.

FILLINGTON (Fm)

Filendene 1241 *Ass* (p)
filindon 1693 *Saunderton Terr*
Fillingden Wood c. 1825 O

'Fila's valley' *v.* **denu**. *Fila* is not found but may be the full name of which *Filica*, preserved only in *Filican slæd* (BCS 1093) and the place-name Filkins (O), is the diminutive.

Green End

atte Grene of Wycombe 1317 Cl (p)

Self-explanatory, but the identification is not quite certain.

Hearnton Wood [heriŋtən]

v. Averingdown *supra*.

Loxboro Wood (6″)

Lockesburwe 1326 FF (*VCH*) (p)

'Locc's burh or beorg.'

Tilbury Wood (6″)

There can be little doubt that behind this name lies the *Tilleberie* of DB, though as noted above (s.n. *Turville*), it is there given as the name of Turville manor. The first element is the pers. name *Tilla*, not actually found in OE, but cf. *Tilli*, and the numerous names in *Til-*, *Tilluc*. Hence, 'Tilla's burh.'

Towerage

Turigge 1208 Winton Pipe Roll (p)

Widdenton Park Wood (6″)

Widinton 1197 Fines (p)
Wydingdona 1228 Bract (p)
Widendon 13th AD i (p)
Wydindon 1301 Winton
Wydinton 1337 Cl (p), 1347 AD i

There is some evidence for an OE pers. name *Wīda*, and this seems to be an *-ingdun* name derived from that pers. name, hence 'Wida's hill,' cf. ingtun, or it may be OE *Widga*, hence 'Widga's hill.' The topography favours a dun.

XVII. BURNHAM HUNDRED

Burneham 1086 DB, 1195 Cur(P), 1232 Fees
Berneham 1086 DB

The exact meeting-place of the Hundred is unknown. For the name *v. infra*.

Amersham

AMERSHAM[1] 106 D 5

Agmodesham 1066 (12th) KCD 824, 1203 Fines, 1218 Bract, 1232 Cl, 1237–40 Fees 1449, 1262 *Ass*, 1282 Ch, 1284 FA, 1299 Fine, 13th AD i, 1317 Pat, 1326 Cl, 1339 AD ii
Elmodesham, *Elnodesham* 1086 DB
Amodesham 1165 P, 1227 *FF*, *Ass*, 1241, 1247 *Ass*
Agemodesham 1176 P (p)
Almodesham R i *P*, 1234 Bract
Angmodesham 1197 Fines, 1284 FA, 13th AD i
Aumodesham 1218 Pat, 1222 WellsR, 1227 *FF*, *Ass*, 1232 Cl, 1235 Fees 465, 1235 Gross, 1247, 1262 *Ass*
Admodesham 1227 *FF*, 1262 *Ass*
Amundesham 1227 *Ass* (p), 1317 Pat, 1326 Cl
Ammodesham 1235 Fees 469
Amondesham 1241 *Ass*, 1338, 1362 Pat, 1373 Cl, 1400 Pat
Augmodesham 1245 Gross (p), 1262 *Ass*, 1275 Ipm, 1340 NI
Agmundesham al. *Agmodesham* 1297 Ipm
Agmundesham 13th AD iv, 1312 Cl, 1366 Cl
Aumundesham 1301 Ipm, 1302 FA, 1331 Cl
Aumomdesham 1318, 1331, 1420 Pat
Aughmodesham 1325 Pat
Aymondesham 1333 Pat
Amondeshom 1340 Cl
Aymundesham 1363 *New* 22 (Weedon)
Amoundesham 1378 Cl
Agmondesham 1348 Pat, 1352 Cl, 1361 Pat, 1414 AD iii, 1455 AD iv, 1477 Pat, 1485 Ipm, 1488 AD v, 1504 Pat, 1519 LP, 1526 LS, Pat, 1535 LDD, 1604 Vern
Amotesham 1414, 1436 Pat, 1440 AD i
Hakmersham 1483 Pat
Egmonsham 1513 LP

[1] The forms in the Lincoln Registers are as follows: *Agmundesham* (1290–1320), *Augmundesham*, *Aughmundesham* (1300–20), *Agmodesham* (1320–42), *Amondesham*, *Agmondesham* (1347–62), *Amondesham*, *Agmundesham*, *Hamundesham* (1363–98), *Amundesham*, *Amondesham* (1405–20), *Amondesham* (1420–31), *Agmondesham* (1452–72, 1480–96, 1496–1514, 1522–47), *(H)amersham* (1522–47), *Agmundisham* al. *Amershams* (c. 1600).

Hamersham 1536 LP
Agmondesham vulgo *Amersham* 1675 Ogilby

The first part of this name is a pers. name and the second element in that pers. name is either *mōd*, or, less probably, *mund*. If the former, the *n* is that intrusive *n* sometimes found in the unstressed syllables of polysyllabic words as in *messenger* and in several p.n. mentioned in PN NbDu 265. The first element of the pers. name is not easy to determine. Forms in *Elm-*, *Alm-*, *Aum-*, *Am-* can be explained on the basis of an OE name in *Aegel-*, whether that is a late form for *Aeþel-* or an entirely distinct element. (For a full discussion of this problem *v.* Zachrisson, *AN Influence*, 101 ff. and Forssner, *Continental-Germanic Pers. Names in England*, 11 ff.) Such a name however would not explain the persistent *Ag-*, *Aug-* forms. For these we must look rather to some name of continental origin in *Agil-* borne perhaps by some 9th cent. holder of the manor. Such continental names in *Agil-* are found in OE. If the name of Amersham was once *Agilmodesham* the existence of OE names in *Aegel-* might soon lead to confusion and one might, side by side with the right name, have a semi-anglicised one arising. Such a theory would explain the curious double development of the name. The *Aug-* forms can only be explained as the result of a conflation of these two types, *Aum-* (from *Alm-*) and *Ag-* (from *Agil-*). Those in *Ang-* may perhaps only be errors of transcription for ones in *Aug-* but they might also be explained as *Angm-* from *Agm-* in the same way that we find ME *Angnes* for *Agnes*, and *Angni* for *Agni*.

Professor Ekwall is inclined to explain this admittedly difficult name by starting from an OE *Ealhmod*, which would explain the DB forms. He adds: 'The early loss of *l* would have an analogy in early forms of Alconbury (Hu), DB *Acumesberie*, RH *Acundberi*, 1303 FA *Aucmundebir*'. The development of the OE *h* is best explained, if we may assume that the *h* was voiced between the consonants surrounding it. For the fricative *g*, Norman hard *g* would be substituted, and before this the *l* would be dropped as it was before the *k*(*c*) in Alconbury. The common early form *Agmodesham* is thus explained. But this spelling must in many instances be a conventional, traditional

one, behind which we have to assume a spoken form with fricative *g*, shown by spellings such as *Augh-* and the early assimilation to *Amm-*. This form is difficult to explain. Possibly it may be looked on as a compromise between genuine English *Alghmodesham* and Normanised *Agmodesham*.'

COKE'S FARM

In 1407 Roger *Koc* had land on the water called Misbourne (HMC xv. App. vii. 130) and his family doubtless gave their name to this farm which is just by that stream.

MANTLES GREEN

The last trace of Turstin Mantel's holding of half-a-hide in Amersham in DB (267 *b*).

QUARRENDON (Fm)

Querendon 1227 *Ass* (p), 1234 Bract (p)

As the forms of this name are derived entirely from pers. names it is impossible to be sure whether this is really a 'mill-hill' (*v.* Quarrendon *supra*) or whether it is a manorial name, when the true modern form would be Quarrendon's.

RAAN'S FARM [reinz]

the fee Le raan 1331 Misc
fee of Raan 1331 Fine
Ranys Fee 1485 Ipm
Rheins Fm 1826 B

This manorial name originates from the *Rane* family. John *de Rane* was a tenant in Amersham in 1235 (*Fees* 465) and Walter *le Ran* in 1312 (Cl).

ROGERS'S WOOD

This may possibly take its name from the *Roger* Koc mentioned under Coke's Farm *supra*. If so the present form is corrupt.

SHARDELOES [ʃɑrlouz]

Shardelowes 1331, 1334 Fine, 1332 Orig, 1333 Cl
Shardelawes 1331 Misc
Sherdlowes 1455 AD iv
Sherdelowes 1464 ib.
Sharlees 1625 HMS 3

The origin of this manorial name is found in Cl (1333) where we find that the messuage and carucate called S. were lately given by Hugh de La More to Adam de Shardelowe. This Adam may have come from Shardlow in Derbyshire.

WEEDONHILL (Fm)

Wodonhull 1364 Pat
Wodynhill 1509 LP
Wedon Hill Eliz ChancP
Wheedon 1826 B

This is a manorial name, the hill taking its name from a family who belonged to Weedon-in-the-Vale *supra*. Ralph de Wedona is mentioned in 1218 (Bract ii. 7) in connexion with Amersham. The association of the family with Amersham goes back however much further for Almar was an undertenant in both Amersham and Weedon (then in Hardwick) in DB (243 *b* and 244 *a*).

WHEATLEY WOOD (6″) [wɪtli]

Witley Wd 1826 B

The true name of the place is clearly 'white clearing.' *v.* **hwit, leah.**

WHIELDEN LANE (6″)

Whilden 1281 Pat (p)
Wheledene 16th *VCH*

OE *hwēol-denu*, 'wheel-valley,' *v.* **denu.** The *wheel* or circle may refer to the very definite curve which the valley makes as Whielden St comes out of Amersham and becomes Whielden Lane leading towards Wycombe. Cf. *hweol-riðig* (BCS 216).

WOODROW

Agmondesham Wodrowe 1520 LP
Agmondesham Wooderew 1535 LP

The meaning of the elements is obvious but that of the compound is not so clear. There is not much likelihood of a 'row' of buildings here.

Ashley Green

ASHLEY GREEN 106 B 5

Essleie 1227 *Ass*
Esselegh in Cestresham 1241 *Ass*
Esseleye 1302 FA
Asscheleye 1346 FA
Assheley grene 1468 BM

Self-explanatory.

GROVE (Fm)

(*de*) *la Grove* 1200 Cur (p)
la Grove in villa de Chesham 1414 IpmR

Self-explanatory.

LYE GREEN

Lye 1550 AD v
Leigh 1766 J

v. leah

PRESSMORE (Fm)

Preesmoor 1826 B

The first element may possibly be the British word found in Welsh *prys*, 'covert, brushwood,' Corn. *pres*, 'meadow,' discussed by Ekwall, PN La 153, and found in Preese (La) and Prees (Sa).

THE THORNE

atte Thorne 1346 FA (p)

Self-explanatory.

WHELPLEY HILL

Welpelie c. 1200 BM
Whelplege 1206 Fines
Hvelpeleghe 1227 *Ass*

Probably *hwelpa-lēah*, 'whelps' clearing,' i.e. where the young animals play, though there is the possibility that we have a pers. name **Hwelpa*. *v.* Kirkwhelpington, PN NbDu.

Beaconsfield

BEACONSFIELD 106 F 4/5 [bekənzfi·ld]

Bekenesfelde 1184 P, 1204 Fines *et passim*
Bekenefeld 1223 Bract, 1241, 1262 *Ass*
Becnefeld 1225 Pat
Bekenfeld 1247 *Ass*
Beckenesfeld 1284 FA

Further forms are unnecessary but we may note

Bekingfeld 1373 IpmR
Beckonesfelde 1529 LDD
Bekyngsfeld 1537 LP

OE *bēacnes-feld*, a genitival compound denoting apparently 'open land marked by a *beacen*.' *v.* feld. This is our word *beacon* but its sense here is uncertain. Beaconsfield stands high and a 'beacon' fire may have been lighted here. The vowel has been shortened in the trisyllable.

BUTLER'S COURT

This probably takes its name from the family of John Botiller who in 1443 (AD i) owned *Hallemore*, now Hall Barn.

COPSHREWS (Fm) (6")

Cops Row 1766 J
Copse Row 1826 B

Apparently so called from a row of trees in a coppice. The modern form is corrupt.

GREGORY'S FARM (6")

Gregorys maner' 1478 ImpR
Gregories otherwise *Butlers Court* Eliz ChancP

The association of the Gregory family with Beaconsfield goes back to the 13th cent. (*VCH*).

HALL BARN

Hallemore 1412 AD i

'Healla's mor.' For this name *v.* Ekwall PN *-ing* 37.

HOLLOWAY'S FARM

Takes its name from the family of *Holweye* of whom Thomas held land in Beaconsfield in 1370 (AD i) and John in 1408 (AD iii).

HYDE (Fm)

This farm-name is the sole survival of the lost manor of *Hide* first mentioned in 1328 (*VCH*).

WILTON PARK

Wyltons maner' 1478 IpmR
Whiltons Park 1766 J

This is a manorial name derived from the family of Thomas de *Whelton* who already in 1344 (Cl) was a witness in Beaconsfield business. He may have come from Whilton (Nth), Northants Survey *Whelton*.

Boveney

BOVENEY 114 A 4

Bovenie 1086 DB
Boveniae 1086 DB
Boueneie 1155 P (p)
Buuenia 1189 P
Boueneya 1201 FineR
Boueneia 1202 Fines
Buueneye 1226 Bract

Probably OE *bufan-ēge*, 'above-island,' for it is just above a small island in the Thames. *v.* eg.

TILSON BRIDGE and LANE (6″)

Tullesdene 16th *VCH*
Tyllstone gate 17th ib.

'Tylle's denu.' This pers. name is not on record but would be a regular formation, side by side with the authenticated *Tulla*.

Burnham

BURNHAM

Burneham 1086 DB, 1164 P
Burnham 1175, 1189 P
Bournham 1405 Pat, 1562 BM

There is no stream of sufficient importance to make derivation from **burna** likely. There is an early pers. name stem *Byrn* (cf. *byrne*, 'corselet') found in *Byrnham* in an original 8th cent. Kentish charter (BCS 199) and in *Byrnhom* the name of the grandfather of the 8th cent. Ealhred, King of Northumbria, and in *Byrngyð*, a nun addressed by Aldhelm in the preface to the *De Laudibus Virginitatis* (pre-Alfredian MS). This would account for the forms of Burnham and also for the pet-names *Bynni* and *Bynna* from earlier **Byrni* and **Byrna*.

The only other reasonable possibility is that the name contains the OE pers. name *Brun(n)a*. This name seems to be the origin of Burnham (Nf). Cf. Stevenson on *Brunemue* (EHR xi. 302–4). The difficulty in the present name arises mainly from the absence of any *Brun-* forms. If the name is really derived from *Brun(n)a* metathesis must have taken place very early. That it might have occurred by 1086 is shown by DB *Burnulfestune* for *Burnaston* (Db) from ON *Bryniólfr*. Association with the common *burna* would materially help the change. If Burnham contains *Byrna* or *Brunna* the name falls into line with Hitcham, Wexham, Loudham's Farm and Cippenham in this neighbourhood, all of which are derived from pers. names.

ALLARD'S FARM (6″)

This takes its name from the family of the Wm. Alard who in 1234 (Cl) held land in Burnham.

BIDDLES FARM

Budewelle, *Beidewelle* 1208 Fines

OE *Bydan-wielle*, 'Byda's spring,' *v.* **wielle**. A well is marked here on the 6″ map. The genitival *s* is corrupt. The name *Byda*, which seems early to have fallen out of use, occurs again in Biddenham (Beds) and Bidford (Wa).

BOTTOM WALTONS (6″) and LOCK'S BOTTOM (6″)

la Batme 13th AD i

v. **botm.**

BRISTLES WOOD (6″)

Bradeshulla 1231 Bract

Bradeshull 1229 *FF*
Brassels Wood c. 1825 O

This points to an OE strong form *Brād* as a pers. name side by side with the more common weak form *Brāda*. 'Broad's hill.' The modern form is corrupt.

BRITWELL (House)

Brutewelle 13th AD i, 1354, 1364 Cl, 1473 Pat
Brittewelle 13th AD iv (p), 1344 Pat
Bretewell 1346 Pat, 1347 Orig
Brytewel 1413 BM

OE *beorhtan wiellan* (dat.), 'bright, clear well.'

BROOKEND

Brok 1235 Bract (p), 1247 *Ass*
le Brok 1275 Ipm

Self-explanatory. It lies on the extreme west of the parish.

EAST BURNHAM

Esburneham 1086 DB
Estburnham 1208 Fines

Self-explanatory.

CAGE'S WOOD (6")

The wood takes its name from the Cage family who in the 17th cent. lived at Britwell Court (*VCH*).

CIPPENHAM [sipənəm]

Sippeham c. 1110 Robinson, *Gilbert Crispin* 41, 1163 P
Chippeham 1218 Bract, 1227 *Ass*, 1249 Gross
Sipeham 1218 Bract
Chipham 1224 WellsR
Scypeham 1227 *FF*
Cipeham 1231 Bract
Cippeham 1237–40 Fees 1448, 1249 Gross
Cipham 1241 *Ass*
Chypeham 1247 *Ass*
Shippeham 1247 *Ass* (p)
Cypeham 1262 *Ass*

Cyppeham 1262 *Ass*
Sipenham 1268 Ch, 1384 Pat
Scipinham 1272 Ipm
Chippenham 1291 Tax, 1300 Ipm, 1305 Cl, 1320 Fine, 1324 Orig, 1325 Cl
Cippenham 13th AD i, iv, 1339, 1364 Cl, 1437 AD vi
Cypenham 1312 Fine, 1535 VE
Sippenham 1313 Pat, 1340, 1385 Pat, 1448 BM
Cyppenham 1322 Misc, 1346 FA
Shippemham 1327 Pat
Sy(p)penham 1429, 1610 BM
Chipenham 1470 IpmR
Chipynghamme 1535 VE
Sippingham 1766 J

OE *Cippan-ham*, 'Cippa's homestead.' *Cippa* is not used independently in OE but is found in Chippenham (C, Gl, W) and a patronymic from this name seems to be recorded in the name *Cipping* which occurs in a south Warwickshire charter of c. 1150 (Radulfus f. Cipping') *HarlCh* 48 C 39. In the Wilts and Gl examples *Cippa* is compounded with hamm. Cf. Crawford Charters 73. The initial *ch* in the present case was, under French influence, modified to *s* and *sh* and the former sound ultimately prevailed, IPN 101. As Cippenham lies immediately to the south of the Bath Road, an important line of medieval travel, and is less than three miles from Windsor, it is easy to understand the modification of the name by French influence.

COCKSHERD WOOD (6″)
Coppyshard 1535 VE

Chalfont St Giles and St Peter

CHALFONT [ʧɑ·fənt]
Ceadeles funtan (dat.) 949 (1200) BCS 883
Celfunte 1086 DB
Celfunde 1086 DB
Chelhunte 1185 Rot Dom
Chaufhunte 1195 Cur(P), 1199 Cur, 1275 Ipm
Chafhunte 1196 FF(P), 1379 Cl

Caufunt 1201 Abbr
Chaufunt 1202 Fines, 1241 *Ass*
Chalfhunte 1220–34 WellsR, 1227 *Ass*, 1229 Pat, Ch, 1232 Cl, 1238 Gross, 1241, 1247, 1262 *Ass*, 1293, 1309 Pat, 1361 Cl, 1368, 1375 Pat, 1490 Ipm
Chalfunt 1220–34 WellsR, 1235 Fees 462, 1284 FA, 1293 Pat, 1509 AD vi
Chalffunte 1227 *FF*
Chaffunte 1229 Bract
Chalfund Sancti Egidii 1237 Cl
Chalfhunte Sancti Petri 1237–40 Fees 1449
Calfunte 1247 *Ass*
Chalfonte 1262 *Ass*
Chafunte 1262 *Ass*
Chaufuntseyntgyle 1262 *Ass*
Calfonte 1297 Ipm
Calfhunte 1324 Pat
Chalfhonte 1330 Pat
Chalfounte 1535 VE
Chawfount 1538 LP
St Giles Cha(l)funt vulgo *Chafforn* 1675 Ogilby
Charlfont 1766 J

'Ceadel's spring,' *v.* funta. The pers. name *Ceadel* in its weak form is also found in *Ceadelanwyrþ* the old form of Chaddleworth (Berks). It is probably of Celtic origin. See Förster, *Liebermann Festschrift* 181, where many local compounds of this name are brought together. The very early loss of medial *d* is noteworthy. The two parishes take their names from the dedication of their parish churches. *v.* Introd. xiv.

Chalfont St Giles

BOTTRELL'S FARM

Boderellis Close 1505 HMC xv. App. vii. 132

Both this and the next name are probably derived from a common pers. name.

DOGGETT'S WOOD (6")

Doggeteshul 1363 HMC xv. App. vii. 129

This probably contains the same surname found in Doggets' Farm *infra*.

GROVE (Fm)

la Grave 1294 Pat (p)

v. graf.

JORDANS

Jurdens 1766 J

This may be a reduction of *Jourdemayns*, a possessive form from the family name *Jourdemayn* found in the district in 1301 (HMC xv. App. vii. 127).

LOUDHAM'S FARM

Ludham 1256 *FF* (p), 1283 *Mert* 404 (p)
Loudham al. *Loutham* 1329 Ipm

OE *Hlūdan-ham*, 'Hluda's homestead.' The strong form *Hlūd* is found in the p.n. *Hlūdes-beorh* (BCS 741). One would have expected the vowel to have been shortened, but cf. Lowdham (Nt). There is evidence of a temporary shortening of the vowel in Lowdham (*Luddeham* 1191–3 (*Cal of Doc France* 16) from an original charter). Probably the influence of the common word *loud* was too strong for the shortening to be permanent. Mutschmann suggests a pers. name *Luda* for Lowdham and such does occur in OE but its vowel must have been short as no OE stem in *lūd-* is known. 'Loud' is also possible as a stream-name in English (cf. *Loud* in Ekwall, PN La 139) but there is no stream here at all. Like the present name, Lowdham (Nt) can hardly be derived from a stream-name, for the brook which runs through the village bore its present name of Cocker Beck already in the 13th cent.

OUTFIELD (Fm)

Otfeld 1303 HMC xv. App. vii. 127

Probably the modern form is corrupt and the true name should be *Oatfield*.

ROUGHWOOD PARK

le Rowewode 1296 HMC xv. App. vii. 127
Row Wood 1826 B

Self-explanatory. The true form would be *Row-wood* (*v.* ruh) but the modern form has been refashioned under the influence of the independent adj.

SUTMER'S COURT (6″)

Sotemere 1319 HMC xv. App. vii. 128 (p)

This is probably a manorial name and the person's original name was *Suthmere*. Cf. Southmere (Nf).

THE VACHE

This is a manorial name deriving from the family of Warnerus de *Vacca* who had land in Chalfont in 1166 (RBE 314). *Vacca* is the latinised form of the family name *la Vache*, of frequent occurrence in Bk. The family probably derived its name from some place in France, the name *Vacca* or *Vache* being perhaps given to some rock or hill which suggested a cow in its outline. In the French *Dictionnaire Topographique* there is a *la Vache* (rock-name) in Morbihan, *La Vache* (Lat. *Vaca*) in La Drôme *la Vache* (Nièvre). We may note also *Les Vaches Noires* as the name of some big rocks near Villers in Calvados (Zachrisson).

Chalfont St Peter

ASHWELL'S FARM

Probably a manorial name from the family of *John de Ashewell* who lived in Chalfont in 1340 (NI). He probably came from Ashwell (Herts).

MUMFORD'S FARM

This farm was held in 1645 by Christopher Mumford (*VCH*).

STAMPWELL (Fm)

(atte) *Stompe* 1296 HMC xv. App. vii. 127 (p)
Stompwell 1766 J
Stumpwell 1826 B
'Spring by the stump' *v.* wielle.

Chenies

CHENIES 106 D 6 [tʃeini], [tʃi·ni]

Isenhamstede R i *P*, 1195 Cur(P), 1232 WellsR, 1241 *Ass*, 1285 Fine, 1352 Ipm

Isenhamtone 1195 Cur(P)
Hiselhamistude 1195 Cur(P)
Iselhamstede 1232 WellsR, 1241 *Ass*
Ysenhamstede 1232 Cl
Hisenhamsted 1235 Fees 463
Hysenhamstud 1235 Fees 466
Hyselhamstud 1235 Fees 556
Islamsted 1247 Ipm, 1309 Ch (*Cheenny*)
Iselehamstede 1277 Pat
Ysenamstud Cheyne 13th AD i
Isnamsted 1315 Abbr, 1378, 1433 Pat, 1467 AD vi
Iselhampstede 1324, 1327 Fine
Esthamstede 1506 Pat
Estnamsteyd 1523 LP
Estmansted 1535 VE
Cheynes 1536 LP
Cheyney 1675 Ogilby
In all the later examples the *Chen(e)y* is omitted for brevity.

The manorial part of the name, now used to the exclusion of the rest, goes back to the family of *Cheyne* who from at least 1232 (WellsR) were associated with it. The history of the other part of the name is not easy. In the first place the first element in it may be either *Isel-* or *Isen-* and it is difficult to say which is the more probable. The actual interchange of the consonants is due to Anglo-Norman influence (cf. IPN 106–8). If the true form is *Isel*, we may compare Islington (Mx), where there is the same variation between *Isel-* and *Isen-*, though the great preponderance of the former (cf. Gover, *PN Mx*) and their ultimate triumph is all in favour of the *Isel-* ones as the original. These would point perhaps to an OE diminutive *Īsel(a)* formed from *Īs(a)* a somewhat doubtful element in OE personal name-compounds (cf. Björkman, NP 194). This p.n. *Isa* may be present in Isfield (Sx). The alternative is to take the true form as *Īsen* for *Īsan* the gen. sg. of this same name *Īsa*. (Those names which Searle gives as beginning in *Isen-* are all of continental origin. *v.* Forssner 164–6.) It should perhaps also be mentioned that in a Sussex charter (BCS 144) we have reference to an *isenan æwylm*, which may point to

Isene as a river-name but is more probably simply a reference to a chalybeate spring (OE *īsen*, 'iron'). If so we should have to take *Isene* as an old name for the Misbourne at this point. According to these various views the name would have to be interpreted as 'Isela's hamstede,' 'Isa's hamstede' or the 'hamstede on the *Isene*.'

DELL (Fm)

(de la) *Delle* 1227 *Ass*

v. dell. Self-explanatory.

Chesham

CHESHAM 106 C 5 [tʃesəm]

æt Cæstæleshamme 1012 (12th) Thorpe 553
Cestreham 1086 DB, 1201 Cur
Cestresham Hy ii (1318) Ch, Hy ii AD, 1199 Cur, 1201, 1212 Fines, 1209–19 WellsR
Cesterham Hy ii AD

The form *Cestresham* is common till the end of the 13th cent. We also have

Chesham 1247 *Ass*, 1268 Pat, 1302, 1312 Fine, 1372 Pat (*in Chiltern*)
Chessham 1302 Ipm, 1355 BM
Chesseham 1325 Cl
Chesham Lecytor, *Chesham Owborn* 1526 LS
Chesum 1675 Ogilby

OE *ceasteles-hamm*, 'the hamm of the *ceastel*,' i.e. marked by such. The word *ce(a)stel* (IPN 148) perhaps denotes a small fort but no such seems to have survived. The later *r* for *l* may be due to AN influence (IPN 106) or it may be due to substitution of the more common *ceaster* for *ceastel*. There were two Chesham manors, one belonging to Leicester and the other to Woburn Abbey.

ASHERIDGE

Esregge 1200 Fines
Asherugge 1535 VE

Self-explanatory.

BARN WOOD and COTTAGES (6″)

(atte) Berne 1338 Misc (p)
the Barne 1606 Rec. ix. 339

v. bern.

BELLINGDON

Belindene 1212 Fines, 1227 *Ass* (p)

Possibly OE *Bellingdenu*, 'Bella's valley,' *v.* denu. *-ing-* is used as in -ingtun. The pers. n. *Bella* may be inferred from *bellan ford* (BCS 454) and other p.n. *v.* Belford (PN NbDu).

BLACKWELL HALL

Blakewell 1227 *Ass* (p), 1275 Ipm (p)
Blakewelle 13th AD i

Self-explanatory.

BOTLEY

Bottlea Helie 1167 P
Bottelag' 1195 Cur(P)
Bot(t)ele 1227 *Ass* (p)
Bottelegh 1241 *Ass*

'Botta's clearing' *v.* leah. The name *Botta* is only found independently once, in the 7th cent., but is a normal short form of such a compound as *Bōtwine* or *Bōtwulf*. Botley (Berks) also represents an OE *Bottan leah*.

THE BURY (6″)

Chesseham al. vocat '*Cheshambury maner*' 1417 IpmR
Chesham Bury 1485 Ipm

The manorial use of burh.

CHARTRIDGE

Charderuge 1191–4 *HarlCh* 57 C 3 (p), 1227 *Ass* (p)
Chardrugge 1200 Fines (p), 1227 *Ass* (p)
Charderugge 1240 AD ii (p), 1262 *Ass* (p), 13th AD vi
Chardrigge 1241 *Ass* (p)
Chartrugge c. 1280 Misc (p)

OE *Cærdan*-hrycg, 'Cærda's ridge,' *v.* Charndon *supra*.

* CODMORE (Fm)

Codmers 1619 *VCH*
Codmer Fm 1766 J

Possibly OE *Cod(d)an-mere*, 'Cod(d)a's mere.' A name *Cod(d)a* may be inferred from Codford (W) (cf. BCS 595 *Codanford*) and Cotheridge (Wo) (cf. BCS 1106 *Coddan hrycg*).

GERMAINS (Great and Little)

Germayns Land 15th *VCH*

From the family name *Germain*.

HIGHAM (lost)

Hegham 1287 Ipm
Heyham 1322 Cl
Hygham 1428 IpmR

'High homestead' *v.* ham.

* HUNDRIDGE (Fms)

Hunderugg' 1199 Cur, 1303 Ch
Hundrigge 1200 Cur
Hundrugge 1284 FA (p)
Hunderigg 1476 IpmR

Either OE *hunda-hrycg*, 'hounds' ridge,' or *Hundan-hrycg*, 'Hunda's ridge,' the pers. name *Hunda* being apparently found in OE *Hundan-denu* (BCS 1213). *v.* hrycg.

HYDE HOUSE

In 1230 Wm de *Hyda* held one carucate of land in Chesham (Cl).

* LATIMER

Yselhamstede 1220 Fees 314
Iselhamstede 1231 Bract
Iselhampstede Botetourte 1325 Pat
Isenhampstede Cheyndust 1346 FA
Isenhampstede Latymer 1389 IpmR
Lattimers 1526 LS

This manor has undergone successive changes of name. It was first a Foliot Manor and is called in the chartulary of

St Mary de Pré, Leicester, *Foliots* in the 15th cent. (*VCH*). It was in the hands of Ralph Cheindut who married the Foliot heiress in 1235 (Fees 463) and is called after that family as late as 1346 (*u.s.*) but in that very passage it is said that it was formerly in the possession (apparently only temporary) of John *Botetourte* and this explains the name given in 1325 (*u.s.*). In 1330 (Pat) it was demised in fee to Wm Latimer, husband of Elizabeth *Latymer*, daughter of John Botetourte and hence came to be known by its last name. For *Isenhamstede* *v.* Chenies *supra*.

LEYHILL COMMON

atte Leyhulle 1337 Cl (p), 1340 NI (p)

'Fallow or unploughed hill' *v.* **læge, hyll.**

PEDNOR (Fms)

Pedenore c. 1200 (14th) *Miss* 68
Padenore 1241 *Ass*, 1363 AD iii, Cl, 1364 Pat
Padenhore 1363 IpmR
Pednore al. *Padnore* 1541 LP
Padnor 1766 J

OE *Peadan-ōra*, 'Peada's bank,' *v.* **ora.** The name *Peada*, borne by a son of Penda King of the Mercians, appears again in Padworth (Berks).

* PEPPETT'S GREEN (6″)

Pippards in Bellingdon 15th *VCH*

This must take its name from a family-name *Pipard*, which is fairly common in the middle ages.

SKOTTOWE POND (6″)

Takes its name from a family who lived hard by in the 18th cent. (*VCH*). They probably came from Scottow (Nf).

* Chesham Bois

CHESHAM BOIS 106 CD/5 [tʃesəm bɔiz]

Boys in Cesteresham 1276 Ipm
Chesham Boys 1339 Cl

This part of Chesham was held by the family of *De Bosco* or *De Bois* already in 1213 (Fines) and the second part therefore is manorial in origin.

Coleshill

COLESHILL 106 E 5 [kousəl]

Coleshulle 1279 (14th) *Miss* 50 (p)
Colshull 1304 Pat
Coleshull 1340 NI (p), 1354 Cl (p)

The pers. name *Cola* is common in OE and *Col* is apparently found in the p.n. *Colesleye*, BCS 586, a late and untrustworthy manuscript. In Coleshill (Wa) the first element is a stream-name *Coll* (BCS 1182), not so in Coleshill (Berks). It is possible that a stream-name *Coll* is the origin of the present name. A well-defined valley lies immediately to the south of Coleshill. It would be a remarkable coincidence if three distinct places named Coleshill were derived from an OE pers. name of extreme rarity, and indeed of doubtful authenticity. The pers. name *Col* contained in Colston Basset (Nt) is certainly ON *Kollr*.

BRENTFORD [breinfəd]

Braynford 1337 Ipm
Westbraynford 1412 AD i
Branford Barns 1766 J

Brentford Grange is far away from any stream. It must have been called *West* Brentford in contrast to the true Brentford which was presumably the original name of the ford, due east of Brentford, at the bottom of the valley, across the Misbourne. The modern form has been clearly influenced by that of the well-known Brentford (Mx). That shows early forms *Breguntford*, *Brentford*, *Brainford*, the modern form being a re-spelling due to the influence of the river-name *Brent* itself. We have no evidence as to whether there was an earlier form *Brentford* for the Bucks p.n. On the whole it seems unlikely for that would compel us to assume that the Misbourne stream had an earlier name *Bregunt*, for which there is otherwise no evidence. Perhaps better we should assume an OE pers. name **Brega*, a pet-form for one of the numerous OE names in *Bregu-*. The name may then be 'Brega's ford' but there is no certainty.

ONGAR HILL

Honger Hill 1766 J

The forms are too late for any certainty. It is probably 'hunger-hill,' a common term of reproach in p.n. but it is just conceivable that it is 'hanger-hill.' *v.* hangra. Ongar St nr. Aymestrey (He) is *Hungerstrete* in 1375.

STOCK PLACE

la Stock 1281 Pat
Stoke 1300 Misc
atte Stocke 1326 Cl (p)

This is probably OE stocc = stump.

WINCHMORE HILL (6")

Winsmore hill 1639 *Terr*
Winshmore hill 1674 *Terr*
Winchmorehill 1706 *Terr*

Possibly OE *Wines-mōr*, 'Wine's mor.'

Dorney

DORNEY 114 A 4

Dornei 1086 DB, 1185 P
Dorney 1209–19 WellsR

The second element is eg, for Dorney is practically surrounded by water. *Dorn* may be the name of one of these streams. Cf. *Dorne* as a river-name in Oxfordshire and Dorne (Wo), *Dorene* in BCS 1135, though the position of the latter does not favour derivation from a lost river-name.

HICKNAHAM

Hikenham 1199 Cur (p)
Jekingham 1766 J
Hickenham 1826 B

Apparently OE *Hiccan-hām*, 'Hicca's homestead.'

Farnham Royal

FARNHAM ROYAL 106 J 5

Ferneham 1086 DB

Farnham 1200 Cur, 1204 Fines, 1230 WellsR, 1235 Gross, 1241, 1247 *Ass*, 1258 Ch
Fernham 1231 WellsR, 1237–40 Fees 1449
Farnam 1274 Ipm
Farneham 1361 IpmR
Farnham Verdon 1391 IpmR
Fernham Riall 1477 IpmR
Farnham Roiall 1478 Pat
Farnam Vardon 1532 BM
Farnehame Ryall 1535 VE

OE *fearn-ham*, 'fern-homestead,' *v.* **fearn, ham**. Verdon, from the Verdon family who were tenants here in DB. 'Royal' because it was held by the grand serjeanty of supporting the king's right arm at his coronation. *riall* represents the AN form *reial*.

Hitcham

HITCHAM 106 H/J 4

Hucheham 1086 DB, 1231 Ch, 1236 Gross, 1241 *Ass*
Hucham 1220 Fees 313, 1227, 1241, 1247 *Ass*, 1284 FA, 1292 Ipm, 1308 FA, 1338 Ipm, 1346 FA
Hugeham Hy iii Ipm
Huccham 1247 *Ass*, 1346 Pat, 1350 Cl, 1405 Pat
Hecham 1338 Cl, 1489 Ipm, 1513 LP
Hiccheham 1382 Pat
Heckham 1480 IpmR
Hycham 1526 LS, 1542 BM
Hutcham 1562 BM

OE *Hycgan-hām*, 'Hycga's homestead,' with the same pers. name as in Hughenden *supra* and the same phonological difficulties. For the forms of the pers. name see that name.

Penn

PENN 106 E 3

Penna de Tapeslawa 1188 P
Lapenne 1197 *FF*(P), 1199 Cur, 1222 Bract

This is probably **penn**, meaning 'enclosure,' though association with Celtic *pen*, 'headland,' is tempting as it stands on a

well-marked hill. As *pen* = headland is not used as an independent word in O or ME it would be difficult to account for the common use of the def. art. *la*, if we assume derivation from that word, though Professor Ekwall points to the Shropshire parallels of *La Munede* for Long Mynd (Sa) and *La Wrekene* for Wrekin (ib.). The def. art. in ME forms of place-names tends as a rule to be used only before significant words (*v.* Zachrisson in *Anglia*, xxii. 308 ff.). For *Tapeslawa v.* Taplow *infra*.

BAYLIN'S FARM

The name of this manor in 1558 (Nicolas, *Testamenta Vetusta* 757) is given as *Bealing's*.

BROOK WOOD (6")

This is *Brock* Wood in the earliest ed. of the 1-in. map and as there is no conspicuous brook here and there may well have been badgers the modern form is probably corrupt.

GATEMOOR WOOD (6")

Gatmoor Hill 1826 B

Probably OE *gāta-mōr*, 'goats' mor.'

GLORY (Fm)

This probably derives its name from the *Glory* family, lords of Glory manor in Wooburn (*v.* Gloryhill *supra*), who held the tenth part of a knight's fee in Penn in the 13th cent. (*VCH*).

HODGEMOOR WOOD

Hoddesmershul 1363 HMC xv. App. vii. 129
Hoddesmore 1592 L. iii. 278

'Hodd's mor' or possibly 'Hodd's mere.'

KNOTTY GREEN

Knocklocks Green 1766 J
Knattocks or *Knotty Green* 1806 Lysons
Knotty or *Knocklock Green* 1826 B

PUTNAM PLACE

This is manorial in origin and takes its name from a family deriving from Puttenham (Herts). In the Close Roll for 1340

we read that Thos. de la Hay held the manor of Puttenham (Herts) and a messuage and carucate of land in *la Penne* with reversion to Roger, son and heir of Roger of Puttenham.

SEAGRAVE'S FARM

Segraves 1400 Pat

A manorial name. There was a Stephen de *Segrave* in Penn in 1230 (FF). This was Stephen de Segrave, Justiciar of England, who derived his name from Seagrave (Lei).

Seer Green

SEER GREEN 106 F 5

la Sere 1223 Bract (p), 1258 Ch
la Cere 1274 Ipm
le Shere 1275 Ipm
la Zere 1276 RH
Sera 1316 FA
Sere 1361 Ipm

Taplow

TAPLOW 106 J 3 [occ. tɔplou]

Thapeslau 1086 DB
Tapeslawe 1186, 1188 P
Tappelawe R i *P*, 1197 FF(P), 1200 Cur, 1213 Fines, c. 1218 WellsL, 1227 *Ass*, 1228 *FF*, 1241 *Ass*, 1252 Ch, 1262 *Ass*
Tepelawe 1194 Cur
Tapplawe 1199 Cur
Tapelawe 1199 Fines
Teppelawe 1227 *Ass*, 1235 Fees 465, 1241, 1262 *Ass*, 1297 Ipm
Toppelewe 1247 *Ass*
Teppelowe 1285 QW
Toppelawe 1346 Pat
Tappelowe 1361 Cl, 1489 Ipm
Toplo 1571 BM
Toplowe 1624 BM
Topler 1675 Ogilby

The second element is OE **hlaw**. The first must be a pers. name *Tæppa* or *Teppa* found also in Tapners (K), *Teppanhyse*

BCS 260. The allied name *Tapa* is found in *Tapahalan* (BCS 993), Tapton (Db) and Tappington (K).

'Tæppa's **hlaw**,' the reference very probably being to the famous barrow in Taplow old churchyard from which came the Taplow hoard of treasures now in the British Museum. There is a single and early example of a pers. name *Tæbba*, which is intelligible as a short form of a compound name consisting of the stem *Tāt*, followed by a second element beginning with *b*. The well-recorded name *Tātbeorht*, for example, would produce a short form *Tæbba*, with shortening and then mutation of the stem-vowel. To such a form *Tæppa* would be related as **Cippa* stands to **Cibba*; such pairs are numerous.

CLIVEDEN [klivdən]

Clivueden' 1195 Cur(P)
Cliveden 1200 Cur, 1211 Abbr
Clifden 1766 J
Cliefden 1826 B

Cliveden stands high above the Thames on top of a steep rise and the first element must be OE **clif** or *cleof* used descriptively of its position. It is commonly compounded with **dun** as in Cleadon (Du) and Clevedon (So) but forms in *don* for Cliveden are rare and late. The second element is clearly **denu** and the reference must be to the valley to the south of the house. 'Steeply sloping valley.'

DILEHURST (lost)

Dileherst 1086 DB, 1163 P

This has commonly been identified with Tyler's Green in Penn, but in the Pipe Roll of 1163 it is associated with Cippenham and this association is confirmed by the grant of the meadow of *Dillepol* with other lands belonging to the manor of Cippenham to Burnham Abbey in 1266 (Dugdale, *Monasticon*, vi. 546). *v.* Baring, *Domesday Tables* 132. It is clear that a wood and a pool in Cippenham must have been named from the same man. The exact form of his name is uncertain.

HARDICANUTE'S MOAT (6″)

(boscus de) *Hurceleye* 1276 RH

Herteleye 1299 Ipm
Hertle 1338 Pat
Hartley Court Mote 17th *VCH*

v. **heorot, leah** for the first part of this name. The whole name is now corrupt. It is also sometimes corrupted to Harlequin's moat (VCH ii. 30).

HUNTERCOMBE HOUSE

A manorial name. In 1346 (FA) John de Huntercombe holds half a knight's fee in Burnham, but the family were already in Bucks in 1262 (*Ass*). The manor is called *Undercombe* in 1422 (IpmR) and *Hundercombe* in 1489 (ib.). The name is doubtless derived from Huntercombe (O).

LENT (6″)

atte Lenthe 1340 NI (p)
atte Liente 1341 AD i
atte Lente 1342 Pat

Professor Ekwall suggests that this is from OE *hlēonaþ*, 'shelter,' and for the change of final *þ* to *t* compares the history of Frant (Sx), earlier *Fernthe*.

PENNLANDS (Fm)

le Penneland 1421 *VCH*

This takes its name from the family of the John de la Penne, presumably of Penn in this county, who in 1278 (Cl) held lands in Burnham.

SUMMERLINS WOOD (6″)

la Somerlese 1344 Pat

'Summer-pasture' *v* **læs**.

WEST TOWN (Fm)

Weston 13th AD i
le Westoun 1347 Orig

'West farm' but why so it is not easy to say. It lies on the West side of the parish and is just west of Burnham Abbey but is hardly west of Burnham itself.

XVIII. STOKE HUNDRED

Stoches 1086 DB
Stokes 1185 Rot Dom, 1195 Cur(P), 1247 *Ass*

The meeting-place of the Hundred was presumably at Stoke Poges, but the exact site is unknown.

Chalvey

CHALVEY 114 A 5 [tʃɑ·vi]

Chalfheye 1227 *Ass*, 1346 FA
Chalfeye 1237–40 Fees 1449
Chalveye 1242 Fees 887, 1255 RH, 1302 FA, 1328 Ch, 1343 AD i
Chauuaye 1247 *Ass*
Chelefaye 1262 *Ass*
Chalueye 1262 *Ass*
Chalfey 1262 *Ass*

As this is almost surrounded by water we must take the second element as OE eg and regard the *h* in certain of the forms as inorganic. The first element is OE cealf, hence 'calf-island.'

Datchet

DATCHET 114 A 6

deccet 10th KCD 693
Daceta 1086 DB
Dachet 1181 P, 1195 FF(P), 1239 Gross, 1241, 1247 *Ass*, 1294 Ch, 1321 Cl, 1327 Ch, 1350 Pat
Dechette 1237–40 Fees 1449
Dacchet 1241 *Ass*
Dachett(e) 13th AD v, 1254 Ipm, 1302 FA, 1335 Ch, 1338 Cl
Dechet 1247 *Ass*
Dachchet, *Dechchet* al. *Dachet* 1276 Ipm
Dochet 1530 LP
Dochett 1547 LP
Dotchatt 1626 Vern

Professor Ekwall inclines to British origin for this name, as suggested by the final *cet* from Brit. *cēt*, 'wood' (cf. Chetwode

supra) but in the absence of evidence that Datchet was early forest ground feels that there is some doubt about this.

RIDING COURT [rediŋ], [raidiŋ]

Rudinges 1197 FF(P)

Rudyng 1344 Cl, 1345 Pat, 1381, 1441 IpmR

'The clearing(s)' *v.* hryding.

SOUTHLEA

Suthle 13th AD i

Southlee 1343 AD i

Sowthlay, *Southle* 1394 BM

Sudley Eliz ChancP

Sudeley al. *Sudley* al. *Southley* FF (VCH)

Self-explanatory, *v.* leah. South in relation to Datchet. The modern form is clearly a spelling one.

Denham

DENHAM 106 G/H 7/8

Deneham 1066 (12th) KCD 824, 1195 Cur(P) (p), 1209–19 WellsR, 1227 Ch

Daneham 1086 DB

Denham 1233 WellsR

Denom 1336 Pat

Denham Durdent 1362 Cl

'Valley homestead' *v.* denu, ham. The *Durdent* family had a holding here already in 1166 (RBE 189).

DOGGETS FARM

Doggatts Eliz ChancP

This must take its name from the family of Walterus *Doget* who in 1311 signs a Denham deed (*HarlCh* 84 F 49). *v.* Lathbury 107.

THE LEA

This name goes back to the late 13th cent. when we have mention of a John de *la Lea* (Lathbury 389).

SAVOY FARM

The manor of Denham Durdens was in 1535 (VE) among the possessions of the Savoy Hospital.

SOUTHLANDS (6″)

Suthlaunde, *Suthlonde* is found as a pers. name in Denham in the 13th cent. (Lathbury 43) and clearly is derived from this farm.

WADLEY COVERT (6″)

Waddelawe 1227 *Ass* (p)

The person bearing this name is associated with Bradenham and the identification of the name is by no means certain. If correct, it means 'Wadda's hill.' *v.* **hlaw.**

Eton

ETON 114 A 5

Ettone 1086 DB, 1176 P, 1202 Fines, 1226 Bract, 1238 Gross, 1255 Ch
Eitun 1155 P
Eiton 1176 P, 1211 Fines
Eton 1207 Fines, 1208 Fees 20, 1229 Bract, 1262 *Ass*, 1312 Fine
Eyton 1211 Fines, 1261 Ch
Eaton 1546 LP

OE *ēg-tūn*, 'island-farm.' It is almost surrounded by water. *v.* **eg.**

BARNES POOL BRIDGE (6″)

This was originally called *pons Baldewin* (RH i. 18). The name still survives in the Baldwin Bridge Trust devoted to its maintenance (*VCH*).

COLENORTON BROOK (6″)

The brook takes its name from a toft called *Coldnorton*, mentioned in 1449 (*VCH*), and called *Colle Norton* in 1572. Norton from its lying to the north of Eton.

TIMBRALLS (not on O.S. maps)

Maxwell-Lyte (*Hist. of Eton College* 16) gives this as the name of a piece of land on the high road to Slough, which takes its name from the *Timberhaw* or *Tymbrehall* which was used for the storage of timber when the College was built.

Eton Wick

ETON WICK 114 H 6

atte Wyk 1340 NI (p)

v. **wic**. The dairy-farm of Eton.

BEGGAR'S BRIDGE (6″)

This was earlier called *Spitelbrigge* (Pat 1443) and must have been so called from some charitable hospital.

BELL FARM (6″)

This should be *Bell's* Farm. It was in the occupation of Matthew Bell in a perambulation of 1605 (*VCH*).

THE BROCAS (6″)

Brocas Crofte 1486 AD v
Brockess 1569 Maxwell-Lyte (*u.s.*) 187

This apparently takes its name from one John Brocas, surveyor of works in Windsor Castle in the 14th cent., who owned land here (cf. Tighe and Davis, *Annals of Windsor*, i. 106).

SOUTH FIELD

le Suthfelde 1440 Pat

Self-explanatory, *v.* **feld**. The word is used here in its later sense.

Fulmer

FULMER 106 H 6

Fugelmere 1198 Fines
Fuegelmere 1202 Fines
Fughelemere 1237–40 Fees 1449
Folemere 1242 Fees 878
Fulmere 1247 *Ass*, 1254 Ipm, 1324 Fine, 1338 Pat, 1509 LP
Fulemere 1262 *Ass*
Folmere 1291 Tax
Fulmer 1294 Ch
Foulmere 1296 Ipm, 1303 AD i, 1333 Ipm, 1338, 1349 Pat, 1375 BM
Fowelemere 13th AD v

Fowelmere 1302 FA
Foulemere 1316 FA, 1344 Cl, 1403 BM
Fullmer 1766 J

'Bird-haunted mere' *v.* fugol, mere. The mere was in the 19th cent. a swamp, laid out for the cultivation of cress (*VCH*).

Gerrard's Cross

GERRARD'S CROSS 106 G 6

Jarrets Cross 1761 Roque

The origin of this name is unknown. *Jarret* is common as a colloquial form of *Gerard*.

BULSTRODE (Park) [bulstroud]

Bolestrode 1195 Cur (p), 1260 AD i, 1329 Fine
Bollestrode 1285 QW
Bolstrode 13th AD iv, 1311 Fine
Bullestrode 1313 Misc

'Bull-marsh' *v.* **bula, strod.**

PRESTWICK (6″)

Prestewic 1224 (15th) *Hist. Mon. St Petri Glouc.* (Rolls Series) ii. 172

'Priests' **wic**,' probably because the farm was used for their endowment.

Hedgerley

HEDGERLEY 106 G 5

Huggeleie R i *P*, c. 1190 (c. 1300) *Miss* 94
Huggelegh 1237–40 Fees 1449
Huggel 1236, 1245 Gross, 1255 RH
Huchele 1242 Fees 879
Hugel 1247 *Ass*
Hugele 1291 Tax, 1342 Cl
Hugelegh 1300 Ipm
Hugeleie 1316 FA
Huggeleye 1336 Ch, 1350 Cl
Huggele 1393 Pat

Hugeley 1470 IpmR, 1490 Ipm, 1538 LP
Hegeley 1509, 1539 LP
Hedgeley 1526 LS, 1540 LP
Hogeley 1535 VE
Hogely 1537 LP
Hegely 1537 LP
Hugely al. *Hedgerley* c. 1560 *Linc*

'Hycga's clearing' *v.* leah. For the later development of *er* cf. Amersham *supra.* This must contain the pers. name found in Hughenden *supra* and Hitcham.

OAK END

Ake 1300 Ipm
Oke 1342 Ipm

Self-explanatory.

Horton

HORTON 114 B 7

Hortune 1086 DB
Horton by Colbroke 1376 Fine

'Dirty farm' *v.* **horh, tun.**

OKEHYDE (lost)

Hochyde 1262 *Ass*
Le Hochyde 1302 FA
Okhide 1346 FA
Okehyde 1350 Cl

Probably a compound of **ac** and **hid**, hence 'hide of land by the oak.'

Iver

IVER 106 J 7

Evreham 1086 DB
Eura 1175 P, Hy i (1267) Ch
Houre al. *Heuere* 1185 Rot Dom
Eure R i P, 1195 Cur(P), 1198 Fines, 1219 Bract, 1227 *Ass*, 1241, 1247 ib.
Evre 1220 Fees 314, 1316 FA, 1340 Ch, 1341 Cl, 1346 FA

Evere 1235 Fees 461, 1300 Ipm, 1302 FA, 1341 Fine, 1350 Ipm, 1377 IpmR, 1422 AD vi, 1491 Ipm
Huure c. 1242 Records of Merton, Appendix XLV
Euere 1249 Gross, 1262 *Ass*, 1402, 1474 BM
Uvere 1284 FA
Ouere 1296 Harl 84 F 47
Eyver 1372 Cl
Iver 1382 IpmR, 1440 AD i, 1468 Pat, 1490 Ipm
Ivere 1383 Cl
Ever 1455 AD iv, 1526 LS, 1535 VE, 1597 D
Ivre 1471 BM
Euer al. *Iver* 1509 LP

The name is difficult but it may be suggested that this is the word yfre and that the slope is that which runs eastward of the village. The *am* of the DB form is probably the Lat. acc. form with inorganic *h*. OE *y* should have become *u* in this part of the county, at least in early times (*v*. Introd. xxiv), but there are only four forms which show traces of that development. The vast majority of the forms show an *e* (cf. Kimble *supra*). This was raised to *i* towards the end of the 14th cent. Cf. the common pronunciation of *ever* as [ivə]. The pron. of *Iver* as [aivə] with a long vowel would seem to be purely a spelling pronunciation, but no trace of any other can now be found though there is a tradition that there was once a somewhat eccentric canon of Windsor who pronounced it *Ivver*. Perhaps this should not really have been reckoned an eccentricity on his part.

DELAFORD PARK

de la Forde 1276 RH (p)
atte Forde of Eyver 1372 Cl (p)

The ford is that on the Coln Brook, the family took its name from it and then the whole family name was attached to the Park.

GALLOW HILL (6″)

Galyhylle 1517 Encl

Self-explanatory. *galy* represents a common colloquial pronunciation of *gallow*.

IVER HEATH

Everheth 1365 Cl

Self-explanatory.

MANSFIELD (House)

This takes its name from the manor for which Lipscomb (iv. 517) quotes forms *Mansfield* al. *Magnesfield* dated 1589. The *g* is a mistake for *y* for this manor was the property of the *Me(y)nevil* family. Seval de *Meynevil* is associated with it in 1249 (*FF*) and we have a John de *Menevill* in connexion with Iver in 1327 (Cl).

RICHINGS PARK

This clearly derives its name from the family of *Richekyng(g)e* of whom Richard is mentioned in the Denham Court Rolls for 1403 and John in a Denham deed of 1423 (Lathbury 151, 113).

SPITAL (Fm) (6″)

le Spittle House 1635 (*VCH*)

Like Spital Bridge *supra* this must have some connexion with an early hospital.

SUTTON

Sutton 1227 *FF* (p), 1422 AD vi

Self-explanatory. It lies in the south of the parish.

THORNEY

Thornig c. 1000 (16th) Ethelweard

'Thorn-island' (*v.* þorn, eg), either from the thorn-bushes there or from some prominent thorn-tree.

Langley

LANGLEY and LANGLEY MARISH[1] 114 A 6

Langeley 1208 Fees 19

Langeleye Mareys 1312 Pat

[1] In the *Hist. S. Petri Glouc.* (Rolls Series, *passim*) there are several entries in which the church of Langley seems alternatively to be called the church of *Laverkestou* (thrice) or *Laverkestoke* (ten times), *Laverkested* (once) and once we have *Langeleia sive Laverkestoke*. It may be noted that *Laverkestoke* has its parallels in the early history of Laverstock (W) and seems to be a compound of 'lark' and *stocc*.

The first part of the name is self-explanatory. The second is manorial in origin the manor having been held by the family of *Mareys* or, in Latinised form, *Marisco*. The normal development would have been to

Langley Maries 1546 LP

and this is the pronunciation indicated by Lipscomb (iv. 531). Confusion with the common word *marsh* or *marish* was however very natural and we find

Langley Marishe 1538 LP
Langley Marsh 1826 B

The same family name has given rise to Huntspill Marsh (So) and Stow Maries (Ess).

ALDERBOURNE (Manor)

Alreburne 1224 (15th) *Hist. Mon. St Petri Glouc.* (Rolls Series) ii. 172
Alderburne 1535 VE

OE *alra-burna*, 'alders' burn,' *v.* **alor, burna.**

COLNBROOK

Colebroc 1146 (c. 1225) Abingd
Colebrok(e) 1337 Cl, 1338 Misc, 1364 Cl
Colbrok 1392 Pat, 1404 AD i
Colbroke 1400, 1505 Pat, 1526 LS
Colbrook 1425 Pat
Cawlbroke 1537 LP
Collebrooke 1608 HMS 224
Col(e)brook 1675 Ogilby

The complete absence of any forms with *n* in early times shows that the name of this brook has been influenced by that of the Colne itself. The first element is really the pers. name *Cola*, hence 'Cola's brook.'

MOUNT FIDGET WOOD (6″)

This must take its name from the holding of Richard de *Munfichet* in Langley in 1247 (Fees 878).

PARLAUNT PARK (Fm)

Parlond 1495 Pat
Perlaunte Park 1524 LP
Perland Park 1533 BM
Parlande Park 1540 LP
Parlaunt Park 1548 BM
Parlaunt 1592 D

The forms are very late but the name is probably 'pear-(tree)-land' with later gallicising of the name.

Slough

SLOUGH 114 A 5/6 [slɑu]

Slo 1195 Cur(P) (p)
le Slowe 1437 Pat
le Slough 1443 Pat

OE *sloh*, 'slough, mire.'

MERTON GRANGE (6″)

Merton Abbey owned property in Upton (WellsL 18).

MIRK (6″)

Merke c. 1242 13th cent. *Records of Merton*, App. xliv
de la Merke 13th AD i (p)
Merk 1248 *FF* (p)

'Boundary' *v.* **mearc**. The farm is just on the boundary of Datchet and Slough parishes.

UPTON

Opetone 1086 DB
Upton c. 1218 WellsL

Self-explanatory. 'Upper' not in relation to Slough but to the low-lying land to the south.

Stoke Poges

STOKE POGES 106 J 5 [poudʒis]

Stoches 1086 DB
Stokes c. 1120 BM, 1228 WellsR, 1237–40 Fees 1449
Stok 1242 Fees 879
Stoke 1284 FA
Stoke Puges, Pogeys 1302 Ipm

Stoke Pougeys 1331 Cl
Stoke Pugges 1420 IpmR
Stoke Pogys 1514 LP
Stoke pewges 1517 Encl
Stokbogies 1526 LS

v. **stoc**. The first mention of the family which has given its distinctive name to the manor is in 1255 when Humbert *le Pugeis* had the custody of the manor (RH i. 34). It may be suspected that the modern pronunciation is purely a spelling one which has replaced the [pjuˑdʒis] that one might have expected.

BERRY (Fm)

Bery ferme 1465 *Bodl*

This is probably the manorial 'bury' from **burh**.

DITTON (Park)

Ditone 1086 DB
Dittun 1205 Fines
Stokes Dutton' 1242 Fees 889
Stokditton 1292 Ipm
Ditton by Colbroke 1370 Cl

OE *dīc-tūn*, 'dyke or ditch-farm,' *v.* **dic**. The 'ditch' is perhaps the moat which still surrounds the house.

Wexham

WEXHAM 106 J 6

Wesham 1211 Abbr
Wexham 1219 WellsR, 1237–1240 Fees 1449, 1241, 1247 *Ass*, 1252 Ch, 1302 FA, 1345 Cl, 1440 BM
Waxham 1247 *Ass*

This may contain as its first element a pers. name derived from the stem *wac-* 'watchful.'

Wyrardisbury

WYRARDISBURY 114 B/C 6 [wreizbəri]

Wirecesberie 1086 DB
Wiredesbur' 1195 Cur (p)
Wyredeberia 1209–19 WellsR

Wyredebiry 1230 *FF*, 1241 *Ass*, 1271 Pat
Wiredebiri 1230 WellsR
Wiredesbir 1237–40 Fees 1449
Wyretesby 1262 *Ass*
Wyrardebury 1274 Fine
Wyradesburi 1275 Ipm
Wyredesburi 1284 FA
Wyrardesbury 13th AD i, 1312, 1324 Fine, 1451 AD i
Wydardesbury 1338 Cl
Wyraudesbury 1348 Pat
Wyrardysbury 1489 Ipm
Wraysbury 1536 LP, 1766 J
Wreysbury 1537 LP
Wrethesbury 1546 LP

'Wigræd's burh.' The second *r* in the spelling forms is clearly due to confusion and there has been a shifting of accent from the first to the second element in the pers. name. Cf. Sherington *supra*.

ANKERWYKE

Ankerwic 1194 BM, 1232 Cl, 1237 Gross
Ancherwich 1200 Cur
Ankerwik 1242 Ch
Ankirwyk 1243 Gross
Auncrewyk 1251 Ipm
Ankerwyk 1257 Ch, 1304 Pat, 1535 VE
Anker(es)wyk 1367 Cl
Ankyrwyk 1491 Ipm

Ankerwyke is the site of a house of Benedictine nuns and the name may record it, the first element being OE *ancor*, 'anchorite.' For the use of this term in ME cf. the well-known *Ancren Riwle*. *v.* wic, 'anchoress-dwelling.'

REMENHAM HOUSE

This represents the manor of Remenhams. John de Remenham held land in Wraysbury in 1289 (*FF*). He must have come from Remenham (Berks).

THE ELEMENTS, APART FROM PERSONAL NAMES, FOUND IN BUCKINGHAMSHIRE PLACE-NAMES

This list, with very few exceptions, confines itself to elements used in the second part of place-names or in uncompounded place-names. Under each element the examples are arranged in three categories, (*a*) those in which the first element is a significant word and not a personal name, (*b*) those in which the first element is a pers. name, (*c*) those in which the character of the first element is doubtful. Where no statement is made it may be assumed that the examples belong to type (*a*). Elements which are not dealt with in the *Chief Elements used in English Place-names* are distinguished by an (n) after them.

ac (a) Oak End, Radnage, Tinick.

æcer Haleacre (?).

æcen (n) *Ekeney*.

æsc (a) Nash, Nashway.

bæc (b) Chisbridge.

***bell(e)** (a) Kimble (?).

beorg (a) Burrow (?), Ellesborough, Grandborough, Lenborough, Redborough, Risborough, Singleborough, Thornborough. (b) Edlesborough, Loxboro (?). (c) Desborough.

beretun Barton Hartshorn.

bern Barn Wood.

bigging *Biggin*.

bocland Buckland.

botl Bottle Claydon, *Newbottle*.

botm Bottom Waltons.

brec (n) *Black Breach*, Bourton Brake, Breaches Wood, Nash Brake.

broc (a) Brookend, Danes Brook, Fulbrook, Shenley Brook. (b) Colnbrook, Dadbrook. (c) Seabrook.

brycg (a) Honeyburge, Ickford Bridge, Kingsbridge, Stonebridge. (b) Touchbridge.

burh (a) Astwood Bury, Berry, Burrow (?), The Bury, Lathbury, Westbury (2). (b) Aylesbury, Bassettsbury, Chilboro, Cholesbury, Loxboro (?), Padbury, Soulbury, Tilbury, Wyrardisbury.

burhsteall Boarstall.

burhtun Bierton, Bourton.

burna (a) Alderbourne, Ledburn, Swanbourne, Wooburn.

byrgen Burn Hill.
ceastel, ceaster Chesham.
cirice Stokenchurch, Whitchurch.
clif (a) Radclive, Whiteleaf.
cnæpp Naphill, Nup End.
cnoll Knowle Hill.
cot(u) (a) *Ascote*, Ascott, Askett, Burcott (2), Caldecote (2), Caldecotte, Foscott, Hulcott, Littlecote, Sheepcothill, *Southcote*, Southcott, Westcott.
(b) Alscot, Boycott, Chelmscott, Pitchcott, Pollicott, Tyrrelcote.
(c) Edgcott, Gawcott.
croh Crafton.
cumb (a) Coombe (2), The Coombe, Coombe's Fm, Coombs, Wycombe.
(b) Liscombe.
(c) *Malecumbe*.
dell Dell.
denu (a) North Dean, Bullington, Cliveden, Crendon Lane, *Ernesdon*, Hampden, Hillesden Wood, Hollingdon, Rowden, Sladen, Whielden, Yewden.
(b) Biddlesden, Fillington, Horsenden, Huckenden, Hughenden, Lavendon, Missenden, Tilson. (c) Hambleden.
dic *Fastendich*, Mulducks.
dun (a) Ashendon, Bovingdon, Claydon Botolph etc., Culverton, Grendon, Hollington, Quarrendon, Shipton, Weedon, Whaddon (2).
(b) Averingdown, Beachendon, Bellingdon, Boddington, Bowden, Charndon, Cheddington, *Copson*, Crendon, Denham, Hearnton, Hillesden, Huckenden, Poundon, Saunderton, Waddesdon, Wavendon, Widdington, Winchendon.
ecg Bradnidge, Hornage.
eg (a) Boveney, Chalvey, Dorney, *Ekeney*, The Rye, Thorney.
(b) *Addersley*, Olney, Towersey.
ende (a) Barley End, Bourne End, Herngate End.
(b) Martin's End, Paine's End.
fald Darrillshill, *Stotfold*.
feld (a) Beaconsfield, Brayfield, Bury Field, Field Fm, Outfield, Portfields, South Field, Whitfield.
(b) *Abfield*, Luffield, Turville.
(c) Marefield.
ford (a) Delaford, Ford, The Ford, Linford, Fenny, Stony and Water Stratford, Tickford, Twyford.
(b) Dadford, Harleyford, Ickford, *Tiddingford*.
(c) Brentford.

funta (b) Chalfont.
fyrhþ Frieth, Oxey Grove.
gafol (n) (c) Gawcott (?).
græf (b) Filgrave.
graf (a) Blackgrove (2), Chilton Grove, Grove (3).
(b) Addingrove, Bedgrove, Filgrave, Marlins Grove, Wingrave.
(c) Arngrove.
grene Bye Green, Green End.
hæcgeat (n) *Hatchetleys*.
ge-hæg (a) Chivery, Nashway.
(b) Balney.
ham (a) Denham, Farnham Royal, Higham, Medmenham.
(b) Amersham, Bragenham, Burnham, Cippenham, Haddenham, Haversham, Hicknaham, Hitcham, Lowdham's, Rowsham, Tyringham, Wexham.
(c) Bradenham.
hamm (a) Chesham, Ham, Sidnums, Woodham, Woolman's Wood.
(b) Buckingham, Dunsham.
hamstede *Ackhampstead*, *Isenhamsted*, Leckhampstead.
hamtun Beachampton.
han (n) Honor End.
hangra (a) Haleacre (?), Solinger.
(b) Collings Hanger.
healh (a) Gorrell, The Hale, Northall, Panshill, Widnell.
(b) Dagnall, Hudnall, Ludgershall, Rignall, Ringshall, Snelshall, Tathall, Worminghall.
heall Waterhall.
hecg (b) Elsage.
heordwic Hardwick.
hid *Deerhide*, Hyde (4), *Hyde* (2), *Okehyde*, Olney Hyde.
hlaw (a) Creslow, Loosley, Rowley, *Shucklow*.
(b) Bledlow, Cottesloe, Culley, Taplow, Winslow.
(c) *Seckloe*.
hleonaþ (n) Lent.
hlinc The Linces, Linslade.
hliþ The Lyde.
hlyde (n) Lude (?).
hlynn Linford.
hoh (a) Hoo Wood, Howe, Howe Wood, Uphoe.
(b) *Fippenhoo*, Ivinghoe, Moulsoe, Petsoe, Tattenhoe.
holt Rockwell, Stockholt.
hrisen (n) Risborough.

hrycg (a) Aldridge, Asheridge, Ashridge, Bledlow Ridge, Dundridge, Hawridge, Oakridge, Sheepridge, Studdridge, Totteridge.
(b) Andridge, Chartridge, Waldridge.
(c) Hundridge, Towerage.

hryding Redding Wick, Riding Ct., Riding Lane.

hyll (a) Brickhill, Brill, Burnhill, Furzenhill, Hill, Great Kingshill, Leyhill, Meadle, Nap Hill, Rhon Hill, Weedon Hill, Woad Hill.
(b) Bristles Wood, Doddershall, Ixhill, Page Hill, Tittershall.
(c) Coleshill.

* **hyrst** Fingest, Gayhurst, Ward's Hurst.

ingas *Halling*, Oving, Wing.

ingtun (b) Addington, Cublington, Cuddington, Dinton, Dunton, Easington, Loughton, Quainton, Shabbington, Sherington, Warrington, Wolverton.

lacu Marlake.

lad Linslade.

læs Lacey Green, Oxley's Fm, Summerlins.

laf (n) Marlow (?).

land Bandland, Greenlands, Newland, Parlaunt, Pennlands, Redland.

leah (a) Apsley, Ashley, Barley End, Chawley, Crawley, Fawley, Green Hailey, Hardicanute's Moat, Harley Field, *Haseley*, Langley, Layland's Fm, Lee, Lillyfee, Loosley Row, Lye Green, *Mesle*, Moorley's, Moseley, Nash Lee, Notley, Oakley, Shenley, Shipton Lee, *Sortele*, Southlea, Stewkley, Trendell's Wood, Wadley, Wheatley, Whorley, Woodleys, Woolley.
(b) Akeley, Bletchley, Botley, Chearsley, Chichele, Chorley, Coppice Lowhill, Cowley, Eakley, Harleyford, Hedgerley, Hemley, Kickle's Fm, Mursley, Peterley, Saunderton Lee, Wormsley, Yardley. (c) Whelpley.

mæd (a) King's Mead, Merrymead. (b) Hardmead.

(ge)mære (a) Marl Copse, Finemere.
(b) Bockmer, Bosmore, Cadmore End, Ilmer (?).

mearc Mirk.

* **mere** (a) *Blakemere*, Fenemore's Fm, Fulmer, Hazelmere, Holmer, Parmoor, Widmere. (b) Codmore. (c) Ilmer (?).

mersc Marsh, Marsh Gibbon, Wycombe Marsh.

mor (a) Finnamore, Frogmore, Gatemoor, Pressmore, Roddimore, Wellmore.
(b) Casemore, Chackmore, Coddimoor, Hodgemoor, Mentmore, Winchmore.
(c) Barmoor.

muga (n) *Lamua*.
ora (a) Denner, Honor End. (b) Ballinger, Hedsor, Pednor. (c) Courns Wood.
penn Penn.
ponde Pann Mill (?), Pond Fm.
port Lamport, Newport Pagnel.
pytt (b) *Ludpits*, Pulpit Wood, Shelspit.
ræwe (a) Potter Row, Woodrow.
(b) Copshrews.
ran (n) Rhon Hill.
sceaga Evershaw, Hogshaw.
slæd *Milnedoneslade*.
slæpe (c) Hanslope.
sloh (n) Rassler Wood, Slough (2).
sperre Holtspur.
stan (a) Stone.
(b) Ibstone, Lillingstone.
stoc Stoke (5).
stocc (a) *Lauerkestoke*, Stock Place.
(b) Adstock.
stocking Stocken, Stocking (2).
stow (a) *Laverkestou*, Stowe.
(b) Bunsty.
strod Bulstrode.
þorn (a) Thickthorn, The Thorne.
(b) Burston, Pitstone.
þorp (a) Eythrope, Sedrup, Westhorpe, Castle Thorpe.
(b) Bigstrup, Colstrope, Helsthorpe.
tun (a) Aston (5), Bierton, Bishopstone, Broughton (2), Calverton, Chilton, Clifton, Colenorton, Crafton, Ditton, Dorton, Drayton (2), Easton St, Water Eaton, Eton, Halton, Horton (2), Littleton, Marston (2), Milton, Monkton, Moreton (2), *Mortons*, Newton (2), Preston, Shipton, Slapton, Stantonbury, Sutton, Thornton, Upton (2), Walton (2), Westlington, Weston (2), West Town, Wotton.
(b) Emberton, Hoggeston, Ravenstone, Shalstone, Simpson, Snelson, Turweston, Woolstone, Wormstone.
v. also **ingtun**, **beretun**, **burhtun**.
twi-ford Twyford.
wæter Loudwater.
weald *Netherweld*, Weald, Westbury Wild.
welig Willen.
wic (a) Ankerwyke, Holywick, Longwick, Prestwick, Eton Wick, Kimble Wick, Terrick.
(b) Collett, Owlswick, Tetchwick, Tingewick.

(c) Terrick.

wielle (a) Blackwell, Bradwell, Britwell, Chadwell, Cranwell, Hartwell, Holywell, Marl Copse, Muswell, Stampwell.

(b) Biddles, Flackwell, Hickwell.

(c) Binwell.

wince (n) Winchbottom.

worþ (b) Littleworth, Marsworth.

wudu Astwood, Bernwood, Chetwode, East Wood, Horwood, New Wood, Kingswood, Prestwood, Roughwood, Snip Wood.

yfre Iver.

NOTE ON THE DISTRIBUTION OF THESE ELEMENTS

Our Survey is not sufficiently advanced for satisfactory comment to be made on the significance of the distribution of these elements but attention may be drawn to a few facts which may ultimately be of significance.

botl. *v.* Introd.

cot. The proportion of places containing this suffix is closely similar to that in Beds, Berks and Northants but much lower than in Oxon.

ham. The great group of these names is in the Thames valley: Bradenham, Medmenham and, very close together, Hitcham, Burnham, Cippenham, Wexham, Farnham Royal, Hicknaham. Amersham carries one up the Misbourne and Denham up the Colne. Besides these we have Haversham and Tyringham on the Ouse, Bragenham on the Ouzel, Haddenham near the Thame and Rowsham on the upper Thame.

ing and **ingham.** *v.* Introd.

ingtun. These names belong without exception to the north of the county.

leah. The proportion is relatively high, more so perhaps than in Beds, Berks and Oxon.

stocc. The Stoke names are relatively very common, agreeing in this respect with Oxfordshire.

þorp. All are clearly *throps* rather than *thorps* and of English origin. They are much more numerous than in Berks and Beds. Northants has a large number, but here the Scandinavian element probably comes in.

tun. Probably much the same proportion as in Berks, and definitely less than Beds, Northants and Oxon.

worþ. Extraordinarily rare though there is some evidence (*v. infra*) that the word survived in independent use in Bk.

PERSONAL NAMES COMPOUNDED IN BUCKINGHAMSHIRE PLACE-NAMES

Names not found in independent use are marked with a single star if their existence can be inferred from evidence other than that of the particular place-name in question. Such names may be regarded as hardly less certain than the unstarred ones. Those for which no such evidence can be found are marked with a double star.

Āca	Akeley
Æbba	*Abfield*
Æddi	Addingrove, Addington, Adstock
Ægel	Aylesbury
Ælf	Elsage (?)
Ælfsige	Alscot (?)
Æþelsige	Alscot (?)
**Agilmod	Amersham (?)
**Balla	Balney
Beald	Ballinger
*Bella	Bellingdon (?)
Bic(c)a	Beachendon
*Bic(c)el	Bigstrup
Blæcca	Bletchley
*Bledda	Bledlow
Boia	Boycott
*Bossa	Bosslane, Bosmore
Bōta	Boddington Hill
Botta	Botley
*Bracca	Bragenham
Brād	Bristles Wood
Brāda	Bradenham
**Brega	Brentford (?)
*Briddel	Burston
Bucc(a)	Bockmer, Buckingham
Buga	Bowden
Buna	Bunsty
Bȳ̆da	Biddles
Bynna	Binwell
*Byrna	Burnham
*Byttel	Biddlesden

Cada	Cadmore
*Cærda	Charndon, Chartridge, Chorley (?)
*Casa	Casemore
*Ceacca	Chackmore
*Ceadela	Chalfont
Cēol	Chilborohill (?)
Cēolmund	Chelmscott
Cēolrǣd	Chearsley
Cēolweald	Cholesbury
*Cetta	Cheddington
Cicca	Chicheley
Cissa	Chisbridge
*Codd(a)	Coddimoor (?), Codmore
*Col	Coleshill (?)
Cola	Collett, Colnbrook
Colman	Colstrope
Copp(a)	Coppice Lowhill, *Copson* Hill
*Cott	Cottesloe
Creoda	Crendon
*Cub(b)el	Cublington
Cūda	Cuddington
Cufa	Cowley
Cūsa	Culley
*Cwēn	Quainton
*Dagga	Dagnall
Dodda	Dadford
**Doder	Doddershall
Duda, Doda	Dadbrook, Dodleyhill, Dunton
Dunn(a)	Denham in Quainton, Dinton, [Dunsham
Ēadhere	*Addersley*
Ēadwulf	Edlesborough
Ealhmōd	Amersham (?)
Ēanbeorht	Emberton
*Eorla	Yardley
**Eorma	Arngrove (?)
Ēsa, Ēsi	Easington
*Fila	Fillington
*Flæcca	Flackwell (?)
*Fygla	Filgrave
*Gafa	Gawcott (?)
*Gicela	Kickle's Fm

Hǣda	Haddenham
*Hæddel	Hedsor
Hæfer	Averingdown, Haversham, [Hearnton
Hāma	Hanslope
**Hamela	Hambleden (?)
*Healla	Hall Barn, *Stoke Halling*
*Help	Helsthorpe (?)
*Helphere	Helsthorpe (?)
Hemma	Hemley
*Heorla	Harleyford (?)
Heoruwulf	Hardmead (?)
Herewulf	Hardmead (?)
*Hicca, *Hicc	Hicknaham, Ixhill (?)
*Hild	Hillesden
Hodd	Hodgemoor
*Hogg	Hogshaw (?), Hoggeston
Horsa	Horsenden
OE Hræfn, ON Hrafn	Ravenstone
*Hring	Ringshall
Hrōðwulf	Rowsham
*Hucca	Huckenden
Hūda	Hudnall
Hunda	Hundridge (?)
*Hwelpa	Whelpley (?)
*Hycga	Hedgerley, Hitcham, Hughenden
Ibba	Ibstone
*Ic(c)a	Eakley, Ickford (?)
Ifa	Ivinghoe
**Īsa, Īsel	*Islehampstead*
*Lāfa	Lavendon
*Lissa	Liscombe (?)
Locc	Loxboro
Luda	*Ludpits*
Luf(f)a	Luffield
Luha	Loughton
*Lutgār	Ludgershall
*Lȳtel, Lȳtla	Lillingstone, Littleworth
*Mænta	Mentmore
*Mǣrling	Marlins Grove
*Mæssa	Marsworth
Mūl	Moulsoe
**Myrsa	Mursley

~~**Myssa~~	~~Missenden~~
*Olla	Olney
Padda	Padbury
Peada	Pednor
*Peohthere	Peterley (?)
*Picca	Pitchcott
Piichil	Pitstone
Piot	Petsoe
Pohha	Poundon (?)
*Pōl	Pollicott
Pratt (ME)	Page Hill (?)
*Rīca	Rignall
*Sǣ(i)ga	Seabrook (?)
**Sandhere	Saunderton (?)
**Sceald	Shalstone, Shelspit
Scobba	Shabbington
Scīra	Sherington
Secgga	*Seckloe* (?)
Sigewine	Simpson
**Smēawine	Smewnes Grange
Snell	Snelson, Snelshall
*Sūla	Soulbury
*Tæppa	Taplow
Tāta	Tattenhoe
Þorólfr (ON)	Turweston (?)
Þoruaster (OSw)	Turweston (?)
Þýri (ODan.)	Turville
Tīda	Tingewick
*Tilla	Tilbury
*Tīr	Tyringham
Tota	Tathall, Tetchwick
*Tyddel	Tittershall
*Tylle	Tilson
Ufa	Oving
Wadda	Wadley
*Wǣrmōd	Wormstone (?)
Wǣrmund	Wormstone (?)
*Wafa	Wavendon

Wealda	Waldridge
*Wearda	Warrington
Weohha (Wuhha)	Woughton
Wīda	Widdenton
*Wīdmund, Wudemund	Wormsley
Wīgrǣd	Wyrardisbury
Wine	Winchmore, Winslow
*Wineca	Winchendon
*Wott	Waddesdon
Wulf (OE), Úlfr (ON)	Owlswick
Wulfhere	Wolverton
Wulfsige	Woolstone
*Wyrma	Worminghall
Ylla	Ilmer (?)
*Ytta	*Tiddingford*

FEUDAL NAMES

Aston Abbots, Clinton, Mullins and Sandford, Chesham Bois, Clifton Reynes, Drayton Beauchamp and Parslow, Eakley Lanes, Farnham Royal, Langley Marish, Lillingston Dayrell and Lovell, Marsh Gibbon, Milton Keynes, Newport Pagnell, Newton Blossomville and Longville, Preston Bisset, Monks and Princes Risborough, Stantonbury, Stoke Goldington, Hammond, Mandeville and Poges, Towersey, Wendover Dean, Weston Turville.

MANORIAL NAMES

In the possessive form. Allard's Fm, Ashwell's Fm (2), Brand's House, Butler's Fm, Chenies, Chequers (2), Drewells, Ginions Field, Gregory's Fm, Holloway's Fm, Hutton's Fm, Limes End, Loakes Hill, Mallard's Court, Mantle's Green, Mantle's Fm, Parrot's Fm, Piggotts, Pophley's Fm, Poynatts, Raan's Fm, Seagraves Fm, Shardeloes, Sutmer's Court, Tyrell's Manor, Vatches Fm, Wardrobes.

Without the distinctive s. Deyncourt Fm, Glory Fm, Horncastle, Huntercombe House, Latimer, Mansfield House, Mount Fidget Wood, Quarrendon, Penn Fm, Putnam Place, Remenham House, Spinfield, Weedon Hill, Wilton Park.

Doubtful. Coombe's Fm, Fenemore's Fm, Woodley's Fm.

Pseudo-manorial. Biddles Fm, Darrillshill, Kickles Fm, Layland's Fm, Loudham's Fm, Oxley's House, Redding's Fm, Sidnums, Standal's Fm, Trendell's Wood, Woolleys, Woolman's Wood.

FIELD AND OTHER MINOR NAMES

In collecting material for the interpretation of the place-names (i.e. those names found on the O.S. maps), a good deal of material has been gathered in the form of field and other minor names, especially those of boundary marks. It is impossible to deal with these exhaustively for more than one reason. In the first place they are too numerous, in the second many of them are without much interest, consisting largely of forms which are common in all field-names: further it is but rarely that one has a succession of forms for an individual name such as is often necessary if any satisfactory interpretation is to be attempted. A selection alone can be attempted.

One of the most important features of interest in these names is the elements that are used in their composition, for a study of these will throw further light on the topographical terms used in Buckinghamshire in early days and help us ultimately to determine the geographical distribution of these terms throughout the country, a matter of the greatest importance in the study of English dialects and language generally.

An analysis of these elements, with illustrations of their use, follows. Those elements that have already been fully illustrated in the true place-names are for the most part left unnoticed.

brech is very common in field-names, *v.* Bourton Brake.

brycg. The compound *Omannebrugge*, 'one-manbridge,' the name of a bridge in Aylesbury, is worthy of note (1398).

OE *bytme*, 'bottom,' is found in *le Bitme* in Beachampton (1258).

croft is very common in field-names.

crundel is found once, in Stokenchurch (1240).

cumb in field-names is fairly widely distributed. Early examples are *Cumbes* in Sherington (1236), *Cumbesbrot* in Northall (1348), *Widecumbe* in North Marston (c. 1230), *Chiscumb* in Hartwell (1320), *Merdescombe* in the S.W. of the county (1305), *Swainescome* in Quainton (1706).

dæl or possibly the Scand. loan word *dale* is found once in *Myrydale* in Stony Stratford (1389).

dal is found in field-names but is not very common.

dell has been noted in *Hertisdelle* in Edlesborough (1235), *Watredelle* in Wendover (14th), *Obindelle* in Burnham (13th), *Optounesdelle* in Chesham (1298).

furlang is the commonest of all field-names and is found in innumerable compounds.

gara, here as elsewhere is common in field-names, e.g. *Poeresgoren* in Westbury in 1280.

garðr has only been noted in *Lingard Pightle* in Bradwell (16th).

geard is found as in *Wodehyerd* in Denham, *le Wingherd* in Maids' Moreton (1236) from OE *wingeard*, 'vineyard.'

geat, with the common dialectal initial *j* is illustrated in *Wudiete* in Stewkley (1218) and *Winniatt feild* in Ellesborough (1639).

holm is fairly common in field-names. Early examples are *Monukesholmes* in Lathbury (1236), *Thacholm* in Ravenstone (1321), *le Holme* in Thornborough (c. 1300), *le Holme* in Northall (1348), *Gatholm* (1373). None seem to be found in the south of the county.

hyll is of very common occurrence. Among various compounds we may note *Hungerhul* in Sherington (1236), *Hungerhill* in Swanbourne (1607), a common term of reproach, *Totehil* in Pitstone (1535), a 'look-out' hill, *Buterhulle*, *Othulle* in Thornborough, *Wethull* in Boveney (13th), referring to the butter, oats and wheat produced there, *Harenhulle* in Thornborough (c. 1255), probably from **har**, refers to its position, *Smethehull* in Tickford (1326), *Smithenhill* in Emberton (1639), *Smethenhull* in Dadford (Hy v) and *Stanethulle* in Thornborough (1270) to the surface, cf. **smeðe** and OE *stāniht*, 'stony.' In *Bernhul* al. *Burihul* in Westbury (1280) we probably have a compound of *byrgen* and *hyll* as in Burn Hill in Stone.

OE *hylde*, 'slope' is probably found in the pers. name *atte Helde* in Chalfont (1330).

lacu is fairly common, as in *Sutlake* and *Brodelake* in Cheddington (c. 1250), *Kerlake*, *Berlake* in Northall (1348), *Norlake* in Slapton (17th), all in one corner of the county and in *Everlake* in Denham (1276).

lǣs is rare as in *Lese* in Wooburn (1340), *Longeleswe* in Longcrendon (1371).

land is very common in field-names. Reference to the crops is made in *Rielond* (1244), *Linlond* (1236), *Flexlond* (1236), *Hemplond* (Hy v), *Benlande* (1674) (*v.* **ryge, lin, fleax, bean**) and to the animals on the fields in several *Goslondes* and *Haverlond* (1283), cf. OE *hæfer*, 'goat.' The shape is described in *Woghelande* (c. 1220), *Naseland* (1680), *Langelond* (1236) (*v.* **woh, næs, lang**), the position in *Hangindelond* (1244), *le Harelond*

(1284) (*v.* **har**), the soil in *Surelond* (1280) from OE *sūr*, 'sour.' See further Bandland Cottage *supra*.

mæd is very common indeed in field-names.

plæsc is found in *Costoweplaihs* in Thornborough (1315), *Waterplassh* in Boarstall (1315).

rod, though not found in p.n. is found several times in field-names. Early examples are *Buggerode* in Stowe (Hy iii), *Tudderode* in Ravenstone (1325), *Stanirode* in Brill (1315).

slæd. This element is one of the commonest in Bucks field-names. The character of a *slæd* is well illustrated by the fact that three times it is compounded with **rysc**, three times with *water*, once each with **mor**, **mos**, **ruh**.

topt is found once in *Burentoft* near Buckingham (1247).

twisel in *Twiselmedue* (1315) in Chilton.

weg. Of compounds with this element we may note *Portwey* in Newport Pagnel (13th), *Ferdwey* in Thornborough in which the first element is OE *fierd*, 'army' (c. 1240) and the common *Merwey*, road or path running along a boundary (**gemære**) and *Chepingwey*, 'market-road,' near Leckhampstead (1276).

worþ which we found was very rare in p.n. is found several times in field-names. Early examples are *la Wurthe* (1235) in Edlesborough, *Betwrthe* (c. 1270) in North Marston, *le Stonwrthe* (13th) in Ellesborough, *Aldewrthe* in Hughenden (1205), *Wernesworth* in Fulmer (1369), *Singleworth* (1280), *Peseworde* in Quainton (1299), *Pebbewrthe* in Risborough (c. 1250).

In addition to these we may note

(i) *la Vente* in Boarstall (1355), *Oxventes*, near Bernwood (1540). This seems to be the word *fent* meaning 'split' or 'rift' which is occasionally applied to a rift in the ground. The initial *v* is dialectal. *v.* Introd. xxv.

(ii) *le Brende* in Stoke Goldington (1328) where we have reference to ground which has been cleared by burning, *v.* **brende**.

(iii) *Swylie* in Maids' Moreton (1236) would seem to be the same as *swilly* noted in the EDD as meaning 'hollow place,' gutter washed out of the soil. If so the word is carried back some six hundred years.

(iv) The field-name *Thertheoxlaydede* in Northall (13th) a picture in miniature of a medieval farming tragedy.

The field-names also throw further light on the personal nomenclature of early Buckinghamshire. In the list that follows personal names of definitely post-Conquest origin have been omitted, e.g. *Walter* in *Waltereshull* (c. 1255).

PERSONAL NAMES IN FIELD AND OTHER MINOR NAMES

OE Aegelmǣr	*Yelmerscroft* (1674)
Aelfsige	*Alsisha'* (1235)
Aescwulf	*Aesculfeswillan* (c. 1200)
Aeþelwine	*Athelynemulne* (1313)
Bēagmund	*Bachemundeswelle* (1335)
Beorhtmǣr	*Britmeresburieles* (c. 1250)
Beorhtric	*Britrichescrot* (c. 1240)
Brūn	*Bruneswude* (1227)
Brunning	*Brunningesacre* (1195)
Bucge	*Buggerode* (13th)
Cada	*Cademade* (1255)
Colling	*Collynggeswyk* (1339)
Cyneweald	*Kynnewaldescroft* (1255)
Dodd	*Doddesmede* (13th)
Dudemǣr	*Dudemereshull* (13th)
Godwine	*Godwinescroft* (1212)
Haþelwold	*Halewoldesdene* (c. 1250)
Heardwulf	*Hardelesmede* (1311)
Heremōd	*Heremodesaltwich* (1212)
*Hūnðrȳð	*Hundryðetreow* (c. 1000)
Lēodwine	*Ledewynslad* (1337)
Lēofrīc	*Levericheshanger* (1281)
*Mentel	*Mentlesham* (1278)
Ōswynn	*Oswynedene* (14th)
Sigeweald	*Siualdes Acre* (c. 1250)
Sigeweard	*Siwardeshull* (1331)
*Toti	*Totysbrege* (c. 1270)
Tūnbeald	*Tumbaldestreow* (10th)
Tudda	*Tudderode* (1325)
*Wern	*Wernesworth* (1369)
Wifel	*Wyuelesgate* (14th)
Wīgbeald	*Wibaldeslake* (1195)
Wīgmund	*Wymundewere* (c. 1275)
Wilbeald	*Wilbaldesham* (13th)
Wulfhere	*Wolfreschobbes* (1315)
Wulfmǣr	*Wlfmeresfeld* (1280)
Wulfrǣd	*Wulfredesmere* (1235)
Wulfstān	*Wulstanesmore* (c. 1210)
ON Dott	*Dottesdun* (1235) in Edlesborough
Gunnhildr	*Gunnildeland* (1240) in Fawley

Kolgrímr	*Colgrimescroft* (1271) in Risborough
**Krakúlfr	*Craculfesberch* (c. 1240) in Thornborough
Ragnhildr	*Rawenildefifacre* (1304) in Westbury
Sveinn	*Swainescome* (1706) in Quainton
	Suenesham (1320) in Steeple Claydon
Tóki	*Tokiescroft* (1218) in Stewkley

INDEX

OF PLACE-NAMES IN BUCKINGHAMSHIRE

INDEX

OF PLACE-NAMES IN COUNTIES OTHER THAN BUCKINGHAMSHIRE

CAMBRIDGE: PRINTED BY W. LEWIS AT THE UNIVERSITY PRESS

CAMBRIDGE
UNIVERSITY PRESS
LONDON: Fetter Lane

NEW YORK
The Macmillan Co.

BOMBAY, CALCUTTA and
MADRAS
Macmillan and Co., Ltd.

TORONTO
The Macmillan Co. of
Canada, Ltd.

TOKYO
Maruzen-Kabushiki-Kaisha

ENGLISH PLACE-NAME SOCIETY. VOLUME II.

THE PLACE-NAMES OF BUCKINGHAMSHIRE

* see amendment in Journal 2, 1970